ISLAND OF JAVA

SKETCHES,

CIVIL AND MILITARY,

OF THE

ISLAND OF JAVA

AND

ITS IMMEDIATE DEPENDENCIES:

COMPRISING

INTERESTING DETAILS

OF

𝕭𝖆𝖙𝖆𝖛𝖎𝖆,

AND AUTHENTIC PARTICULARS

OF

THE CELEBRATED POISON-TREE.

———————

Illustrated with a MAP of JAVA and PLAN of BATAVIA, from
actual Survey.

———————

LONDON:

PRINTED FOR J. J. STOCKDALE, 41, PALL-MALL.

1811.

ISLAND OF
JAVA

John Joseph Stockdale

WITH AN INTRODUCTION

BY JOHN BASTIN

PERIPLUS

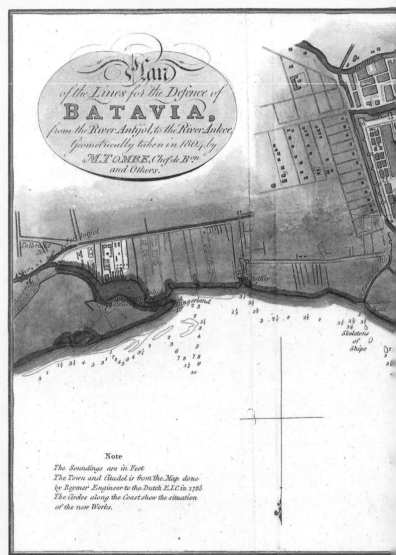

Plan
of the Lines for the Defence of
BATAVIA,
from the River Antijol, to the River Ankee,
Geometrically taken in 1804, by
M. TOMBE, Chef de B.on
and Others.

Note

The Soundings are in Feet
The Town and Citadel is from the Map done
by Reymer Engineer to the Dutch E.I.C. in 1785
The Circles along the Coast shew the situation
of the new Works.

Published Sep.r

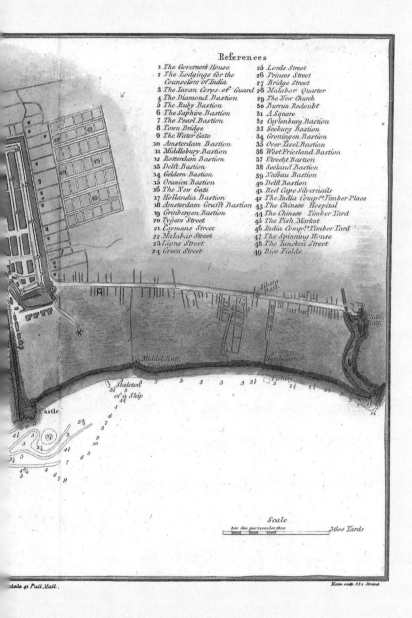

References

1 The Governor's House
2 The Lodgings for the Counselors of India
3 The Javan Corps of Guard
4 The Diamond Bastion
5 The Ruby Bastion
6 The Saphire Bastion
7 The Pearl Bastion
8 Town Bridge
9 The Water Gate
10 Amsterdam Bastion
11 Middlebury Bastion
12 Rotterdam Bastion
13 Delft Bastion
14 Geldern Bastion
15 Oranien Bastion
16 The New Gate
17 Hollandia Bastion
18 Amsterdam Graft Bastion
19 Grinbergen Bastion
20 Tygers Street
21 Caymans Street
22 Malabar Street
23 Lions Street
24 Green Street
25 Lords Street
26 Princes Street
27 Bridge Street
28 Malabar Quarter
29 The New Church
30 Burun Redoubt
31 A Square
32 Cuylenburg Bastion
33 Seeburg Bastion
34 Groningen Bastion
35 Over Issel Bastion
36 West Friesland Bastion
37 Utrecht Bastion
38 Seeland Bastion
39 Nassau Bastion
40 Delft Bastion
41 Red Cape Silvernails
42 The India Compy. Timber Place
43 The Chinese Hospital
44 The Chinese Timber Yard
45 The Fish Market
46 India Compy. Timber Yard
47 The Spinning House
48 The Juncken Street
49 Rice Fields

Scale
3600 Yards

Map
of the
ISLAND OF JAVA,
prepared from the Actual Surveys
of
M. d'APRES de MANNEVILLETTE,
Gen. C. F. Tombe.
Engineer &c. &c.
for
Sketches Civil & Military,
by
J. J. STOCKDALE.
Publish'd at 41, Pall Mall 5, October 1811.

J   A

Tree I.
Dr Rachit

CRAWANG

Meerlenaars

Pamanoekan
Koranglawir
Jati
Barong
Kira
Tsilandok
Groodak
Koret
Babakan
Mijarang
Tsiamboe
Lawoek
Sipadawa
Parang
Tsikanpi
Tsikapi
Doeko
Pandadan
Tsiklape
Tsipappan

Keloor
Paartang
Rajajang
Indramaijoe
Lelin
Ponkape
Widasari
Bajawak
Bantarvan
Tsiboedas

Docka
Poeren
Tolohagon
Pamdian

Indermaye
Singara
Logiekase

Intramaijoe

Inpanagara

Pagadeen
Kandvsoli
Parrocha
Tsigonter
Pariak
Bindone
Sindawan
Passer
Magara

Sammadang
Kilimenk
Samadang
Samer
Tsiangua
Tsibodas
mpan Ganten

Qualang
Dok
Opette
Tsibado
Sikap
Tsieptek
Kadawang

Hauris

Derma
Winnagara

GABANG

LEDOX
POMARDEEN

ROMO

Tsibeger
Tsironsa
Vumange

Prakamapaß

OETAME

Sipeet
Hoegyring
Madura

LIMBANGA

PANJOEMAG

BA

Pondajang
Lagoera
Dorrawati
Tsigentel
Asakal

Sibusang
Kawongan
Sasokarti
Linkombasan
Tsigoeger

Tsibobong
Dammajong
Tsikankaese

land Pagger
Goenong

POURA

Koedawan
Tsilimkon
Cadjan
Lomeri
Tsialok
Tsikallong

Sagaro
Noekan
B.

Soessa Canhang

UKA

A

N

O

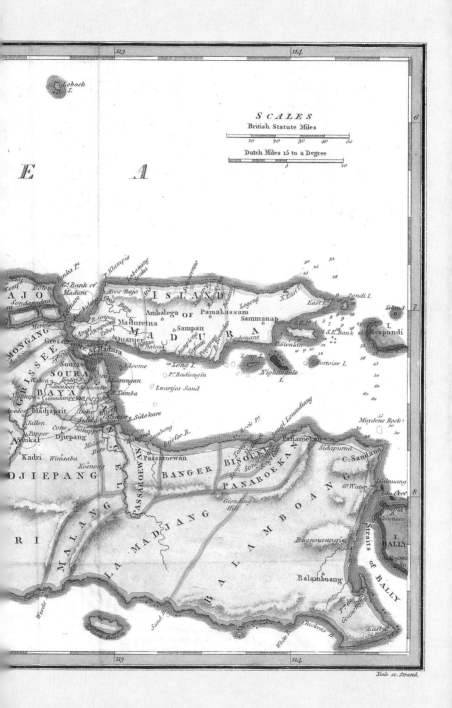

Lebock I.

E A

SCALES
British Statute Miles

| 10 | 20 | 30 | 40 | 50 |

Dutch Miles 15 to a Degree

| 5 | 10 |

6°

AJO
Sondanadan

Temp. Doton
R. Klampis
G.t Bank of
Madura
Kabonang
Sedka
Aros Baja

Bona

ISLAND OF MADURA

Kemp

Sampani
R. Serpan
R. Balega

Merina
Gresse
L. of Madura

MONGANG
CRISSEE

Souras

SOURA
BAYA

Waton
Sidang
Teteloon
Soemenko

Matanpa
Guadampessa

Madjapait
Doks
Sidoa
Kalatjen

wedoe!
Tallon
Cotto
Bakapper

Papper

Asinkai

Djiepang

Kadri   Winisaba
Koenong

DJIEPANG

RI

Wesels

Ambalega
Sampan

Madureina
Quarter
Tebel

Eloome
Long I.
P.t Badiengin
Zwartjes Sand

Tamba

Winon
Bond
Pombong

Djenbong

Malang
Boto

Passaroewan

PASSAROEWAN

MALANG

LA MADJANG

Pamakassam
Sammanap

Logeng
Ladouaini

Sivalan

Long I.

R. Sidekare

Sidekare
R.
Rejefse R.

Rock Pt.
Town
Gowai Loewidiang
Sonar

Faharoekan

BISOUKA
Sonar

PANAROEKAN

BANGER

Glending
Hill

N. East I.
East I.
Pondi I.

Island
Respondi
I.

S.E. Bank

Fortoise I.

Nightingale
I.

Sidapurna

C. Sandan

Muydens Rock

G.t Water Pt.

Teueuang
Tau Cert

Barota
B.
Cocotiers

I.
BALLY

Straits of BALLY

BALAMBOANG

Bagnouvangis

Balamboang

P.de
Grounon

Sand R.

Chickeus B.

White R.

East I.

Noele sc. Strand.

Dedicated to the memory of Mike Sweet,
whose love of books was only surpassed by his love of people

Originally published as Sketches, Civil and Military,
of the Island of Java and Its Immediate Dependencies, &c.
by J. J. Stockdale, London, 1811

Reprinted by Periplus Editions (HK) Ltd, in association with
Antiques of the Orient Pte Ltd, Singapore, 1995

Reprinted in paperback by Periplus Editions (HK) Ltd, 2003

Introduction © John Bastin, 1995

ISBN 962 8734 23 7

DISTRIBUTORS

Indonesia
PT Java Books Indonesia,
Jl. Kelapa Gading Kirana, Blok A-14/17, Jakarta 14240
Tel (021) 451 5351; Fax (021) 453 4987
Email: cs@javabooks.co.id

Asia Pacific
Berkeley Books Pte Ltd, 130 Joo Seng Road,
#06-01/03, Singapore 368357
Tel (65) 6280 1330; Fax (65) 6280 6290
Email: inquiries@perplus.com.sg
www.periplus.com

Japan
Tuttle Publishing, Yaekari Building, 3rd Floor,
5-4-12 Osaki, Shinagawa-ku, Tokyo 141-0032
Tel (03) 5437 0171; Fax (03) 5437 0755
Email: tuttle-sales@gol.com

North America, Latin America & Europe
Tuttle Publishing, 364 Innovation Drive,
North Clarendon, VT 05759-9436
Tel (802) 773 8930; Fax (802) 773 6993
Email: info@tuttlepublishing.com
www.tuttlepublishing.com

05 06 07 08 09 6 5 4 3 2
Printed in Singapore

Introduction

Tʜɪs was the first book to be published in England relating to the British conquest of Java in 1811. The Preface makes clear that it was compiled when news reached London of the projected invasion of the island by British forces in India: 'The following work owes its origin to the expedition, under that brave and experienced soldier Sir Samuel Auchmuty, against the last settlement remaining in the hands of an European power hostile to Great Britain'.

The compiler and publisher of the book was John Joseph Stockdale (1770–1847), the eldest son of the publisher John Stockdale (1749–1814). He was admitted to the Stationers Company in London in 1802, and he began publishing books shortly afterwards. He was undoubtedly something of a rogue, and is mainly remembered as the publisher, and probably the author, of the notorious *Memoirs* (1825) of the courtesan Harriette Wilson (1789–1846), written in revenge on the Duke of Beaufort for breaking his promises to her. The publication was something of a blackmailing affair, since those who paid up had their names removed from the text. It prompted the Duke of Wellington's famous remark, 'Publish and be damned'. Stockdale issued from his premises at No. 41, Pall Mall, London, an extensive list of publications, including books on military history, and he advertised his willingness to execute 'gratefully' even 'the smallest orders' for books published by himself or others, and for newspapers, magazines and stationery. He also offered for sale prints, paintings and secondhand books.

It was typical of Stockdale that he should have decided to publish something on Java when news reached London of the projected British invasion of the island. He put the book together in an 'unprecedentedly' short space of time by reprinting four long sections, or 'Books' as he describes them, from S.H. Wilcocke's English translation of J.S. Stavorinus' *Voyages to the East-Indies* (London, 1798), and from an English translation he had made of parts of C.S. Sonnini's edition of C.F. Tombe's *Voyage aux Indes Orientales, pendant les années 1802, 1803, 1804, 1805 et 1806* (Paris, 1810). The book was printed by Samuel Gosnell of No. 8, Little Queen Street, London.

The publication dates of 24 September and 5 October 1811 on the two maps in the book, and the date of 9 October of the Dedication, suggest that the book was put in hand shortly after news reached London of the departure of the British invasion force from India in the previous March. The first edition was published in November or early December 1811, judging by a notice in the book advertising the issue of a second 'enlarged' edition at 14s.6d., since this contains an additional chart of the Strait of Madura by the Dutch East India Company engineer M. Loriaux, which is dated 30 November 1811. The two maps in the first edition, and the chart of the Strait of Madura in the second edition, were offered for sale separately, the first at 2s.6d., and the other two at 1s. each.

The publication date of 30 November 1811 on the chart of the Strait of Madura clearly indicates that Stockdale decided to publish a second enlarged edition of the book before news reached England in mid-December 1811 of the landing of the British forces in Java, and of their victory over the combined Dutch and French forces at Meester Cornelis on 26 August. As well as the chart, the second edition of the book contains an additional chapter, or 'Supplement', taken from John Barrow's *A Voyage to Cochinchina* (London, 1806). The Supplement was printed by Francis Vigurs of No. 5, Princes Street, Leicester Square, London, and was published separately, together with the chart, under the title: *An Account of the Island of Java, from Anjerie, in the Strait of Sunda, to Batavia; containing its Natural History, Customs, &c. Intended as a Supplement to "Sketches, Civil and Military". Illustrated with a Chart of the Strait of Madura, from Actual Survey, Shewing that Part of Java Where the Final Conquest of the Island was Effected by Sir Samuel Auchmuty* (London, 1812), pp. iv, 407–50, price 2s. An 'Advertisement' printed on a separate leaf after the title-page reads:

The following Supplement, published separately, to complete the First Edition of "Sketches, Civil and Military, of the Island of Java", is almost wholly taken from Mr. Barrow's elegant Voyage to Cochin China.

The Chart of the Strait of Madura should face page 391.

1st February, 1812.

The date of this Advertisement is odd considering that the 'Advertisement to the Second Edition', which appears in the various issues of that edition, bears an earlier date of 23 January 1812:

ADVERTISEMENT to the SECOND EDITION

THE surrender of the Island of Java and its dependencies having now taken place, and created such a demand for this humble compilation as seemed to justify the Publisher in bringing forward a new edition of it; he has annexed a Chart of the Strait of Madura, which is intended to be placed opposite page 391; and has added another Chapter, for which he is almost wholly indebted to Mr. Barrow's elegant and interesting "Voyage to Cochin China".

23 January, 1812.

This date of 23 January corresponds closely with the publication two days earlier of reports in *The London Gazette Extraordinary*, and in the British press, of the conquest of Java and the acceptance by the Governor-General, Jan Willem Janssens (1762–1838), of the Articles of Capitulation submitted to him by the British Commander-in-Chief, Sir Samuel Auchmuty (1756–1822), on 18 September 1811. What Stockdale appears to have done, in order to make up a second edition of the book, was initially to issue copies of the first edition with a cancel title-page, and separate Supplement and chart; and, subsequently, copies with the Supplement and chart bound in. The text of copies of the first issue of the second edition thus ends at p. 406, as in the first edition, but with an added final leaf, 'Advertisement to the Second Edition', whereas in copies of the second issue this Advertisement precedes the bound-in Supplement and chart. Some copies of the second issue contain an engraved portrait of Sir Samuel Auchmuty by A. Cardon (1772–1813) bound in before the Preface.

The first and second issues are printed on the identical thick paper as the first edition; the final Contents page (p. xix) is the same as in the first edition, and the error in the numbering of p. 59 is uncorrected from the first edition. The third issue of the second edition, on the other hand, is printed on different paper; pp. v–vi of the Dedication has been re-set, with added text dated 3 February 1812; and there is an addition to p. xix detailing the contents of the Supplement. The numbering of p. 59 is also corrected, and the 'Advertisement to the Second Edition' is printed on a leaf following the title-page. In this third issue the inclusion of the engraved portrait of Sir Samuel Auchmuty is optional.

The portrait is lettered: *Brigadier General Sir Samuel Auchmuty, K^T Commander in Chief of his Britannic Majesty's Forces, at the taking by assault of Montè Vidio, in South America, on the 3d of February, 1807. Abbot pinxit. A. Cardon sculpsit. Published 11th May 1808 by I.I. Stockdale 41 Pall Mall.* In the list of publisher's advertisements at the end of the first edition of the book, the portrait is offered for sale separately at 3s. It was first published in Stockdale's *Notes on the Viceroyalty of La Plata in South America; with a Sketch of the Manners and Character of the Inhabitants. To which are added, a History of the Operations of the British Troops in that Country, and Anecdotes, Biographical and Military, of the principal Officers employed. With a portrait of Sir Samuel Auchmuty, and Plans* (London, 1808), price 10s. 6d. Stockdale alludes to this work in the Preface to *Sketches, Civil and Military, of the Island of Java.* The portrait also illustrates a 'Life of Sir Samuel Auchmuty' in the *Royal Military Chronicle* (London, 1811), II, facing p. 217, where it is lettered: 'Engraved for the Military Chronicle', with the date, London 1 July 1811. An acknowledgement that it was published by Stockdale is given on p. 277.

In publishing his book on Java, Stockdale was aware that little was known about the island in Britain apart from the one subject that had intrigued the reading public for nearly thirty years—the Upas, or poison tree, which had been described in blood chilling terms by the German surgeon J.N. Foersch in *The London Magazine: or, Gentlemen's Monthly Intelligencer* in December 1783, and which had later been popularized by Erasmus Darwin (1731–1802) in his epic poem *The Botanic Garden* (London, 1789–1791), where it is dramatically described as 'the Hyrdra-Tree of death'. Stockdale was not one to miss the opportunity of pursuing such a popular subject, and he included in his book the text of Foersch's account (pp. 311–22), as well as other related matter (pp. 323–46), and made reference to the 'celebrated' poison tree on the title-page.

According to Foersch's account, his curiosity was aroused by various accounts of the poison tree and the violent effects of its poison when he was stationed at Batavia (Jakarta) in 1774 as a surgeon in the service of the Dutch East India Company. He applied to the Governor-General P.A. van der Parra (1714–1775) for permission to travel through the country to investigate the poison tree, which was situated in mountainous country about 27 leagues from Batavia, 14 from Surakarta, and 20 from Jogyakarta. The country round the tree to a distance of between 10 and 12 miles was entirely barren, and Foersch made a tour round this dangerous spot some 18 miles from the tree and found the country desolate. He met near the foot of the hills an 'old ecclesiastic' from whose house criminals were sent to collect the valuable poison for use on spears and other warlike instruments. These criminals had been sentenced to death by the Susuhunan of Java, and their only chance of escaping with their lives was to attempt the task of collecting the poison. However Foersch was told by the old ecclesiastic that during thirty years more than 700 criminals had made the attempt but only two in twenty had returned. He showed him the list of criminals, and Foersch later saw a corresponding list when he visited Surakarta in 1776 and witnessed the execution of thirteen of the Susuhunan's concubines for infidelity by a lancet dipped in Upas poison. He subsequently witnessed other executions by the same method at Semarang.

Foersch's sensational account was reprinted in *The Universal Magazine of Knowledge and Pleasure* in January 1784, and in other publications in succeeding years. So much circumstantial detail was contained in the account that many were inclined to believe it. However, the Upas tree (*Antiaris toxicaria* Leschenault) was already well known to seventeenth and eighteenth century travel and scientific writers on Indonesia, including Rumphius, who gave an account of the poison or Spatter tree of Macassar (*Arbor toxicaria* Latin) in his *Herbarium Amboinense* (Amsterdam, The Hague, Utrecht, 1741–1755). Scientific opinion in Europe and Indonesia was therefore highly sceptical of Foersch's account, and shortly after its publication the Directing Members of the Batavian Society of Arts and Sciences in Jakarta instigated enquiries through two of its members, Jan Matthijs van Rhijn, Chief Resident at Yogyakarta, and Willem Ardiaan Palm, Chief Resident at Surakarta, and their principal findings were published in 1789 in the *Nieuwe Algemeene Vaderlandsche Letter-oefeningen* by Lambertus Nolst, M.D., a member of the Batavian Society of Experimental Philosophy at Rotterdam. The report, which refutes Foersch's statements in such detail as essentially to deny the very existence of the Upas tree in Java, contains the text of letters exchanged between Palm and the Susuhunan of Surakarta, Pakubuwana III, in November 1785 in which the latter denied all knowledge of Foersch and the Upas tree, and, by implication, the latter's claim to have witnessed at the *kraton* in 1776 the execution of thirteen concubines by Upas poison.

Further detailed enquiries about the Upas tree were made when members of Lord Macartney's embassy to China visited Java in 1793. Sir George Staunton (1737–1801), Secretary to the embassy, found that at Batavia Foersch's account was regarded in the same light as the fictions of Baron Munchausen, but he confirmed the existence in the island of a vegetable poison which on a Javanese *keris* rendered wounds incurable. Dr. Hugh Gillan (?–1798), Physician to the embassy, also learned from one of the Keepers of the Hortus Medicus at Batavia that there was a tree in the garden which distilled a poisonous juice but that it was kept secret for fear that slaves might get their hands on it. Staunton obtained a copy of Palm and Van Rhijn's report in refutation of Foersch's account and sent a copy of it to the President of the Royal Society in London, Sir Joseph Banks (1743–1820).

Another member of the Macartney embassy to China, the comptroller of the Household, John Barrow (1764–1848), also made particular enquiries about the Upas tree in Java in 1793, and he concluded that there was 'little favourable to the truth of *Foersch's* relation'. Indeed, Barrow arrived at the somewhat negative conclusion that Upas was 'the appellative' for every poisonous tree in the island and that the word was applied equally to the poisonous plants as well. 'In this sense', he wrote, 'the *Bohun* or *Boon Upas* of *Foersch* would imply neither more nor less than a *poisonous* tree, and not any particular species of tree, much less an unconnected individual *sui generis*, bearing the name of *Upas*'.

More positive results were achieved by the French naturalist Louis Auguste Deschamps (1765–1842) who, as a member of the expedition of Joseph Antoine Bruni D'Entrecasteaux (1739–1793) in search of Jean François de Galaup La Pérouse (1741–1788), escaped internment in Java in 1793 by entering Dutch service and spending nearly nine years in the island as a physician engaged in botanical research. During his extensive travels Deschamps came upon the Upas tree growing in the forests of Blambangan in eastern Java where he was able to confirm the deadly effects that the resin had when used as a poison on weapons. He rejected, however, the fiction that the tree poisoned the atmosphere as alleged by Foersch, attributing the story to the fact that there was a high mortality rate among those persons exiled to the marshy and unhealthy regions of eastern Java. He indicated that the representation of the flowers in Rumphius' *Herbarium Amboinense* was incorrect, and he described the characteristics of both the male and female flowers, and produced drawings which survive among his collections in the Natural History Museum, London. Deschamps' account of the Upas tree was published by Conrad Malte-Brun (1775–1826) in Volume I of his *Annals des Voyages* (Paris, 1808), and the substance of the account was printed again by Malte-Brun in the French edition of John Barrow's *A Voyage to Cochinchina* (London, 1806), which was published in Paris in 1807. This, together with Foersch's account of the Upas tree, extracted from a version in *The Monthly Repertory* (?), was appended by C.S. Sonnini (1751–1812) to C.F. Tombe's *Voyage aux Indes Orientales* (Paris, 1810), and reprinted by Stockdale in his book.

In 1810 Jean Baptiste Louis Théodore Leschenault de la Tour (1773–1826), who had made his way to Java from Timor where he had been left because of ill-health by Nicolas Baudin (1754–1803) on his voyage of exploration to Australia, published his 'Mémoire sur le *Strychnos tieute* et *l'Antiaris toxicaria*, plantes vénéneuses de l'île de *Java*', based on his own observations of the two plants in Banyuwangi in eastern Java and on experiments he had made with the poisons. Equally important, he brought back to France in 1807 a great quantity of the poisons collected and prepared in Java, Borneo and Macassar, which enabled François Magendie (1783–1855) and Alyre Raffeneau-Delile (1778–1850), physician and botanist on Napoleon's Egyptian expedition, to conduct extensive experiments which were recorded in a series of papers read before the Faculty of Medicine in Paris in 1809.

Stockdale included an English translation of Leschenault de la Tour's 'Mémoire' in his book (pp. 323–44), as well as part of a paper by (Sir) Benjamin Collins Brodie (1783–1862) on 'Experiments with the Upas Antiar' (pp. 344–6), which was read to the Royal Society on 21 February 1811 detailing the experiments he had carried out with a quantity of the poison supplied to him by William Marsden (1754–1836), author of *The History of Sumatra* (London, 1811). Marsden indicates in his book that

the original source of this supply of the poison was Dr. William Rox-
burgh (1751–1815), who had brought to England in 1806 a small branch of
the Upas tree with some of the poisonous gum from a specimen transplanted from Sumatra in the Botanic Garden, Calcutta. Marsden does
not refer to the Upas tree in the first and second editions of his book,
which were published in London in 1783 and 1784, but he was almost certainly responsible for publishing, probably at Sir Joseph Banks' request,
an English summary of Palm and Van Rhijn's refutation of Foersch's
account in *The Gentleman's Magazine* of 1794. He added a paragraph on
the subject of the Upas tree to the third edition of *The History of Sumatra* of 1811 in which he dismisses Foersch's fables and cites in support of
his view a report by Dr. Charles Campbell of the East India Company's
medical establishment at Fort Marlborough in west Sumatra.

It would appear that at the proof stage of his book Marsden learned
of the experiments which had been carried out on the Upas poison by
Raffeneau-Delille in Paris because he added a hastily written footnote
on the subject. At about the same time, in a letter dated 11 April 1810, he
wrote to Thomas Stamford Raffles (1781–1826) at Penang asking him to
make further enquiries about the Upas tree which, he stated, was 'again
becoming the subject of general conversation, in consequence of experiments…by the French on the effects of the poison'.

The Upas tree was among the first subjects which Raffles discussed
with Dr. Thomas Horsfield (1773–1859) at Surakarta in December 1811,
shortly after his appointment as Lieutenant-Governor of Java. He asked
the American naturalist for an early report, and this was sent to him on
21 March 1812 under the title, 'An Essay on the Oopas or Poison Tree of
Java'. After recounting what Rumphius had to say on the subject, and
giving details of the discovery of the tree by Leschenault de la Tour and
himself in eastern Java during 1805 and 1806, Horsfield described the
methods employed by the Indonesians in the preparation of the poison
and recorded his own experiments with it on live animals at Surakarta.
The 'Essay' was written in ignorance of the information which was by
then widely known about the Upas tree in Europe, and Marsden, to
whom Raffles sent a copy on 22 October 1812, had the embarrassing task
of informing Raffles that much of the novelty and importance of Horsfield's experiments had been pre-empted. In his letter Marsden also
recorded the highly interesting information that at the time he published

his sensational account of the Upas tree, Foersch was a visitor at Sir Joseph Banks' house in Soho Square, and that he had been assisted in the publication by a medical man of Marsden's acquaintance. The latter was almost certainly the naval surgeon James Lind (1716–1794), physician to the Haslar Naval Hospital and author of *An Essay on Diseases Incidental to Europeans in Hot Climates* (London, 1768), which passed through five editions during the author's life-time.

Marsden's letter is of considerable importance not only in placing Foersch in London at the time when he published his account of the Upas tree but also at the very heart of the British scientific establishment. Very little is known about Foersch, apart from the misleading statements contained in his account. He was not, as stated there, a Surgeon at Batavia in 1774 in the employ of the Dutch East India Company, but a Surgeon Third Class stationed at Semarang in 1775 and 1776, after which he rose to the rank of Senior Surgeon. He travelled in Java but never visited Surakarta, as he claims to have done. That he left Java in the employ of the British was already established by the Dutch in the mid-1780s, but the fact was overlooked in succeeding years as misinformation piled up about him. Already in December 1783, in printing his account of the Upas tree, *The London Magazine* assigned to him two different sets of initials, 'N.P.' at the beginning of the account, and (correctly) 'J.N.' at the end. Inevitably, the first set of initials tended to predominate in later statements about him, and the matter was made worse when *The Monthly Repertory* (?) reprinted his account under the initials 'C.H.', stated to be an Englishman. The error was perpetuated by C.S. Sonnini in his edition of C.F. Tombe's *Voyage aux Indes Orientales* (Paris, 1810), and although Stockdale took Sonnini to task in his *Sketches, Civil and Military, of the Island of Java*, for giving an incorrect reference to the title of the journal, and for not knowing that Foersch was the author of the account (p. 311n), readers of Tombe's book were bound to be misled.

Indeed, Stockdale's correction of Sonnini passed unnoticed by many later writers on the subject of the Upas tree, including D.M. Campbell, who in reprinting Foersch's account in his *Java: Past & Present* (London, 1915) avers that it was written by an 'English surgeon called C.H.', and, in further confused explanation, states: 'It was in 1773, at the time an English doctor named C.H. was living at Batavia, and issued a treatise on vegetable poison, that the so-called imaginative Dr. Foersch, a sur-geon to the Dutch East India Company stationed at Samarang, startled the world and made the blood grow cold with his description of *Gunúng Upas'*. Campbell made enquiries to discover the name of the English surgeon named C.H., but he had little chance of success as the initials were those of the translator of Foersch's account from Dutch into Eng-lish, who is simply described in *The London Magazine* of December 1783 as 'Formerly a *German bookseller* near Temple Bar'. His name, in fact, was Charles Heydinger, who lived in The Strand and at other addresses in London between 1771 and 1778. That he was interested in botanical and horticultural matters is indicated by the appearance of his name on the title-page of a catalogue of plants and seeds by Conrad Loddiges (1739?–1826): *C. Heydinger, Buchhhändler, No. 6, Bridges-street, Covent garden*. According to the printer, John Nichols (1745–1826), he issued other catalogues during the 1770s but was unsuccessful in business and died in distressed circumstance in about 1778, obviously an error, as he must have lived on into the early 1780s when Foersch was in London writing his account of the Upas tree.

For Stockdale, the inclusion of material relating to the celebrated poison tree proved highly successful, and created a popular demand for his book. It was essentially the first book in English to focus exclusively on the island of Java, and to this extent it is historically and bibliograph-ically important. It was succeeded in 1815 by Major William Thorn's *Memoir of the Conquest of Java . . . To which is subjoined, A Statistical and Historical Sketch of Java*, and in 1817 by Raffles' monumental two volume work, *The History of Java*, which laid the foundation of British historical knowledge of Indonesia for more than a century. Java itself remained under British control until 1816, when, in accordance with the political arrangements made at the end of the Napoleonic wars, the island and its dependencies were returned to the Netherlands. These three books were the product of the British conquest and occupation of Java, and today stand as reminders of that singularly important event in the modern his-tory of South-East Asia.

JOHN BASTIN
Eastbourne, East Sussex, England
June 1995

TO

JAMES AMOS, ESQ.

ST. HELEN'S PLACE.

———————

MY DEAR SIR,

I HOPE I shall neither offend you by having prefixed your name to the following pages, nor by stating the motives, beyond those of a private and personal nature, which influenced my selection.

The disposition which you evinced, at an unusually early period of life, to render yourself extensively useful to society, and in which disposition you so strenuously persevere, would, of itself justify my choice, and, I hope, be sufficient ground to induce your acceptance of this public testimony, from a consciousness that, not being unworthily offered, on the one part, neither will its reception be derogatory on the other. The long connexion of your respected family with the East Indies, and your own well-known extensive concerns with that rich portion of the globe, have also combined to direct you to acquaint yourself with details which give you more than an individual interest in what relates to it.

You have already availed yourself of many opportunities to display your zeal in promoting every useful political and commercial knowledge; and the advancement of commerce and of literature, as best calculated to promote the general good, has frequently been seen to be near to your heart.

Although it may seem presumptuous, in such an individual as myself, to attempt to confirm you in the truly beneficial and laudable sentiments you have adopted on, I doubt not, the most mature and studied conviction of their utility, yet the vanity will, I trust, be venial, which impels me to hope that even this inconsiderable meed of applause may prove an incitement to your progress towards giving them an universal expansion.

To you, Sir, pre-eminent in the commerce of a country " WHOSE MERCHANTS ARE PRINCES," I now presume to dedicate these hasty " Sketches," and have the honour to subscribe myself, with most respectful esteem,

My dear Sir,

Your sincere, though very humble friend:

JOHN JOSEPH STOCKDALE.

London,
9th October, 1811.

A

PREFACE.

THE following work owes its origin to the expedition, under that brave and experienced soldier Sir Samuel Auchmuty *, against the last settlement remaining in the hands of an European power hostile to Great Britain. The subject, in itself interesting, is rendered much more so by the probability of the many new sources of enterprise, which will now be opened to the view of that liberal, extensive, and spirited commerce, which has so highly contributed to enable this kingdom to present itself an insurmountable barrier to the atrocious schemes of that enemy of the human race, Napoleon Buonaparte.

* A biographical memoir and portrait of this gentleman is contained in " Notes on the Vice-Royalty of La Plata," &c. which also includes an account of his military operations in South America.

The portion comprised in the first three Books, is selected from the Voyages of John Splinter Stavorinus, rear-admiral in the service of the States General; into which is incorporated the substance of the notes of his well-informed English translator, Mr. Wilcocke, with occasional reference to the early labours of the celebrated Valentyn, Sir George Staunton's Account of the Embassy to China, &c. &c.

Although the plan of comprising each separate account in one Book subjects the reader to some repetition; yet, as it is calculated to do more justice to the respective travellers, the editor hopes it will not be imputed to him as a fault.

The remaining part of the work acquires much value, as the actual observation of an intelligent traveller, C. F. Tombe *, an officer of engineers, and general in the French service, whose information is most recent, and in a great measure entirely new.

From the same source is derived the first actual survey of the island of Java and its im-

* Voyage aux Indes Orientales, edited by Sonnini.

mediate dependencies, which has been made public in this country, or indeed in Europe, and the plan of the line of defence of Batavia ; with the addition of the city, to the plan, and some necessary details to the interior of the map, principally from Valentyn's book ; for the loan of which, and the ready access afforded to the invaluable stores contained in the museum and library of the Right Hon. Sir Joseph Banks, Bart. the editor must, in common with every votary of literature and science, acknowledge his warmest obligations.

The authorities for the other additions are in every case duly quoted. The particulars of the celebrated poison-tree will, he cannot doubt, be considered highly important.

In a space of time, perhaps unprecedentedly short, the editor has translated, selected, and compiled, the subsequent " Sketches," and, to avow " the head and front of his offending," he has been guilty of *making a book*, which he ventures to hope will be found to contain amusement, interest, and information. The effort, at

any rate, is not very ambitious; and, although
it cannot entitle him to literary reputation, he
trusts that its avowed production on the spur of
the moment, will shelter him from the severity
of that criticism, which has often shown itself
indulgent to his lowly endeavours. He has
little, indeed, to apprehend from the huge Levia-
than of criticism, The Edinburgh Review *,
which, singular as it may appear, has studiously
avoided, except in one instance †, noticing any
works of which he is the publisher, although
some of them are the productions of the first
characters of the time :—personal offence he can
scarcely have given to these mighty arbiters of
public taste, not having individual knowledge of
any one of them.

* It would be more consistent with that grammatical accuracy on which these critics occasionally love to descant, to
substitute the word Essayist for that of Review; but, even
waving this objection, how can the general title of Review be
fairly assumed by a work which does not notice, foreign literature included, in the course of its whole yearly series, as
many English books as issue from the London press alone in
one quarter of the time?

† Mr. Petrie's Statement of Facts relative to the Disturb-
ances in India.

Whatever may be the fate of the present performance, he feels confident that, as rather an uncommon exertion of industry in his own calling, it will attach no blemish to his humble name.

No. 41, *Pall Mall.*

CONTENTS.

BOOK I.

BOOK II.

CHAPTER I.

CHAPTER II.

BOOK III.

CHAPTER I.

CHAPTER II.

BOOK IV.

ON

THE ISLAND OF JAVA

1768—1771.

BOOK I.

CHAPTER I.

Situation of Java.—Straits of Sunda.—Prince's Island.—Dwars in den Weg.—Bay of Anjer.— Claim of the Dutch East India Company to the Sovereignty of the Straits of Sunda.—Bay of Bantam.—Road of Batavia.—Kingdom of Bantam—tributary to the Company.—Speech on the Appointment of a Successor to the Throne.—Empire of Jaccatra.—Cheribon.—The Soesoehoenam, or Emperor of Java.—The Sultan.—Principality of Madura.—Political Conduct of the Company towards the native Princes.

THE island of Java, which is one of the largest of those constituting the great Oriental Archipelago, is situated between 6° and 9° south latitude, and extends from 120° to 131° east longi-

tude from Teneriffe, being one hundred and
sixty-five Dutch miles in length. It lies nearly
in the direction of east and west; to the south
and west its shores are washed by the southern
Indian Ocean ; to the north-west lies the island
of Sumatra ; to the north, Borneo ; to the
north-east, Celebes ; and to the east, that of
Bali : from which last it is separated by a narrow passage, called the Straits of Bali.

The arm of the sea which runs between Java
and Sumatra, is known by the appellation of
the Straits of Sunda. The length of this channel is, on the Sumatra side, taken from the
Flat Point, to Varkens, or Hog Point, fifteen
German miles; and, on the Java side, from the
first point, or Java Head, to the point of Bantam, full twenty. In the mouth of the strait
lies Prince's Island, about a league and a half
from the coast of Java, and full six leagues from
Sumatra.

Prince's Island is low, and only about four
leagues in circumference. It has, however, two
hills, one at its east end, and the other a little
more to the south, which make it visible at a
moderate distance, especially the hill which lies
at the east end, and which is accordingly, by
navigators, called the High Hill ; the English
call it the Pike. At its s. w. side is a stone reef,
which, according to the charts, extends a league

and a half out to sea, and is dangerous for ships going through the passage between this island and Java. The island is covered with trees, and affords an agreeable prospect to the passing seamen : it is inhabited by Javanese, who subsist by fishing.

By the situation of Prince's Island, at the entrance of the Straits of Sunda, are formed two passages ; the one, running between Prince's Island and Java, has been called the Behouden, or Secured Passage, and is made use of, for the most part, by those ships which have to pass the straits during the south-east monsoon, in order that, sailing close in with the shore of Java, they may soon get within anchoring-depth, and not be in danger of being driven out to sea again, by the currents, which at that time of the year set strongly out of the straits to the westward.

The other passage, which is called by seamen Het Groote Gat, or the Great Channel, sometimes serves also as an entrance to the straits during the south-east monsoon; but it is with the greatest difficulty, and after a continued struggling with the south-easterly winds, and the currents, that this can be effected ; and not unfrequently five or six weeks are spent in working up a distance, which, in the west monsoon, is often sailed over in twice as many hours.

Notwithstanding the difficulty of entering the straits on this side, when these contrary winds and currents are in force, almost all the ships which fall to leeward, upon the west coast of Sumatra, as well as those which come from the west of India, are obliged to pass through this channel, as it is scarcely possible to reach the windward shore of Java, in the teeth of the south-east monsoon; and they therefore cannot generally avail themselves of the other passage.

The entrance of the straits, on this side, affords an uncommonly pleasing prospect, near the Sumatran shore. First, the Flat Point, which is low, and covered with trees, and behind it the majestic mountains of Sumatra, rising with a gradual ascent to the clouds; a little more forward, the Keizers, or Emperor's Island, lifts its high and spiry summit; farther on, the islands Kraketau, Slybzee, and Pulo Bicie, or the Iron Island, show their mountains covered with evergreens. The opposite coast of Java is not inferior to this, and improves continually in appearance, affording at the same time good anchorage, which is not to be met with on the Sumatra side. The numerous groves of cocoa-nut-palms, and the rice-fields in the back-ground, give the most pleasing ideas of the fertility of its soil.

Twelve or thirteen leagues from Prince's Island,

in the most narrow part of the strait, and opposite to Varkens, or Hog Point of Sumatra, lies
an island, which, on account of its situation,
exactly in the middle of the channel, has, with
great propriety, obtained the name of Dwars in
den Weg, Thwart the Way, or Middle Isle.   It
is low, and of little extent, with some small
reefs, which stretch out from it here and there.
Like all the islands in these seas, it is covered
with wood, and is believed to be uninhabited.

A strong current always runs through the passages on either side this island, setting, with the
prevailing easterly or westerly winds, either to
the north-east or to the south-west, although it
sometimes happens, that the current runs contrary to the direction of the wind, for a short
time.   Between Dwars in den Weg and the coast
of Java, and farther on to the point of Bantam,
there appears to be a settled current, independently of the wind.

Ships passing out through the Straits of Sunda,
often anchor in the bay of Anjer, in order to
take in their last supply of fresh water, from a
rivulet which runs from the mountains into the
sea, at this place, close to a little grove of cocoa-
nut-trees.   There is likewise a Javanese village,
which is under the jurisdiction of the king of
Bantam, and which has erroneously been reckoned, by some travellers, among the large cities

of Java, though it has nothing which can be construed into a town.

Not far from this is an islet or rock, entirely overgrown with brushwood; it is called the Brabandsch-hoedje; and a little farther to the north, a similar one, called the Toppers-hoedje * : this last is steep and bold, having fifty fathom depth close to it.

The Dutch East India Company claim an absolute sovereignty over the Straits of Sunda, and this is acknowledged by all the other powers. The Company require the salute, and have the right of interdicting this passage to all other nations, though they prudently do not enforce such right. The right is maintained as proceeding from the circumstance, that the land on both sides of the straits is tributary to the Company; viz. the kingdom of Bantam on the Java shore, and on the other side the land of Lampon, with that which lies farther westward, being conquered provinces belonging to Bantam. There is a resolution, on this subject, of the council of India, and articles are included in the secret orders which are given to the Company's ships bound to the west of India, respecting the salute to be required of the ships of other nations; but

* They are called the Cap and Button by English navigators.

which order is not to be opened, unless they chance to meet with such.

From Anjer to the point of Bantam, the country appears, in general, with high mountains inland, and a foreland more level. From this point, which is the northernmost extremity of Java, the land declines to the south-east, and makes a deep bay; and in the farthest part of the bight is situated the city of Bantam.

From the point of Pontang, which forms the eastern extremity of the bay of Bantam, as that just mentioned does the western, the land is every where very low; yet there are high mountains inland, among which the Blue Mountain towers above the rest. Although this mountain lies at a great distance, towards the south side of the island, and south-east from Batavia, yet it is seen before Bantam. It was formerly, as is related, a volcano; but nothing of this kind is at present perceivable.

The navigation from this place to the road of Batavia affords the most agreeable prospects, by the numerous small islands, covered with perpetual verdure, and which are strewed, as it were, along the sea. The anchoring ground is every where very good; but there are many rocks, from ten to eighteen feet under water, and which sometimes occasion much damage to the vessels which do not carefully avoid them. The

Batavian government, however, have caused buoys to be placed upon them, moored by heavy anchors; and upon some of them beacons are erected; but when these are washed away by the currents, the navigator must avoid the rocks by taking the bearings of the several islands.

The road of Batavia is justly esteemed one of the best in the world, as well with regard to the anchoring-ground, which consists of a soft clay, as to the safety it affords the ships which anchor in it, and to the number which it can contain. Although the road is open from the N.W. to E.N.E. and east, yet ships lie as secure and quiet as if they were landlocked, on account of the numerous islands which lie on that side, and break the force of the waves. Ships are never obliged to moor stem and stern here; and the current which runs within the islands is not strong, but without them it is very violent.

In the road, nearest to the town, lies a guard-ship, commonly called the admiral-ship, with an ensign at the top, from which, both in the day and in the night, such signals are made to the other ships in the road, as the commanding officer thinks requisite. For several years past it has been regulated, that one of the captains of the ships in the road should keep guard on board this ship, in order that, in case of accident, by fire or otherwise, some one may be always at hand, to give the necessary directions, as the other captains of the vessels generally pass the night in the city. On such occasions a signal is made from the admiral-ship, to give information, in order that the necessary assistance be immediately sent from the shore.

Before saying any thing of Batavia, it will not be improper ro relate how far the power of the East India Company extends over the whole island of Java, which is divided into four empires, or kingdoms, either wholly or in part subject to the dominion of the Company.

The first, to begin from the west, is the kingdom of Bantam; this is governed by its own kings, with full power of life and death over their subjects; yet they are tributary to the Company, paying a yearly acknowledgment of a hundred *bhars* of pepper, or 37,500 pounds weight; besides which, a strict engagement is entered into by the king, not to sell either pepper, or any produce of his country, to other nations. It must all be delivered to the Company, for a certain stipulated price; and this does not solely regard the pepper produced in his dominions in Java, but likewise all which is grown in his other territories, his conquered provinces, situated in the great island of Borneo, and in Sumatra, which likewise yield much pepper; and the Company have accordingly residencies

established, in the first, at Banjermassing, and
in the last, at Lampon Toulabouwa, which serve,
in the same way as Fort Speelwyk at Bantam,
to enforce the fulfilment of the treaties, and to
prevent a contraband trade.

The king of Bantam is also deprived of the
power of appointing his own successor, and the
Company nominate one of the royal family to
succeed him, as latterly took place in the year
1767.

The speech made, on that occasion, by Mr.
Ossenberg, ordinary counsellor of India, who
was deputed thither from Batavia, to represent
the united Dutch East India Company, as lord
paramount, from its peculiarity, is well worthy
of being inserted literally in this place, translated
out of the Malay, the language in which it was
delivered.

" His excellency the governor-general, and the
honourable the council of India, having thought
fit and resolved to appoint me commissary plenipotentiary to the court of Bantam, in order, at
the request of the king, to propose and appoint
his majesty's eldest son Pangorang (prince)
Gusti, hereditary prince, and successor to the
empire of Bantam ; and this desirable period
being now arrived, in consequence, I, the commissary aforesaid, in the name and behalf of the
general East India Company of the Nether-

lands, appoint the said pangorang, to be pangorang ratoo, or hereditary prince, and heir to
the crown and the whole empire of Bantam,
by the title of Abdul Mofagir Mohamed Ali
Joudeen.

" The commissary expects, that the said pangorang ratoo will, at all times, consider this his
important promotion, as a peculiar favour, and a
great benefit conferred upon him by the honourable Company; being adopted from this moment, as the grandson of the East India Company of the Netherlands; and that he will
henceforth, on all occasions, and in all times,
behave with integrity and gratitude towards
them, obeying the commands of the honourable
Company, and of the king his father, during
his whole life."

After the appointment, this harangue was again
read, by order of the commissary, in the Malay
language, in the presence of the king his father,
of all the grandees of his court, and a number
of the Company's servants, who had come from
Batavia, and belonged to the retinue of the
commissary; and the ceremony concluded with
playing of *gomgoms*, and other demonstrations
of joy.

The second empire in Java is that of Jaccatra, which is bounded, to the east, by that of
Cheribon, and to the west, by the kingdom of

Bantam. Jaccatra was formerly governed by its own kings; but the last of these having been subdued by the arms of the Company in the year 1619, they have ever since possessed it, by the right of conquest, as sovereigns. It is under the immediate government of the governor-general and council of India, and all the Javanese of Jaccatra are therefore born the Company's subjects. Before this revolution, Jaccatra was the capital of the empire; but Batavia, which is built very near the former, is now the chief place.

The third empire is that of Cheribon. This is under the dominion of three different princes, who are independent of the Company, and sovereigns in their respective districts. Yet they are their allies, and, in the same manner as the king of Bantam, they are bound, by treaty, to sell all the produce of their territories, exclusively to the Company, and not to permit any other nation than the Dutch to enter their dominions; for the due maintenance of which conditions, the Company likewise take care to guard and garrison their seaports.

These would be the only princes in Java, who possessed not only nominal, but also real sovereignty, were it not for the situation of their dominions, which lie between Jaccatra, and the empire of the Soesoehoenam, or emperor of Java, who is also a dependant on the Company; of whom they must of course stand in awe, and whose wishes they must in every respect observe; for if they do not, the Company make no scruple of dethroning one prince, and establishing another in his stead.

The Company exercised their power in this respect, in the commencement of the year 1769. One of these Cheribon princes, not treating his subjects well, was put under arrest, by orders from the council of India, and banished to the castle Victoria, in the island of Amboyna; while another prince of the blood was elevated to the vacant dignity, upon condition, however, of his furnishing a certain annual sum of money, for the support of his imprisoned predecessor.

The fourth empire is that of the Soesoehoenam, or emperor of Java, which is often called Soesoehoenam Mataram, from the place of his residence. This empire comprehended, of old, the greater part of the island: that of Cheribon once formed part of it, and it was then very powerful; but, since the Dutch have been established here, it has lost much of its lustre and importance. Yet it remained undivided till about the middle of the present century, when the emperor found himself so much embarrassed, in consequence of the rebellion of Manko Boeni, a prince of the blood, that he made a cession of his territories to the Company, who, in return, granted him the half back again as their vassal, and promised him their protection, engaging at the same time, never to make an emperor of Java, who was not a prince of the imperial family.

The empire being thus split into two parts, the other half was, in like manner, given to Manko Boeni, as the Company's vassal, under the title of Sultan, with a similar promise of protection, and engagement never to nominate any other than princes of his family, as suc-cessors to his dignity. This other half consti-tutes the fifth empire of Java.

To these may be added a sixth, though it does not properly belong to Java; being a separate island, but close to it: the island and princi-pality of Madura, which is divided from Java by a narrow strait. It is under the government of a prince, who is equally a vassal of the Com-pany, who also dispose of the succession.

All these princes are under engagements to deliver the produce of their respective countries to the Company alone, and not to sell any of it to another nation; likewise, not to enter into any connexions, or treaties, with other powers; and great care is taken to enforce these con-ditions, by the Company, whose numerous forts and garrisons, along the whole north coast of

Java, render the contravention of them extremely difficult, if not wholly impossible, to the native princes. Were they, however, all to unite against the Company, the latter would be in a very disagreeable predicament; but their mutual and unceasing jealousies and animosities are safeguards against this. Though the Company's government do not perhaps foment, yet they do not extinguish the flames of discord; which being always kept smouldering, make one native prince prevent whatever another may design against the Company.

It was likewise for very solid political reasons, that the empire of Java was allowed, or rather contrived, to be divided into two states; for such an extent of territory as it formerly comprehended, would always have made, whoever was its sole master, a dangerous neighbour to the Company, whereas, being under the dominion of two men, who are irreconcilable enemies, it is easily kept in entire subjection.

CHAPTER II.

Climate of Java.—Land and Sea Winds.—Mon-
soons.—Thunder-storms.—Rivers.—Productions.
—Pepper.—Rice.—Sugar.—Coffee.—Cotton-
yarn.—Salt.—Indigo.—Timber.—Fruits—Vast
Variety of them.—The Natives.—Their Cha-
racter.—Dress.—Customs.—Dwellings.—Food.
—Diversions.—Religion.—Physicians.—Agri-
culture.

JAVA is situated to the south of the equator, in
a climate which was thought uninhabitable by
the ancients, who believed that the scorching
heat rendered the land there so arid and barren,
as to be unable to produce any thing for the
subsistence of man.   This opinion originated
from their total ignorance of the interior parts of
Africa, which lie between the tropics, as well as
respecting the Indies, and the great peninsula
beyond the Ganges.   The improvements of navigation, in modern times, have exploded this
error, and proved that the lands near the equinoctial line, far from being barren and uninhabited, yield the palm in nothing, to less torrid
regions, and are able to feed full as many inha-

bitants, as the most fertile country in the temperate climates.

The idea, that the heat must be utterly insup-
portable in these parts, is not so absurd, for the
sun is twice a year vertically over them, and its
rays shoot almost always in a perpendicular line ;
so that it would be nearly as bad as was supposed,
if Nature herself did not come to their assistance,
by the refreshing land and sea breezes, which
blow here alternately throughout the year, and
so far moderate the heat, as to make it tolerable
to most men. As the rising and setting of the
sun is likewise always nearly at the same hour,
and scarcely differs more than a few minutes, the
long nights consequently cool the air so much,
that in the morning, for an hour or two before
daybreak, it may be rather said to be cold than
warm, especially by such people as have resided
here for some time.

From the month of July to November, the
thermometer of Fahrenheit was always, in the
hottest part of the day, between 84° and 90°,
excepting only one day, when it rose to 92°;
and in the greatest degree of coolness in the
morning, it was seldom lower than 76°. This
thermometer was placed in the open air, in the
city of Batavia, shaded both from the rays of the
sun, and from their reflection.

The barometer undergoes little or no variation,

and stands for a whole year at twenty-nine inches
ten lines, according to daily observations.

The warmth of the air decreases greatly, on
approaching the mountains, which lie towards
the southern parts of the island. At the country-
seat of the governor-general, called Buitenzorg
(rural care), situated full sixteen Dutch miles
south from Batavia, at the foot of the Blue
mountains, the cold is so great in the morning,
that not only thick clothes are requisite, but it is
difficult to become warm even with them. Dr.
Thunberg, who visited both Buitenzorg and
the Blue mountains, says, that the climate is
very healthy and refreshing, and the air, especially in the morning and evening, absolutely cold,
insomuch that, not having brought a great-coat
with him, he was " chilled, and perfectly
shivered with the cold evening air, in a country
that lies almost directly under the equator."

The land and sea winds blow here every day
without exception. The sea-breeze, which in
the east monsoon is generally confined between
E. N. E. and north, but in the west monsoon runs
as far as N. W. and farther, begins to blow about
eleven or twelve o'clock in the forenoon. It
increases gradually in the afternoon till evening,
and then dies imperceptibly away, till about
eight or nine o'clock, when it is perfectly calm.
The land-wind begins at midnight, or just be-

fore, and continues till an hour or two after sunrise, when it generally again falls calm, till the sea-breeze comes on at its accustomed hour.

The year is divided into two seasons, one of which is called the east monsoon, or dry season, and the other the west monsoon, or rainy season.

The east, or good monsoon commences in the months of April and May, and ends in the latter end of September, or the beginning of October. The trade-winds then blow, about four or five leagues off shore, and through the whole of the Indian seas to the south of the line, from the s. e. and e. s. e. , at times, however, running as far as s. s. e. with fine dry weather, and a clear sky.

The west, or bad monsoon, generally begins in the latter end of November or beginning of December. The wind often blows with great violence, and is accompanied by heavy torrents of rain, which render this season very unhealthy, and a time of the greatest mortality. The same winds are likewise found to prevail every where to the south of the line. They continue till the latter end of February or the beginning of March, and are very variable till April; in which month the easterly winds begin to blow: hence these months, as likewise October and part of November, are called the shifting months; and the times of the breaking up of the mon-

soons are esteemed, at Batavia, the most unhealthy of all.

It is very remarkable, that, when the westerly
winds blow as far as nine or ten degrees south of
the line, the contrary takes place, at the same
time, and to the same distance, to the north of
it; and *vice versa,* when the westerly winds prevail to the north, the easterly winds blow to the
south of the line; which alternation is greatly
helpful to the navigation westward of Java.

For some years past, it has been observed at
Batavia, that the commencement of the mon-
soons begins to be very uncertain, so that neither
their beginning nor their end can be depended
upon with so much certainty as formerly; the
cause of which has not hitherto been discovered.

Thunder-storms are very frequent at Batavia,
especially towards the conclusion of the mon-
soons, when they occur almost every evening.
They, however, seldom do much damage.

There are no large rivers in Java navigable by
vessels of even a moderate burden, but many
small ones, which, flowing from the mountains
in a northerly direction, run into the sea, all
along the northern coast; they are, however,
mostly choked up at the mouth by sands or
mud-banks, which render their entrances, at low
water, very difficult to the smallest vessels.

On the bank, or bar, before Batavia, the flood

rises about six feet, though at spring-tides, as every where, it is more. High and low water, likewise, only occur once in four-and-twenty hours.

The productions of the island are considerable, and of great importance to the Company ; more particularly for the last .thirty years, in which period the cultivation of coffee and other articles has been assiduously prosecuted and encouraged.

The chief produce is pepper, which is mostly grown in the western part of the island. This spice is produced from a plant of the vine kind, *piper nigrum,* which twines its tendrils round poles or trees, like ivy or hops. The pepper-corns grow in bunches close to each other. They are first green, but afterwards turn black. When dried they are separated from the dust, and partly from the outward membranous coat, by means of a kind of winnow, called a harp, and then laid up in warehouses. This winnow, or harp, is an oblong frame, with a bottom of iron wire closely twisted, so that the pepper-corns cannot pass through it ; this is set sloping, and the ungarbled pepper rolling along it, frees itself from most of its impurities.

The empire of Bantam, with its dependencies at Lampon, yield annually to the Company more than six millions of pounds of this spice. This pepper is esteemed the next best to that which comes from the coast of Malabar. That from Palembang, of which likewise a very considerable quantity is delivered to the Company, as well as that of Borneo, is of a much inferior quality.

The price for which the king of Bantam is obliged to sell all the pepper produced in his dominions, is fixed at six rixdollars, or fourteen gilders and eight stivers per picol of one hundred and twenty-five pounds, nearly two-pence half-penny per pound.

It has been the opinion of many, that the white pepper is the fruit of a plant distinct from that which produces the black ; this, however, is not the case ; they are both the same production ; but the white is manufactured by being laid in lime, which takes off its outer coat and renders it whitish. This is done before the pepper is perfectly dry.

Rice, *oryza sativa*, is the second product of Java, and is collected in large quantities, especially in the empire of Java proper. It grows chiefly in low fenny ground. After it has been sown, and has shot up about two or three hand-breadths above the ground, it is transplanted by little bundles of six or more plants, in rows ; then by damming up the many rivulets which abound in this country, the rice is inundated in the rainy season, and kept under water till the stalks have attained sufficient strength ; when the land is drained, by opening the dams, and it is soon dried by the great heat of the sun.

At the time of the rice-harvest, the fields have much the same appearance as our wheat and barley fields, and afford an equally rich scene of golden uniformity.

The sickle is not used in reaping the rice, but instead of it a small knife, with which the stalk is cut about a foot under the ear; this is done one by one, and they are then bound into sheaves, the tenth of which is the reward of the mower.

The *paddee*, which is the name given to the rice whilst in the husk*, does not grow, like wheat and barley, in compact ears, but, like oats, in loose spikes. It is not threshed, to separate it from the husk, but stamped in large wooden blocks, hollowed out; and the more it is stamped the whiter it becomes when boiled. The native Indians throughout the East use this grain as bread, and as their principal food.

Java has been called the granary of the East, on account of the immense quantity of rice

---

* The following, besides many others, are names applied to rice, in its different stages of growth and preparation : *paddee*, original name of the seed : *oossay*, grain of last season; *bumee*, the rice-plants before transplantation ; *bras* or *bray*, rice stripped of its husk; *charroop*, rice cleaned for boiling ; *nassee*, boiled rice, &c.

which it produces. The other islands in this neighbourhood yield little or none, except Celebes, where enough is grown to provide Amboyna with this staff of life.

In the year 1767 the quantity of fourteen thousand tons of rice was required, and furnished, for the consumption of Batavia, Ceylon, and Banda, from the island of Java.

Sugar is produced in large quantities in Java, and brought to Batavia. The quantity of thirteen millions of pounds, manufactured in the year 1768 in the province of Jaccatra alone, is sufficient to show with what luxuriance the sugar-cane, *saccharum officinarum*, flourishes here. Much of it is exported to the west of India, to Surat and the coast of Malabar and the rest to Europe. Most of the sugar-mills are kept and worked by Chinese.'

A fourth production of the island is coffee. The plantations of it are, however, peculiarly confined to the provinces of Cheribon and Jaccatra. The tree, *coffea*, which produces this berry, was first introduced into Java in 1722 or 1723, under the government of the governor-general Zwaardekroon, who greatly encouraged the cultivation of it among the Javanese. It is so much multiplied, that in 1768 Jaccatra furnished 4,465,500 pounds weight to the Company, who paid four rixdollars per picol, being

equal to about 14*s*. 5*d*. sterling per cwt. ; but
other accounts make this article stand them in
the same proportion as the pepper, two-pence
halfpenny per pound, or about 1*l*. 2*s*. per cwt.:
the first is probably what is paid to the cultivators, and the last the invoice value, with the addition of the charges.

Cotton yarn is likewise an important object of
trade, which Java furnishes to the Company.
It is spun by the Javanese from the cotton produced, in great plenty, in the interior parts.
The province of Jaccatra yielded, in 1768, no
more than 133 picois, or 16,225 pounds, which
was 1875 pounds less than ought to have been
delivered by the Indians, according to the quota
imposed upon them ; but this deficiency was occasioned by a season of uncommon drought, by
which the cotton crop had been materially injured.

Salt, much of which is brought from Rembang to Batavia, is also an article of trade for
the Company, who dispose of it for a handsome
profit at the west coast of Sumatra.

Another product is indigo, which is mostly
shipped to Europe. The culture of the plant
which produces this dye, *indigofera tinctoria*, is
prosecuted with vigour in the province of Jaccatra. In the year 1768 the natives were as-

sessed at 6125 pounds, though they only furnished 2875 pounds.

Large quantities of heavy timber are also
brought from the north-east coast of Java to
Batavia. This is not, in reality, a branch of trade
for the Company; but it is of great importance
for ship-building, and other purposes.

The great importance of this island to the
Company is very apparent. It produces some of
their most considerable articles of commerce,
and provides the greater part of their Indian
possessions with food, besides furnishing materials for ship-building.

The island is extremely abundant in fruit-
trees. First is the cocoanut-palm, *cocos nucifera*,
which is well known; the *suri*-tree, which yields
the palm-wine, or toddy; china-oranges, *citrus
aurantium*, of which there are two sorts, one of a
large, and the other of a smaller size; the tama-
rind-tree, *tamarindus indica*, the fruit of which
consists in pods, containing the tamarind, a
spungy substance, in which the beans or stones
are inclosed: the *pompelmoes*, or shaddock, *citrus
decumanus*, the fruit of which is most wholesome,
on account of its refreshing quality and taste.
It is a large lemon, of the size of a child's head;
the juice is moderately acid, and quenches thirst;
it is cooling, antiseptic, and antiscorbutic.

Next the *durioon*, or *drioon* tree, the fruit of

which is inclosed in a hard shell, of the size of a
man's head, and sometimes larger; it has a most
disagreeable smell, which is extremely offensive
to those who have never eaten of it; when once,
however, the fruit is tasted, the loathing which
its odour is apt to excite is quickly overcome,
and use makes it, in the end, so familiar, that
it is generally preferred beyond all other fruits.
It is a strong stimulative, and is therefore much
prized by the Chinese. The tree is large and lofty;
the leaves are small in proportion, but in themselves long and pointed. The blossoms grow in
clusters, on the stem and larger branches. The
petals are five, of a yellowish white, surrounding
five bunches of stamina, each bunch containing
about twelve, and each stamen having four antheræ. The pointal is knobbed at top. When
the stamina and petals fall, the empalement resembles a fungus, and is nearly the shape of a
Scotch-bonnet. The fruit is not unlike the bread-
fruit, but larger and rougher on the outside. It
has by some been confounded with the bread-
fruit. It is considered as diuretic and sudorific,
and serviceable in expelling wind.

The *sursak*-tree has a fruit similar to the *durioon*,
but it is not accompanied by such a fetid smell; it
seems to be the *nanca*, or jakes, of Cook, and the
boa nanca (radermachia) of Thunberg; or what is
commonly called the jack, by the English: at

Batavia, it is generally of the size of a large melon ; its smell somewhat resembles that of mellow apples, mixed with garlick ; the outer coat is covered with angular prickles, and contains a number of seeds, or kernels, which, when roasted, eat like chesnuts, inclosed in a fleshy substance, of a rich, but, to strangers, strong flavour, but which gains upon the taste.

The *mango* tree, *mangifera indica*, deserves equally to be noticed ; its fruit, when ripe, is of a thin, oblong shape, and about the size of a goose's egg. Its coat is not thick, of a yellow colour, and soft. When peeled, it has a fleshy substance. Within it is of an orange colour, like a melon, to which its flavour has some analogy ; but a good mango is much more delicious. In the centre is a large kernel. When green it is made into *attjar* (a common name for all articles preserved in vinegar with spices) ; for this the kernel is taken out, and the space filled up with ginger, pimento, and other spicy ingredients, after which it is pickled in vinegar, and is sent to all parts.

The *mango-tanges*, or mangosteen, *garcinia manganosta*, is esteemed the most delicious fruit of the Indies. It is generally of the size of an apple, and resembles a pomegranate in appearance, only it is larger and thicker, and its coat is not so tough. The fruit, when stripped of

the outward rind, appears like a little apple, of
a snow-white hue, composed of six or seven
lobes, of the size of the joint of a finger, with
a black stone in the inside ; they are very soft
and juicy, and their flavour is delightfully refreshing beyond description.   The taste approaches nearest to that of the peach ; but it is
rather more mellow.   The tree is about the size
of that of a common plum.   Some assert that
they have been cured of a dysentery of long
standing by eating large quantities of this fruit;
though others are of opinion, that it produces
a contrary effect.   The rind has a strong astringent power, and might perhaps be used as a dye
for a fine deep red colour.   The Chinese use
the rind of the mangosteen for dying black.

Lemon, *citrus medica*, and lime trees, are in
great plenty, as is also a certain fruit called *ka-
tappa*, *terminalia catappa*, like our walnuts, but
better tasted.   It grows upon a high tree, which
affords an agreeable shade, and is inclosed in a
green husk, where it lies in rolls, and is as white
as milk.

Pinc-apples, *bromelia ananas*, are produced in
large quantities, and are therefore little esteemed
at Batavia ; they are generally sold for the value
of a stiver (penny) apiece, and sometimes for
less.

Besides these, the fruits most worthy of remark are the *pisang*, or bananas, *musa paradisiaca*, of which there are several sorts; the best, *pisang radja*, is delicious and wholesome, with a thin coat and an inner pulp, which is sweetish, and somewhat mealy; it is eaten both raw and dressed in various ways. The *jamboo, eugenia malaccensis*, is of a deep red colour and oval shape; the largest not bigger than a small apple; it is pleasant and cooling, though it has not much flavour. The *jamboo-eyer-mauer, eugenia jambos*, both smells and tastes like conserve of roses. The *papaya, carica papaya*, is as large as a small melon, and the yellow pulp within has nearly the same taste. The sweetsop, *annona squamosa*, consists of a mass of large kernels, from which the surrounding pulp, which is very sweet and mealy, is sucked. The custard-apple, *annona reticulata*, derives its English name from the likeness which its white and rich pulp bears to a custard. The *rambutan, nephelium lappaceum*, grows in large clusters, and very much resembles a chesnut with the husk on; the eatable part is small in quantity, but its acid is rich and pleasant, and perhaps more agreeable than any other in the whole vegetable kingdom. The *bilimbing, averrhoa belimbi*, the *bilimbing besse, averrhoa carambola*, and the *cherimelle, averrhoa acida*, are three species of one genus, and though they differ in shape, are nearly the same in taste: the first is oblong, of the thickness of a finger, and so sour that it cannot be eaten alone ; the *bilim-bing besse* is an egg-like pentagonal fruit, about the size of a pear, and is the least acid of the three ; the last is extremely acid, and of a small roundish irregular shape, growing in clusters close to the branch, and containing each a single seed; they all make excellent pickles and sour sauce. The *guava, psidium,* is well known in the West Indies. The *boa bidarra, rhamnus jujuba,* is a round yellow fruit, about the size of a gooseberry ; its flavour is that of an apple, but it has the astringency of a crab. The *nam-nam, cynometra cauliflora,* in shape somewhat resembles a kidney ; it is about three inches long, and the outside is very rough ; it is seldom eaten raw. The *suntul, trichilia,* within a thick skin, contains kernels like those of the mangosteen, but which are both acid and astringent. The *madja, limoni,* has, under a hard brittle shell, a lightly acid pulp, which cannot be eaten without sugar. The *salac, calamus ro-tang zalacca,* is the fruit of a prickly bush, and has a singular appearance, being covered with scales, like those of a lizard ; it is nutritious and well-tasted, in flavour somewhat resembling a strawberry. The *fokke fokkes, solanum melongena,* is of a purple-blue colour, shaped like a pear, and of various sizes ; it has an agreeable taste when

boiled. Water-melons, *arbuses,* are in great
plenty and very good. Grapes, melons, pumpkins, promegranates, and figs, appear to be the
only European fruits at Batavia, though straw-
berries and some others are said to thrive in the
interior parts of the country.

The native inhabitants are all commonly called
Javanese, whether they belong to the kingdom
of Bantam or to any other part of Java; those
of Madura bear the name of their island. They
are of a middling size, and in general well-
proportioned, of a light brown colour, with a
broad forehead and a flattish nose, which has a
small curve downwards at the tip. Their hair is
black, and is always kept smooth and shining,
with cocoanut-oil. They are in general proud,
lazy, and cowardly. Their principal weapon is
kris, a kind of dagger, like a small hunting-
knife, and which they always carry with them.
The handle or hilt is made of different materials,
more or less valuable, according to the wealth or
dignity of the wearer. The blade is well-
hardened steel, of a serpentine shape, and thus
capable of making a large and wide wound. It
is often poisoned, and in that case causes immediate death. Arrogant towards their inferiors,
they are no less cringing to their superiors, or
those from whom they have any favour to expect.
Their dress consists in a piece of cotton, which

they wrap round the waist, and drawing it between the legs, fasten it behind. They are otherwise naked, except that they wear a small cap. This is the dress of the common people. Those of more consideration wear a wide Moorish coat of flowered cotton, or other stuff, and in general turbans, instead of caps. They suffer no hair but that of the head to grow, and eradicate it carefully wherever it appears elsewhere.

The dress of the women is little better than that of the men : it consists in a piece of cotton-cloth, which they call *saron*, and which, wrapping round the body, just covers the bosom, under which it is fastened, and hangs down to the knees, and sometimes to the ancles : the shoulders and part of the back remain uncovered. The hair of the head, which they wear very long, is turned up, and twisted round like a fillet, fastened with long bodkins of different sorts of wood, tortoise-shell, silver, or gold, according to the rank or wealth of the lady. This head-dress is called a *condé*, and is also in vogue among the Batavian ladies. It is often adorned with a variety of flowers.

The men and women are very fond of bathing, especially in the morning. Children of both sexes go entirely naked, till about eight or nine years of age; twelve or thirteen is their age of puberty.

The Javanese are polygamists; they marry as many wives as they can maintain, and take their female slaves for concubines. This, however, of course, does not occur with the common people, who must be content with one wife, because they cannot afford to keep more. The women are proportionally more comely than the men, and are very fond of white men. They are jealous in the extreme, and know how to make an European, with whom they have had a love-affair, and who proves inconstant, dearly repent his incontinence and his fickleness, by administering certain drugs, which disqualify him for the repetition of either. People of the utmost credibility at Batavia have related too many examples of this refinement of female revenge, to render the circumstance doubtful.

Their dwellings may, with greater propriety, be called huts, than houses. They are constructed of split bamboos, interlaced or matted, plastered with clay, and covered with *attap*, or the leaves of the cocoa-nut tree. The entrance is low, and has neither door nor shutter. The whole house usually consists of but one apartment, in which husband, wife, children, and sometimes poultry, of which they keep a great many, pig together on the ground. They always choose a shady place for building, or plant trees all round. Such as possess more property, are provided with a little more comfort and convenience; but it is always in a wretched, paltry manner.

Their chief food is boiled rice with a little fish, and their drink water. They do not, however, reject arrack, when they can obtain it. They are almost continually chewing betel, or *pinang*, and likewise a sort of tobacco produced here, and therefore denominated Java tobacco, which they also smoke, through pipes made of reed : they sometimes put opium into their pipes, with the tobacco, in order to invigorate their spirits; but the continual use of it rather deadens them : some, who have been too immoderate in this indulgence, sit like statues, with open fixed eyes, and speechless.

They have no tables nor chairs, but sit upon the ground, or upon mats, with their legs crossed under them. They neither make use of knives, forks, nor spoons, but eat with their fingers. They have a certain kind of musical instruments, called *gomgoms*, consisting of hollow iron bowls, of various sizes and tones, upon which a man strikes with an iron or wooden stick; their harmony is not disagreeable, and they are not unlike a set of bells.

Cockfighting, for which they keep a peculiar breed, is a favourite diversion. Though never so poor, they will sooner dispose of every other part of their property, than their game-cocks. They are, besides, obliged to pay a tax to the Company for these fowls; and this duty is yearly farmed at Batavia, and forms part of the revenues of the province of Jaccatra. In the year 1770 it amounted to about 35*l.* 10*s.* per month; it is, however, peculiar to that province.

A kind of tennis-play is also a favourite diversion among them, and they are very handy and dexterous at it. They strike the ball with their feet, knees, or elbows, whither they choose, and receive it back; thus keeping it for some time in continual motion, without its touching the ground: the ball is generally of the size of a man's head, hollow, and made of matted reeds.

Their manner of salutation consists in touching the forehead with the right hand, accompanied by a slight inclination of the body.

The Mahomedan religion is predominant over the whole island. It is said, that far inland, over the mountains, towards the south side of the island, some of the aboriginal idolatrous natives are still to be met with. Mosques, or places of prayer of the Mahomedans, are erected all over the island; there is a very famous one near Cheribon. They are very particular about the tombs of their saints, and will suffer nothing unbecoming to be done upon or near them.

They have both male and female physicians, who have been known to effect very surprising cures by their knowledge of the medicinal and vulnerary herbs produced in their country. They have sometimes greater practice among the Europeans at Batavia, than those physicians who have been regularly bred, and come from Europe; but they know nothing of anatomy. Much friction of the affected parts, is one of their chief means of cure. This is done with two fingers of the right hand, which are pressed down by the left, and passed continually downwards, after having first anointed the part with water mixed with fine ground wood or oil.

For the purposes of agriculture, they use buffaloes instead of horses, of which, however, there are plenty, but of a diminutive size. The buffaloes are very large animals, bigger and heavier than our largest oxen, furnished with great ears, and horns which project straight forward, and bend inwards. A hole is bored through the cartilage of the nose, and these huge animals are guided by a cord which is passed through it. They are generally of an ash-grey colour, and have little eyes. They are so accustomed to be conducted three times a day into the water, to cool themselves, that without it they cannot be brought to work. The female gives milk, but it is little valued by the Europeans, on account of its acrimonious nature.

CHAPTER III.

Batavia.—The River of Jaccatra.—Water-fort.— Bar at the Mouth of the River.—The Castle.— Buildings in and near it.—Walls of the City.— Gates.—Admiralty-wharf.—Quarter for Workmen.—Churches.—Houses.—Chinese Houses.— Massacre of the Chinese.—Assessment on Rents. —Bank of Batavia.—Suburbs.—Chinese Campon.—Character of the Chinese.—Their Appearance.—Dress.—Religion. — Temples. — Divination.—Tombs.—Environs of Batavia.—Roads. —Streets.

The city of Batavia, styled the Queen of the East, on account of the beauty of its buildings, and the immense trade which it carries on, is situated very near the sea, in a fertile plain, in the kingdom of Jaccatra, upon the river of that name, which, running through the middle of the town, divides it into two parts. To the north of the city is the sea-shore; behind it, to the south, the land rises with a gentle, and scarcely perceptible, acclivity to the mountains, which lie fifteen or sixteen Dutch miles, or leagues, inland; one of these, which is very high, bears the name of the Blue mountain.

In 1619, the governor-general, John Pieter-

sen Coen, took the town of Jaccatra, which he
in a great measure destroyed, and founded another city, not exactly on the same spot, but very
near it, to which he gave the name of Batavia,
though it is said, that he much wished to have
called it New Horn, from the place of his nati-
vity, Horn, in North Holland. Although then
an inconsiderable place, in point of strength and
beauty, he declared it the capital of the Dutch
settlements in India: his choice of the situation
was so just, his plan so well contrived, and every
thing throve so fast under his care, that Batavia
rose with unparalleled rapidity to that magnifi-
cence and importance, which have rendered it the
admiration and the dread of all the more eastern nations of the Indies; and which still dazzle
and overawe them, although the city has, for
these last fifty years, greatly declined, both as to
opulence and population.

The city is an oblong square, the shortest sides
facing the north and south, and the longest the
east and west. Through the middle of it, from
south to north, runs the river of Jaccatra, over
which there are three bridges, one at the upper end
of the town, another at the lower part, near the
castle, and the third about the middle, and thence
called the Middle-point bridge. Two of these
are built of stone. Close by the middlemost is
a large square redoubt, provided with some

pieces of cannon, which command the river, both up and downwards.

The breadth of the river, within the city, is about 160 or 180 feet. It runs into the sea, past the castle and the admiralty-wharf. On both sides of the mouth are long piers of wood and brick-work, about 3800 feet in length, taken from the moat of the city. The eastern pier, which was repaired, and in a great measure rebuilt, a few years ago, cost the Company 36,218 rixdollars in timber, and 36,320 rixdollars in masonry, making, at forty-eight stivers, $f.174,091,4$, about 16,000l. sterling; a large sum, when it is considered, that the timber costs the Company but little money, as it is produced in abundance in Java.

The vessels belonging to the free merchants are laid up and repaired between these piers on the west side; but along the east side, the passage remains open for the lighters, which go in and out of the city, with the cargoes of the ships.

At the outward point of the eastern pier is a shed for the horses which draw the small vessels and boats up and down the river.

Opposite to this is a hornwork, commonly called the Water-fort, built during the government of the governor-general Van Imhoff, at an immense expense to the Company; for several large ships were obliged to be sunk, on account of the depth of water on the spot, in order to lay a good foundation for building the fort. It is constructed of a kind of coral-rock, and defended by several heavy cannon * : within it are barracks for the garrison ; and there is no other approach to it than along the western pier. It is at present very much out of repair, and the walls begin to sink and fall in many places.

The objects for which this fort was erected, seem to have been the defence of the road, and of the entrance of the river ; yet in both these respects it is now of little advantage, for the anchoring-place is so far removed from this fortification, by the increase of the mud-bank which lies before the river, that, although its guns might reach the ships in the road, little damage could be done on either side, at such a distance † ; and as to what regards the defence of the river's mouth, that is of very trifling importance ; for the daily and continual increase of the bar

* In 1793, when Lord Macartney visited Batavia, this fort had, mounted and dismounted, fourteen guns and two howitzers.

† Ary Huysers, who wrote an account of the Dutch settlements in India, in 1789, and had been at Batavia a few years before, says, that in his time a trial had been made of the heavy artillery at the mouth of the harbour, and that it was found sufficient to command and protect the whole extent of the road.

renders the water much too shallow for large vessels, and an enemy would never seek to effect a landing there, but would always prefer an easy, firm sea-beach, such as is to be met with beyond Ansjol *.

The above-mentioned bank or bar lies directly before the mouth of the river, and extends a great way to the west, and but a little to the east; for which reasons, such vessels as are deeply laden, must go round by the east side, close along the eastern pier, in order to get within the bar. It is continually increasing towards the road, by which the place where the ships lie is more and more removed from the city. To the westward it is dry in some places.

Right before the mouth of the river, from which the most shallow part of the bank is distant about 600 or 650 feet, there is at low water no more than a foot or a foot and a half, so that a common ship's boat cannot get over it, but must also go round its east end. When the

---

* At Ansjol, and at Tanjongpoura, to the eastward of the city, on the sea-coast, are strong forts, and to the westward, at Ankay, Tangorang, and the Kwal. On the land-side, Batavia is further covered by the forts at Jaccatra, the Watering-place, Ryswick, &c.; though these are merely defences against the natives, and are most of them little better than fortified houses.

sea-breeze blows fresh, it makes a troublesome
and cockling sea ; and a west or bad, monsoon,
seldom passes, without the loss of some vessels
upon it.

This shoalness of the water is said to be the
consequence of a violent earthquake which took
place in Java in the latter end of the last century, and by which the river of Jaccatra was
partly stopped up; yet the greatest increase of
the bank has been since the year 1730 ; and it
is to be apprehended that the river will in time
become wholly unnavigable and useless.

The castle, or citadel, of Batavia, which
forms the north boundary of the eastern division
of the city, is a regular square fortress, with four
bastions, which are connected by high curtains,
except on the south side, where the curtain was
broken down during the government of Baron
Van Imhoff. The walls and ramparts are built
of coral-rock, and are about twenty feet in
height. It is surrounded by a wet ditch, over
which, on the south side, lies a drawbridge.
Between the moat and the buildings within the
fort, on this side, is a large area or esplanade.
In the centre of the buildings looking towards
the city, is a great gate and broad passage, with
warehouses on each side, leading to another
esplanade on the north side, inclosed between

the ramparts and the buildings, all which is appropriated to the use of the Company *.

The government-house, which forms the left wing of the buildings to the south, is provided with numerous and convenient apartments, but is at present uninhabited. In it is a large hall, where the council of India generally assemble twice a week; this is adorned with the portraits of all the governors-general since the establishment of the Company.

Close by is a little church, or chapel, usually called the Castle-church; and somewhat more forwards a guard-house, where a party of dragoons always mount guard.

Over the castle-bridge there is a great plain, or square, planted with tamarind-trees, which afford a very agreeable shade. The entrance to it from the city is over a bridge, through a large and stately gate. This is surmounted by a bold

---

* Captain Parish's account of this fortress, in Macartney's Embassy to China, 1793, is as follows:—" A little above was the castle; a regular square fort, but without ravelins or other outworks. It had two guns mounted on each flank, and two, or sometimes three, on each face; they were not *en barbette*, nor properly *en embrasure*, but in a situation between both, having both their disadvantages, without the advantages of either. The wall was of masonry, about twenty-four feet high. It had no ditch, but a canal surrounded it at some distance. It had no cordon. The length of the exterior side of the work was about 700 feet."

cupola, from which rises an octagon turret,
containing the only public clock to be met with
at Batavia.   It was built under the government
of Baron Van Imhoff, as appears by an inscription over the gateway, and forms no trifling em-
bellishment of the city.

On the left side of the gate is a large building,
used as a guard-house, having in front a long
gallery, resting upon a row of pillars, and where
a captain's guard of grenadiers is generally
posted.

On the west side of the square stand the
Company's artillery-house, and the dispensary,
or provision-magazine, both of which reach
back to the river-side, so that the goods are taken
in and out of the lighters with the greatest ease.
This is an advantage which is possessed by almost
all the Company's warehouses and repositories in
Batavia.

On the opposite side are the iron-magazine, and
what is termed the grass-plot, being the place of
execution for criminals : this is an artificial
square eminence, upon which are a gallows and
some posts ; behind it is a small building, with
windows looking towards the place of execution,
whence the counsellors of justice behold the
completion of their sentences.   It is customary
throughout Holland and its dependencies, for
the magistrates, or judges, who have passed

sentence upon criminals, to preside at the execution of it. This is, in Europe, generally done
upon some open place before their town-halls,
from the windows of which the magistrates,
dressed in their robes of ceremony, behold the
execution.

A number of pieces of artillery, iron and brass,
and of all sorts and sizes, together with other
warlike implements, are ranged upon the plain.
Any one may ride through the gate just mentioned, as far as the drawbridge of the castle,
but not over it, unless he have the rank of senior
merchant.

The city is encircled by a wall of coral-rock *,
defended by twenty-two bastions, or bulwarks,
all provided with artillery, and surrounded by a
broad moat, in which there is seldom any want
of water, that being conveyed into it from the
river.

Batavia has five gates; one at the east side,
which is called the Rotterdam gate; two to the
south, the New gate, and the Diest gate; one
to the west, the Utrecht gate; and one on the
north side, west of the river, called the Square
gate.

* Sir George Staunton says, that part of the town-wall is
constructed of lava, which is of a dark blue colour, of a very
hard dense texture, emits a metallic sound, and closely resembles
some of the lava of Vesuvius.

Near the last-mentioned gate, and opposite to the castle, is the admiralty-wharf; and not far off, the warehouses for naval stores, as likewise the workshops of the carpenters, coopers, sail-makers, and smiths, with other offices connected with the shipping. Here are also the houses of the commandants and comptrollers of equipment, who were formerly obliged to reside upon the wharf; but for some years past this regulation has not been observed, and they now live in more pleasant parts of the town.

In the south-east corner of the city, close to the ramparts, lies the *Ambagtskwartier,* or the workmen's quarter, in which all the mechanics and labourers who are employed by the Company in their buildings, have their abode. The journeymen work here under masters of their respective trades, carpenters, smiths, plumbers, braziers, masons, and others, who are all accountable to the chief of the quarter, who is called *fabriek,* or head workman, and has generally the rank of merchant. Besides a great number of Europeans who are employed here, there are full a thousand slaves, by whom the Company incurs an enormous expense, with little benefit from their labour, which generally turns to the advantage of individual members of the government.

Within the city are three churches for the reformed religion, in which service is performed in the Dutch, Portuguese, and Malay languages; and one without the gates, which is called the outer Portuguese church. Besides these a Lutheran church was built during the government of Baron Van Imhoff, not far from the castle; this is provided with a fine organ and a very handsome pulpit.

There is a town-hall, with other public buildings. The houses are mostly of brick, run up in a light airy manner, and stuccoed on the outside, with sash windows. Within they are almost all built upon a similar plan, the fronts being in general narrow, though there are a few which are more extended.

On entering the door there is a narrow passage, and on one side a parlour; then you come into a large long room, lighted from an inner court, which trenches upon this apartment, and renders its form irregular. This is called the gallery, and is the place where the family usually live and dine. The floors are of large, square, dark red stones. No hangings are to be seen, but the walls are neatly stuccoed and whitened. The furniture consists in some arm-chairs, two or three sofas, and a great many looking-glasses, which the Europeans, in these regions, are very fond of. Several chandeliers and lamps are hung in a row, along the length of the gallery, which

are lighted up in the evening. The stairs leading
to the upper rooms are generally at the end of
this apartment. Six or seven steps up, is one
which stands over the store-room, or cellar, where
the stock of wine, beer, butter, &c. is kept. Up
stairs the houses are distributed almost the same
as below. They are in general but poorly provided with furniture; and the setting out of
rooms is not so much in vogue here as in Holland; nothing is added which is superfluous,
or more than is wanted for use. Behind the
gallery are the lodgings for the slaves, the kitchen, &c. Few houses have gardens, and there
are not even the least vestiges of there ever having been gardens behind the houses. In several,
the windows are closed with a lattice-work of
rattans, instead of being glazed, for the sake of
air.

The above relates only to the houses of Europeans, which are the greatest in number. The
few Chinese who live at present within the city,
have very wretched houses, the inside of which
is very irregularly distributed. They mostly
dwell in the southern and western suburbs,
called the Chinese Campon. Before the revolt
of the year 1740, they had the best quarter of
the city allotted to them, to the west of the great
river; but when, in that commotion, all their

houses were burnt to the ground *, the whole
quarter was made into a *passar*, or market, where

* The following account of this massacre, extracted from
a very recent and intelligent Dutch writer, Ary Huysers, who
was long resident at Batavia, may not be unacceptable —" A
little before the perpetration of this massacre, several thousand
Chinese adventurers and fortune-hunters had resorted to Batavia, allured by the prosperity of their countrymen already
settled there. The great number of these new colonists, together with the robberies and murders which were committed
by them, excited no little degree of just apprehension. The
famous Van Imhoff, who was at that time a member of the
council, proposed, in order to get rid of these useless and dangerous new-comers, that every Chinese who could not prove
that he had an honest livelihood, should be seized and transported to Ceylon, there to be employed in mining, or other labour, for the service of the Company. This advice was approved and immediately followed. A great number of Chinese
were seized and put in irons; but imprudently several Chinese
of property were secured by the under-officers charged with
the execution of the order, and were only liberated on paying
large sums of money. This occasioned great murmurs, and led
the rest of the nation to credit a report which was spread
abroad, that those who were unable to pay would be drowned
or otherwise put to death. They in consequence retired by
thousands from the city towards the interior parts, and strengthened themselves so much as to render the fate of Batavia itself
precarious. In this dilemma the council first offered an am-
nesty to the discontented Chinese, but this they rejected with
scorn; and purposing to exterminate the whole Christian settlement, began by ravaging the country in the wildest manner,
burning the sugar-works, and marching down to the gates of
the city. Here however they met with a severe repulse. The
civil and military inhabitants united in resisting them, and

all kinds of provisions are now daily exposed to
sale.

---

drove them back again into the country. During these commotions the Chinese who resided within the town kept themselves perfectly quiet; and in order that these innocent people
might not be exposed to insult, the government issued an order,
prohibiting them from leaving their houses after six o'clock in
the evening, and ordering them to keep their doors shut. This
prudent precaution was not, however, sufficient to protect
them from the fury of the irritated soldiery and sailors who
were in the city, and had witnessed the devastations of the
Chinese without the gates. Suddenly and unexpectedly an
instantaneous cry of murder and horror resounded through the
town, and the most dismal scene of barbarity and rapine presented itself on all sides. All the Chinese, without distinction,
men, women, and children, were put to the sword. Neither
pregnant women nor sucking infants were spared by the re-
lentless assassins. The prisoners in chains, about a hundred
in number, were at the same time slaughtered like sheep.
European citizens, to whom some of the wealthy Chinese had
fled for safety, violating every principle of humanity and morality, delivered them up to their sanguinary pursuers, and em-
bezzled the property confided to them. In short, all the
Chinese, guilty and innocent, were exterminated. And whence
did the barbarous order by which they suffered emanate ?
Here a veil has industriously been drawn, and the truth will
probably never be known with certainty. The governor-
general, Valkenier, and his brother-in-law Helvetius, were accused by the public voice of directing the massacre; but it was
never proved upon them." It is remarkable, that, when Valkenier was afterwards condemned to imprisonment for life at
Batavia, among the numerous charges brought against him for
mal-administration during his government, no notice was

The poundage, or assessment, which is paid annually by every house, consists in half a month's rent. This money is expended in dragging and cleansing the canals, and in repairing the town-hall and other buildings belonging to the city. Permission must be requested, every year, of the Company's government to levy this assessment in behalf of the city, which is seldom refused.

The houses are not let by the year, but by the month; the rents run from five to forty rix-dollars per month. A good house, in an agreeable situation, may be hired for twenty or twenty-

---

taken of his presumed instrumentality in this dreadful massacre.

Much apprehension was entertained that this occurrence would excite the indignation of the emperor of China, and deputies were sent to him the following year to apologize for the measure. The letter written to the emperor on the occasion is given at length by Huysers; the only remarkable circumstance in which it differs from the above relation, is the allegation that some Chinese within the city had set fire to it in different places, and were preparing to rise upon the Europeans; but the extermination of the innocent with the guilty is acknowledged, and attempted to be excused on the plea of necessity. These deputies were agreeably surprised on finding that the emperor calmly answered, that " he was little solicitous for the fate of unworthy subjects, who, in the pursuit of lucre, had quitted their country and abandoned the tombs of their ancestors."

five rixdollars.   A rixdollar, at Batavia, is worth forty-eight stivers, or about 4*s*. 4*d*. sterling.

The churches are repaired out of the duties levied upon funerals.

A bank of circulation has been established here for some years, which is united with the lombard, or bank for lending money on pledges. It is under the administration of a director, who is generally a counsellor of India, two commissaries, a cashier, and a book-keeper.

A fee of five rixdollars is given at the opening of an account; and stamped bank-bills, signed by the director and commissaries, are delivered for the money placed in the bank.   Its capital is computed to amount to between two and three millions of rixdollars; between 435,000*l*. and 650,000*l*. sterling.

The suburbs of Batavia are remarkable on account of their considerable extent, uncommon pleasantness, and great population.   They are inhabited by Indians of various nations, and by some Europeans.   The Chinese quarter is the most populous, and seems itself a city, with numerous streets; yet their houses are mean and small.   It is crowded with shops, containing all kinds of goods, as well those of their own manufacture, and such as they receive annually from China, as what they buy up of those imported from Europe.   The number of the Chinese who live both within and without the walls of the city, cannot be determined with precision; but it must be very considerable, 'as the Company receive a poll-tax from them of more than 40,000 rixdollars.

Every Chinese who has a profession is obliged to pay a monthly poll-tax of half a ducatoon, six shillings; women, children, and those who have no trade, are exempted from the tax; so that their number can only be guessed at. They are under a chief of their own nation, who is known by the appellation of Chinese Captain; he lives within the walls, and has six lieutenants under him in different districts. A flag is hoisted at his door, on the first or second day in every month, and the Chinese, liable to the tax, are then obliged to come to him to pay it.

Like the Jews in Europe, they are very cunning in trade, both in the largest dealings and in the most trifling pedlary. They are so desirous of money, that a Chinese will run three times from one end of the city to the other, if he have but the prospect of gaining one penny. In doing any business with them, the greatest care must be taken to avoid being cheated.

Their stature is rather short than tall; they are in general tolerably square, and not so brown as the Javanese. They shave their heads all round, leaving a bunch of hair on the middle of the crown, which is twisted with a riband, and hangs down the back. Their dress consists in a long robe of nankeen, or thin silk, with wide sleeves, and under it they wear drawers of the same, which cover their legs.

In every house there is a niche, or place where the image of one of their *joostjes*, or idols, painted on Chinese paper, is hung up. Before it they keep one or more lamps always burning, as also a kind of incense, which is made into little thin tapers. This idol is generally depicted as an old man with a square cap upon his head, and a female, designed for his wife, by his side. About an hour's walk out of the city, just beyond Fort Ansjol, they have a temple, standing in a grove of cocoa-nut trees by the side of a rivulet, and in the midst of most pleasant scenery. The building is about twenty feet in length, and twelve or thirteen in breadth. The entrance is through a railing into a small area, and then into a hall, behind which is the sanctuary. In the middle, just within the door, is a large altar, on which tapers made of red wax are kept burning night and day. There is also an image of a lion richly gilt In a niche behind the altar are representations of an old man and woman, both with crowns upon their heads, and about two feet in height, which are their idols; and as they look upon their *joostje* to be an evil spirit, they

continually supplicate him not to do them any
harm. In their adorations they prostrate themselves before him, and endeavour to express the
awe and reverence they entertain by striking
their head continually against the ground.

They likewise consult their idol when they are
about any important undertaking. This divination is done by means of two small longitudinal
pieces of wood, flat on one side and round on
the other. They hold these with the flat sides
towards each other, and then letting them fall
on the ground, augur of the effect of their
prayers, and the good or bad result of their pur-
posed enterprise, by the manner in which they
lie, with the round or flat sides upwards. If the
presage be favourable, they offer a wax candle
to their god, which the priest, or bonze, who
attends at the temple, immediately turns into
ready money.

In this temple I saw a Chinese, who let these
little sticks fall above twenty times before they
promised him success : he seemed to be but very
little pleased with these repeated evil prognosti-
cations, and shaking his head, at every time,
with a most discontented look, he threw himself
upon the ground, and thumped his head against
it, till at last the omen proved agreeable to his
wishes; and he then joyfully lighted a thick

wax candle, and placed it upon the altar of his *joostje.*

Besides this temple, the Chinese have several others, which are tolerated by the government; but it is worthy of observation, that whilst the practice of the most abominable idolatry is allowed, the exercise of the Roman Catholic religion is obstinately prohibited.

The Chinese are of a very lustful temper. They are accused of the most detestable violations of the laws of nature; and it is even said, that they keep swine in their houses, for purposes the most shameful and repugnant.

Their tombs, on which they expend a great deal of money, are partly built above, and partly under ground. They are arched over. The entrance, which is made like a door-way, is closed with a large stone, covered with engraved Chinese letters. They are to be seen in great numbers, about half an hour's walk from Batavia, on the road to Jaccatra.

They visit the graves of their ancestors and relations from time to time, strew them with odoriferous flowers; and when they depart, leave a few small pieces of silk or linen, before the entrance, and sometimes boiled rice, or other victuals, which is speedily made away with at night.

The environs of Batavia are very pleasant, and

are almost every where intersected with rivulets, by which the circumjacent rice-plantations are inundated, and fertilized in the proper season.

There are five principal roads which lead from the city towards the country, and which are all planted with high and shady trees.

That which runs to the eastward, to Ansjol and the sea-coast, is laid along the side of a rivulet, the stream of which running down an imperceptible slope, is very slow, which makes it resemble the canals in Holland. Both sides of it are adorned with gardens; but they are beginning to be neglected, save one or two, belonging to the director-general.

At no great distance from the sea-shore, whither this road finally leads, is an oyster-bed; and on the beach stands a house of entertainment, which is resorted to by the Europeans, for the purpose of eating this shell-fish.

The second road has the appellation of the Mango-doa, from its having been formerly planted with a double row of mango-trees. This runs more south than the former one, and farther inland. Along this road are likewise many gardens, but they are not so splendid and pleasant as those which border and embellish the road to Jaccatra; for there the finest picture which can be conceived, presents itself to the delighted eye, both with respect to the grandeur of the buildings and the elegance of the grounds. Most of the houses belonging to them, have their fronts towards the road, and from the back rooms they have a prospect of the river of Jaccatra.

This road is nearly two hundred feet broad, and is closely planted with trees. I do not know that I ever beheld a more delightful avenue. It terminates at a small fort, which is called Jaccatra, situated about half a Dutch mile from Batavia ; and, though the road is continued to Weltevreeden, the country-seat of the governor-general, and beyond it farther into the country, it assumes on the other side of Jaccatra the name of Goenong Sari.

The fourth is called the Molenvliet, or Mill-drain, because part of the water of the great, or Jaccatra river, is diverted through a channel along this road, for the purpose of turning a powder-mill, which stands scarcely ten minutes walk from the city. The road leads along the canal, for full half a Dutch mile up the country, and is equally adorned on both sides, with handsome houses and pleasant gardens. It then proceeds to Tanabang, where a large market is held every Saturday, for all kinds of provisions which are brought thither from the interior.

The fifth road leads through the Chinese Campon, also along a river, to Fort Ankay, and is, in like manner, bordered on both sides with gardens.

None of these roads, nor any of the streets in the city, are paved ; the ground consists of a hard clay, which is made very smooth and plain ; only in the city, along the sides of the streets, by the houses, are stone footpaths, of about three or four feet in breadth.   The streets and canals are planted on each side with large trees; generally the *onophyllum, calophyllum,* and *calaba,* the *eana-rium commune,* and some others which are still more rare.

CHAPTER IV.

Government of Batavia.—Council of India.—Governor-General.— Director-General. — Counsellors of India.—Council of Justice.—Board of Scheepens. — Punishments. — Impalement. — Mucks.—Orphan-Chamber.—Opium-Company.— Chief of the Marine.—Commandant and Upper Comptroller of Equipment.—Vice-Commandant. —Military.—Militia.—Ranks and Precedency.— Sumptuary Laws.—Clergy.—Coins.—Weights. —Measures.

THE chief government of Batavia, and of all the possessions of the Dutch East India Company in Asia, is vested in the council of India, with the governor-general at their head.

This council consists, besides the director-general, of five ordinary counsellors, including the governor of the Cape of Good Hope, nine extraordinary counsellors, and two secretaries.

Five of the extraordinary counsellors are governors of the out-factories of the north-east coast of Java, Coromandel, Amboyna, Ceylon, and Macasser.

This council determines affairs of every kind, those which relate to the administration of justice, alone excepted. Yet in civil matters, an appeal may be made from the sentence of the council of justice, to the council of India.

All appointments and promotions to offices are effected by the council of India, not excepting that of the governor-general; but this must be confirmed by the assembly of seventeen, in the Netherlands. Ecclesiastical preferments, and the appointment of the ministers of justice, proceed immediately from the direction in Holland. In the council of India, the governor and director general, and the five ordinary counsellors, alone, conclude upon most matters which are brought before them; the other nine members are properly only assessors, who may give their advice, but have no votes, except on war or peace with the Indians, pardoning criminals condemned to death, in the election of a governor-general, and in a few other important points. The power and influence of this body in the Indies, are unbounded. It is the representative of the state and of the Company, and millions of Indians are subject to its sway. Kings and princes are crowned and dethroned by its mandates. " I have been witness," says Ary Huysers, " to the deposition of two powerful kings of the Moluccas, and the hereditary prince of Tidore. One of these died miserably in a little village, near the place of my residence. I saw

the venerable old man before his death ; he was
seventy-two years of age. When I expressed
my commiseration at the deep humiliation he
had undergone, he answered with a sigh, in the
Malay language, pointing to heaven, ' It is the
will of God.' "

The authority of the governor-general is almost unbounded; and although he is obliged to
give cognizance to the council, and consult
them on some matters, he possesses a most arbitrary and independent power in all : for there
are few or no members of the council, who do
not stand in need of his good offices, in some instance or other, for example, in order to obtain
lucrative employments for their relations or favourites * ; and if this be not sufficient to make
them obey the nod of the governor, he is not
destitute of the means of tormenting them in
every way, under various pretences; nay, of

* By the second article of the oath taken by the governor-
general and counsellors of India, on their appointment, they
engage " never to receive any gifts or presents, directly or
indirectly, from any one under their authority; neither in
respect, or in the hope or expectation thereof, nor of any
advantage, favour, or other private consideration, either of
relationship, friendship, or otherwise, to appoint or cause to
be appointed, any other individual to an office, place, or
station, than such as they believe and find to possess the most
experience, the most integrity, the most fidelity, and the most
ability for the same."—So much do men regard oaths!

sending them prisoners to Europe; as was done with respect to MM. Van Imhoff, de Haaze, and Van Schinnen, in the year 1740, by the governor-general Valkenier *. As, therefore, those who are immediately next to him in rank, depend upon, and stand in awe of him, it follows that the inferior servants of the Company feel still deeper reverence, and tremble before him, as in the presence of one upon whose arbitrary will and power their happiness or misery wholly depends.

The governor-general usually resides at his country-seat, called Weltevreeden, about an hour and a quarter's walk from Batavia, and which is a superb mansion.

He gives public audience here every Monday and Thursday; and on Tuesdays and Fridays at another seat, situated nearer to the city, on the Jaccatra road. On the other days of the week he is inaccessible to every body, and cannot be spoken to unless on affairs of the greatest importance and urgency. Nobody goes thither without having some business; for it would be taken extremely ill if any one were to pay a visit

* He was the personal enemy of those gentlemen, and so tyrannically abused his authority, that when the council refused to sanction this arbitrary measure, he surrounded the council-table with a body of armed men, and thus constrained them to assent to his wishes.

F

of mere ceremony.   The time of audience is
from six o'clock in the morning till eight.   Every
one waits in the open air, in the court before the
house, till he is called in by one of the body-
guards.

   When the governor rides out, he is always accompanied by some of his horse-guards.   An
officer and two trumpeters precede his approach,
and every person who meets him, and happens
to be in a carriage, must stop and step out of it
till he has ridden by.   This humiliating homage,
as well as that paid to the *edele heeren*, or counsellors of India, as will be presently noticed, are
equally required from foreigners.   These ceremonies are generally complied with by the captains of Indiamen, and other trading ships :
" but," says Captain Carteret, who was at
Batavia in 1768, " having the honour to bear
his majesty's commission, I did not think myself
at liberty to pay to a Dutch governor any homage
which is not paid to my own sovereign : it is,
however, constantly required of the king's
officers ; and two or three days after my arrival,
the landlord of the hotel where I lodged told me,
he had been ordered by the *shebandar* to let me
know that my carriage, as well as others, must
stop if I should meet the governor, or any of
the council ; but I desired him to acquaint the
shebandar that I could not consent to perform

any such ceremony; and upon his intimating something about the black men with sticks, who precede the approach of these great men, I told him, that if any insult should be offered me, I knew how to defend myself, and would take care to be upon my guard; at the same time pointing to my pistols, which happened to lie upon the table: upon this he went away, and about three hours afterwards returned, and told me he had orders from the governor to acquaint me that I might do as I pleased." Since that time the English officers have never been required to comply with this degrading custom; yet when they have been in an hired carriage, nothing has deterred the coachman from stopping and alighting, in honour of the Dutch grandee, but the most peremptory menace of immediate death.

A company of dragoons always mount guard at Weltevreeden. He has besides some halberdiers, who are employed in carrying messages and commands, and who always attend on the governor's person wherever he goes. They are dressed in short coats of scarlet cloth, richly laced with gold, and are next in rank to the junior ensign in the Company's service.

When his excellency entered the church, all persons, both men and women, the counsellors

of India not excepted, stood up in token of respect; but this etiquette was abolished upon the
accession of R. de Klerk to the government in
1777. His lady receives the same honours, and
is equally escorted by a party of horse-guards
when she rides out.

The director-general, who is the eldest counsellor of India, is the next in rank. The direction and control over the trade of the Company,
throughout all India, and to Europe, together
with every thing relative to it, is exclusively
intrusted to him. The governor-general does
not in the least meddle in these matters if the
director has ability for it.

Next in order are the ordinary and extraordinary counsellors of India. Those who reside at Batavia are also usually presidents of
different boards or courts. Every counsellor of
India has likewise the correspondence with one
of the out-factories allotted to him; the general
himself has that of one or two settlements; and
no one is excused in this respect but the director,
on account of his multifarious other avocations.

Although every member lies under this obli-
gation, there are but few who take the trouble
upon themselves; most of them transfer it to
persons of a lower rank.

When a counsellor of India, or his lady,
enters a church, all the men stand up, in the

same manner as for the governor-general, but the women remain sitting. On meeting one of them in a carriage, every body must stop, rise up, and bow to them, and stay till they are gone by. When they go out, they have two slaves, who run before them with sticks: other people are allowed but one.

There are always two secretaries of the government, who take down in writing the propositions, or resolutions, which have been discussed in the council, and lay them before the governor-general when the assembly breaks up. He examines them, and gives directions what is to be made into decrees, and what is only to be inserted in the journals. The resolutions being then drawn up in writing by the first secretary, are again presented to the governor, who makes such alterations in them as he thinks fit; and at the ensuing session of the council they are read over and approved.

The salary of a counsellor of India is a thousand rixdollars per annum; besides which he has six hundred rixdollars for house-rent, seven hundred for his trouble in signing dispatches, three hundred towards providing his table, together with a considerable allowance of provisions from the Company's warehouses. Taking every thing together, he can reckon upon a yearly income of four thousand rixdollars, 875*l.*

Besides the above, the first secretary has the emoluments of making out the commissions, which do not amount to a trifle, especially when many appointments of governors, directors, or commandants occur, who pay liberally for their commissions; sometimes giving fees to the amount of a thousand rixdollars. None of them can save any thing from this income, which they amply want for their household expenses; for which reason they are generally favoured with the government or directorship of an out-settle-ment, after they have been three or four years in the council.

The private secretary of the governor-general is usually promoted to be secretary to the council, upon a vacancy.

Thirty-six, or forty, clerks are daily employed in the secretary's office, which is next to the government-house, in the castle. They have for the most part the rank of junior merchants; nevertheless they are not able to earn more than a bare subsistence.

Justice is administered to the servants of the Company by an assembly, having the appella-tion of council of justice. This body is by its constitution independent of the council of India; but, as the members of which it consists have many wants and wishes to be fulfilled, they likewise endeavour to be near the fountain-head of promotion and advantage; and, as well as all others, follow the inclinations of their sovereign ruler in all cases that are brought before them. This council consists of a president, who ranks next to the junior counsellor of India, eight ordinary members, and two adjutors, taken from the Company's servants. Their salary is no more than two thousand two hundred rixdollars; which is scarcely sufficient for the support of their establishments: they are besides obliged to serve the office of counsellor of justice, for the space of ten years, before they may be candidates for any other office.

There are two fiscals belonging to this council, one of which bears the title of advocate-fiscal, or attorney-general, but whose office relates only to the persons in the Company's service. The other is styled the water-fiscal, through whom all indictments relative to navigation are made. This was formerly one of the most lucrative employments of all India, and it is still very advantageous, though not so much as formerly, because the private trade is not so flourishing as it was in former times. The methods by which fortunes were made in this office will easily be conceived by seafaring people. The secretary of the council of justice has the rank of merchant.

The citizens and free merchants of Batavia, who are not in the Company's service, are amenable to a separate municipal court of justice, being what is called the board of *scheepens*, or aldermen, who are eight in number, with a president, who is a member of the council of India.

To this court belong a sheriff, for the matters which relate to the city, and a constable of the territory of Batavia; both of which are very lucrative offices, and are never bestowed but on great favourites.

The punishments inflicted at Batavia are excessively severe, especially such as fall upon the Indians. Impalement is the chief and most terrible.

In the year 1769 there was an execution of this kind, of a Macasser slave who had murdered his master. The criminal was led in the morning to the place of execution, the grass-plot, and laid upon his belly, being held by four men. The executioner made a transverse incision at the lower part of the body, as far as the *os sacrum*; he then introduced the sharp point of the spike, which was about six feet long, and made of polished iron, into the wound, so that it passed between the back-bone and the skin. Two men drove it forcibly up along the spine, while the executioner held the end, and gave it a proper direction, till it came out between the neck and shoulders. The lower end

was next put into a wooden post and rivetted
fast, and the sufferer was lifted up, thus impaled, and the post stuck in the ground. At
the top of the post, about ten feet from the
ground, there was a kind of little bench, upon
which the body rested.

The insensibility or fortitude of the miserable
sufferer was incredible. He did not utter the
least complaint, except when the spike was
rivetted into the pillar; the hammering and
shaking occasioned by it, seemed to be intolerable to him, and he then bellowed out for pain;
and likewise again when he was lifted up and
set in the ground. He sat in this dreadful situation till death put an end to his torments, which
fortunately happened the next day about three
o'clock in the afternoon. He owed this speedy
termination of his misery to a light shower of
rain, which continued for about an hour, and he
gave up the ghost half an hour afterwards.

There have been instances at Batavia, of criminals who have been impaled in the dry season,
and have remained alive for eight or more days
without any food or drink, which is prevented to
be given them by a guard who is stationed at the
place of execution for that purpose. None of
the vital parts are injured by impalement, which
makes the punishment the more cruel and intolerable; but as soon as any water gets into the

wound, it mortifies and occasions a gangrene, which directly attacks the more noble parts, and brings on death almost immediately.

This miserable sufferer continually complained of intolerable thirst, which is peculiarly incident to this terrible punishment. The criminals are exposed, during the whole day, to the burning rays of the sun, and are unceasingly tormented by numerous stinging insects.

About three hours before he died he was in conversation with the bystanders, relating to them the manner in which he had murdered his good master, and expressing his repentance of the crime he had committed. This he did with great composure; yet an instant afterwards he burst out in the most bitter complaints of unquenchable thirst, and raved for drink, while no one was allowed to alleviate, by a single drop of water, the excruciating torments he endured.

This kind of punishment, notwithstanding its great cruelty, is asserted by many to be of the highest necessity, in a country where a treacherous race of men, unrestrained by any moral principles from the perpetration of the greatest crimes, perform the daily menial and household services of the Europeans. The slaves who come from the island of Celebes, and especially the Bouginese, are guilty of the most horrid murders:

most of those who run *mucks* belong to that nation.

These acts of indiscriminate murder are called
mucks, because the perpetrators of them, during
their frenzy, continually cry out *amok, amok,*
which signifies *kill, kill.* When, by swallow-
ing much opium, or by other means, they are
raised to a pitch of desperate fury, they sally out
with a knife or other weapon in their hand, and
kill, without distinction of sex, rank, or age,
whoever they meet in the streets of Batavia ; and
proceed in this way till they are either shot or
taken prisoners. Their intoxication continues
till death ; they run in upon the arms opposed
to them, and often kill their opponents even
after they are themselves mortally wounded.

In order, if possible, to take them alive, the
officers of justice are provided with a pole ten or
twelve feet in length, at the end of which is a
kind of fork, made of two pieces of wood, three
feet long, stuck on the inside with sharp iron
spikes; this is held before the wretched object of
pursuit, who runs into it, and is thus taken.

If he happen to be mortally wounded, he is
immediately broken alive upon the wheel, without any form of trial, in the presence of two or
three of the counsellors of justice.

It is remarkable, that at Batavia, where the
assassins, when taken alive, are broken on the

wheel, with every aggravation of punishment
which the most rigorous justice can inflict, the
mucks yet happen in great frequency ; whilst at
Bencoolen, where they are executed in the most
simple and expeditious manner, the offence is
extremely rare.   At Batavia, if an officer take
one of these *amoks*, or mohawks, as they have
been called by an easy corruption, alive, his reward is very considerable ; but if he kill them,
nothing is added to his usual pay : such is the
fury of their desperation, that three out of four
are of necessity destroyed in the attempt to secure
them.

The orphan-chamber at Batavia serves at the
same time for the whole of the Dutch possessions
in India.   Every out-factory has, it is true, its
own orphan-chamber, but they must render account of their administration to that of the capital, and remit the effects which are not claimed,
or the heirs to which do not reside on the spot.
That of Batavia corresponds with the orphan-
chambers of the different cities where the chambers of the East India Company are established.
These *weeskamers*, or orphan-chambers, are establishments which are dispersed throughout the
United Provinces for the administration of the
estates of all who die intestate, and the appor-
tionment of them among the heirs.

The board consists of a president, who is a

counsellor of India, and six *weesmeesters*, or regents, who are appointed by the council of India, with a secretary, and a sworn clerk. The capital stock remaining in the hands of the orphanchamber amounted, in the year 1766, to about 220,000*l.* sterling.

There are several other courts, or boards, as the commissioners of dikes or sluices, of bankruptcies, a court of common pleas, a board of control over marriages, and others.

A company was established at Batavia, during the government of Baron Van Imhoff, for the opium-trade, which is still in existence. The stock is divided into shares of two thousand rixdollars each, on which half only has hitherto been furnished, but the remainder may be required at any time. The dividends are unequal, yet very large, and the shares sell at a high premium; they are generally in the hands of the counsellors of India. The management of this trade is intrusted to a director, who is a counsellor of India, two acting proprietors, a cashier, and a book-keeper.

Every chest of opium stands the Company in two hundred and fifty, and sometimes three hundred rixdollars, and is delivered to the society for five hundred, and sometimes more. On the other hand, the Company is bound to sell this drug to no other. The retail of it produces large

profits, as eight or nine hundred rixdollars, and
more, are made of every chest. The gain would
be more considerable, if this monopoly could be
strictly enforced for the whole quantity of opium
consumed in the eastern parts of India ; but, notwithstanding the Company have interdicted this
trade to their servants, and especially to the seamen, upon pain of death, and have prohibited
the importation into any of their possessions, by
foreign nations, upon pain of confiscation of
ship and cargo, yet very great violations of these
laws are daily practised, on account of the important profit it affords ; by which the society
is much injured, although on their part they do
all they can, on the arrival of ships from the
Ganges, to discover if any contraband opium be
on board : but those who engage in this illicit
trade, take too many precautions to incur much
risk of detection. The smuggling trade which
the English carry on in this article in the eastern
islands, and by way of Malacca, is also extremely detrimental to the society.

When any ships arrive in the road of Batavia,
from places whence contraband goods can be
brought, two of the members of the council of
justice, with the water-fiscal, and the provost-
marshal, are dispatched the next day, in order
to examine whether any prohibited wares are on
board; the examination, however, is only per-

sonally done by the last-named officer, who reports the result to the others.

A chief of the marine, or port admiral, has been established at Batavia since the year 1762. His rank is equal to that of a counsellor of India, but he takes place after the junior counsellor. He has the same privileges; has equally the style of *edele heer*, and may be present at their assemblies; but cannot deliver his sentiments, except in matters relative to his department. His chief occupation consists in superintending the repairs of ships, examining the ships' journals, signing sailing-orders, and warrants for delivery of stores to the ships; and further, in keeping whatever relates to maritime affairs in due order.

Upon this officer, follows the commandant and upper comptroller of equipment, to whom the management of the stores is confided. He likewise superintends the discharge, loading, manning, and furnishing the ships with provisions. This is one of the most lucrative, but, at the same time, most troublesome employments at Batavia; since he has had a head placed over him, however, the emolument has greatly decreased, while the fatigue remains in its full extent. He is assisted by a vice-commandant, and under comptroller of equipment, who ranks as post-captain, to whom he generally leaves the superintendence of loading and unloading the ships, and who supplies his place in cases of sickness or absence.

The Company have granted to these three officers as an emolument, the privilege of shipping some tons of 'goods, not contraband, by every ship which sails to India, according to the size of the vessels; and if the ships' captains do not buy up these goods at a very high rate, they are sure to find but scanty opportunities of disposing of their own.

The commanders of vessels, with their lieutenants and mates, rank next; the first equal with merchants: in 1770 there were thirty-nine of them who resided there, or commanded country-ships.

The whole of the Dutch land-forces in India are under the command of one head, who was formerly styled captain-major, but has now the title of brigadier, and ranks after the chief of the marine. He has two lieutenant-colonels under him; one of whom has the command of the military at Batavia, and the other at Ceylon; there are, besides, six majors, two of whom reside at Ceylon, one on the Malabar coast, one at the Cape of Good Hope, and two at Batavia: one of the last is also chief of the artillery.

There is a regiment of dragoons, which serve as a body-guard to the governor-general. The infantry are divided into two battalions, and are quartered in the city and suburbs.

Besides these regular troops, there are two companies called *pennists*, consisting of merchants, junior merchants, book-keepers, and assistants. One company is called *pennists* of the castle; the other, *pennists* of the city. The former is commanded by the first secretary of the government, and the latter by one of the senior merchants of the castle. They are reviewed once a year by the governor-general and council; and each company has a distinct uniform.

The other Company's servants are also formed into two companies; one consists of the marines and others belonging to the admiralty-wharf, with the commandant and upper comptroller of equipment at their head; the other, of the workmen of the *ambagts kwartier*, with the *fabriek*. Independently of these, all the free inhabitants, or citizens, are enrolled into two companies of horse and of foot, which are commanded by a counsellor of India, as colonel, and mount guard every night at the town-hall.

All the practitioners of surgery are subordinate to a chief, who has the control over all the surgeons and surgeon's mates as well on board ships as in the hospitals; and who has the rank of senior merchant.

Every individual is as stiff and formal, and is

G

as feelingly alive to every infraction of his privileges in respect to precedency, especially in public companies, as if his happiness or misery depended wholly upon their due observance. Nothing is more particularly attended to at entertainments, by the master of the house, than
the seating of every guest, and drinking their
healths, in the exact order of precedency.
The ladies most tenaciously insist upon every
prerogative attached to the station of their
husbands : some of them, if they conceive themselves placed lower than they are entitled to, will
sit in sullen and proud silence during the whole
entertainment. It does not unfrequently happen,
that two ladies of equal rank meeting each
other in their carriages, neither will give way,
though they may be forced to remain for hours in
the street.

To provide against these disputes on the subject of precedency, the respective ranks of all the
Company's servants were ascertained by a resolution of government, which was renewed in 1764;
and a regulation respecting the pomp of funeral
processions was added to it, which is still in
force. Regulations were likewise introduced
with respect to dress during the government of
the governor-general Mossel; by which persons
of a certain condition were alone allowed to wear
embroidered or laced clothes; but this is

little attended to at present, for almost every one
who chooses dresses in this forbidden finery.
Velvet coats are however not common, and they
are absolutely prohibited to be worn by any
under the rank of senior merchant.   The act by
which these regulations were established, is composed of a hundred and thirty-one articles.   It
enters into the most minute detail respecting the
carriages, horses, chairs, servants, dress, &c. of
the Company's servants, and exhibits a strange
picture of meanness and illiberality.   By the 8th
article, little chaises for children, drawn by the
hand, must not be gilt or painted, but in the
exact proportion of the rank of the parents.   By
the 31st no one inferior to a merchant shall use
a parasol or umbrella in the neighbourhood of
the castle, except when it rains.   Ladies whose
husbands are below the rank of counsellors of
India, may not wear at one time jewels of greater
value than six thousand rixdollars; wives of
senior merchants are limited to four thousand,
others to three and one thousand.   Article 49th
permits ladies of the higher ranks to go abroad
with three female attendants, who may wear
" ear-rings of single middle-sized diamonds, gold
hair-pins, petticoats of gold, silver, or silk cloth,
jackets of gold or silver gauze, chains of gold,
or beads and girdles of gold, but neither pearls
nor diamonds, nor any other kind of jewels, in

the hair." Wives of inferior merchants may have two, and ladies in an inferior station one maid, who may wear " ear-rings of small diamonds, gold hair-pins, a jacket of fine linen, and a chintz petticoat, but no gold nor silver stuffs, nor silks, jewels, real or artificial pearls, nor any ornaments of gold." By article 65, none but persons of the highest rank are allowed to have trumpets, clarions, or drums among the music with which it is customary to entertain guests during dinner. There is a wise recommendation in the 83d article, to the officers of the Company in Bengal, not to surpass their predecessors in pomp of dress nor appearance, and especially not the governors or chiefs of the other European settlements. Perhaps the 110th article is the most curious of all. It allows to the director at Surat, when he goes in state, among other things, four fans, made according to the fashion of the country, with the feathers of birds of paradise, and cow-hair, with golden cases and handles. It likewise fixes the duties to be paid upon all carriages, horses, &c. It is worthy of observation, that those upon carriages increase downwards from the higher to the lower ranks : members of the government pay 50 rix-dollars per annum ; captains of the military, merchants, &c. 100 ; junior merchants, &c. 125 ; book-keepers, &c. 180; citizens of no special rank, and native inhabitants of consideration, 200 ; and the common natives, 300 rixdollars for keeping carriages. Fines are the penalties attached to the infraction of almost all these sumptuary regulations.

There may be twelve clergymen of the reformed religion at Batavia, six of whom preach in the Dutch, four in the Portuguese, and two in the Malay languages ; likewise three Lutheran ministers, who preach in Dutch.

Service is performed every Sunday in the above languages ; in Dutch at two churches in the morning, but only at one in the afternoon. An examination of catechumens takes place every Wednesday evening. So that, upon the whole, these reverend gentlemen need not complain, when their number is complete, of too severe labour. The morning service commences at half past eight o'clock, and is generally over by ten, when the greatest heat of the day begins.

Ecclesiastical disputes are never heard of here. The Company's government, who are extremely anxious to avoid every thing which could interrupt the public tranquillity, would soon terminate the quarrel by the summary argument of force.

It is much to be wished that upright and learned clergymen were alone sent out ; yet that

this is not always the case, appears from a resolution of the government in the year 1768,
earnestly requesting that the assembly of seventeen would dispatch some ministers of the Gospel,
possessed of virtue and learning, to Batavia, with
an augmentation of salaries and emoluments.
Their salary was then one thousand eight hundred gilders per annum; but with their allowances for house-rent, board, &c. they could
reckon upon three thousand, about 275*l.*; which
is certainly not enough to live upon at Batavia
with a family, and on an equal footing with the
senior merchants.

Once in every year, or sometimes only once in
two years, one of the clergymen of Batavia goes
upon a visitation to the Company's possessions
on the west coast of Sumatra. Some of them
well know how to turn such occasions to the advantage of their pockets, by taking with them as
much merchandise as they can find room for.

The coins current at Batavia are the milled
Dutch gold ducat, worth six gilders and twelve
stivers: the Japan gold *coupangs*, of which the
old go for twenty-four gilders, and the new for
fourteen gilders and eight stivers: the Spanish
dollar or piaster rises and falls according to the
quantity in circulation, or the degree of demand;
its value is generally between sixty-three and
sixty-six stivers: the milled silver ducatoon,

which is the current coin of the Company throughout their possessions, except on the continent of India ; its proportionate value according to the other
coins is sixty-six stivers ; but in Indian money
it goes for eighty, at which rate it is current at
Batavia ; at the Cape of Good Hope it is worth
seventy-two, and at Cochin seventy-five stivers :
the unmilled ducatoon is two stivers less at Batavia : the milled Batavia rupee, called the silver
derham d'Java, which was formerly coined at
Batavia, is made good in the Company's books at
twenty four stivers, and in circulation it is taken
at thirty ; it is the only rupee which goes for so
much at Batavia, and is current at Amboyna,
Banda, Ternate, Macasser, and Malacca, at the
same rate, but on the coast of Malabar it is eight
per cent. less in value than the Surat rupee : all
other rupees generally go for twenty-seven
stivers ; the Persian rupees are the most current ;
there are also half and quarter rupees in circulation. The smaller coins are skillings, *dubbeltjes*,
or twopenny-pieces, and doits : there are two
sorts of skillings ; the old, which are current in
Holland, go for six stivers, but the new, here
called ship-skillings, are worth seven and a half :
twopenny-pieces which are old and worn go for
two stivers, but the new for two stivers and a
half : no other doits are taken in change than
those stamped with the mark of the East-India

Company, and these are equal to a farthing. The rixdollar, which is the money used for accounts in private trade, is worth forty-eight stivers; thus, three new or milled ducatoons are equal to five rixdollars*.

Most merchants' goods are calculated at Batavia by *picols* of one hundred and twenty-five pounds, Amsterdam weight†; and these are subdivided into a hundred *cattis*, each weighing one pound and a quarter.

Rice and other grain is measured by *coyangs*, which differ in weight. On the receipt of the rice by the Company at Java, they must weigh three thousand five hundred pounds. They are shipped at Batavia for three thousand four hun-

---

* The following is a table of the value in sterling money of the above coins at the par exchange of *f.*11 per pound; viz.

				£.	s.	d.
The old Japan gold coupang	*f.*24	0	or	2	3	7¾
The new ditto	14	8		1	6	2¼
The milled Dutch ducat	6	12		0	12	0
The silver milled ducatoon	4	0		0	7	3¼
The unmilled ditto	3	18		0	7	1
The Spanish dollar from	3	3		0	5	8¾
to	3	6		0	6	0
The rixdollar	2	8		0	4	4¼
The Batavia rupee	1	10		0	2	8¾
Other rupees, about	1	7		0	2	5½

† Ricaud, in his Traité de Commerce, makes the *picol* at Batavia equal to 118⅓*lb.* Amsterdam weight.

dred, and landed there for three thousand three hundred. The warehouse-keepers dispatch them for the out-factories for three thousand two hundred, where they are unloaden for three thousand one hundred; and finally, they are delivered for consumption for three thousand pounds at the out-factories, namely, those which receive their rice from Batavia, as Malacca, the Cape of Good Hope, Ceylon, the western coast of Sumatra, &c.: thus every *coyang* loses five hundred pounds in weight. This deficiency is an allowance which is made to the Company's servants, who respectively have the management of the rice; for instance, for every 3300 received at Batavia, the warehouse-keepers are only bound to deliver 3200, &c. Out of this difference they must make good all loss by dust, &c. and what they can keep over is a perquisite to themselves. Similar allowances are made on most of the goods in which the Company trade, and they are all fixed by a resolution of the council. They form a very material part of the income of the Company's servants; who, however, are bound to sell again to the Company what they have gained in this way, of all spices, coffee, saltpetre, japan, copper, and tin; the other articles they are allowed to dispose of as they please.

Sugar is taken by *canassers* of three *picols*, or

three hundred and seventy-five pounds neat each : the gross weight is about four hundred, or four hundred and five pounds.

The *ganting* is a small rice-measure, of thirteen pounds and a half in weight.

Every bag of coffee shipped from Batavia to Holland, weighs two hundred and fifty-two, and a bale of cinnamon eighty pounds.

CHAPTER V.

European Mode of Living at Batavia.—Women.—
Their early Marriages.—Complexion.—Temper.—
Manners.—Education of Children.—Bathing.—
Excessive Jealousy of the Indian Ladies.—Cruelty
to their female Slaves.—Short Widowhoods.—
Dress.—Diversions.—Carriages.—Norimons.—
Carts drawn by Buffaloes.—Management of the
Company's Trade.—Senior Merchants of the
Castle.—Warehouse-keepers.—Commissaries at the
Warehouses.—Exportation of Gold and Silver to
India.—Decay of Batavia by Increase of private
Trade.—Province of Jaccatra.—Imports at Ba-
tavia.—Islands of Onrust—De Kuiper—Purme-
rend—Edam.

Europeans, whether Dutch or of any other
nation, and in whatever station they are, live
at Batavia nearly in the same manner.   In
the morning, at five o'clock, or earlier, when the
day breaks, they get up. Many of them then sit
at their doors; others stay in the house, with
nothing but a light gown, in which they sleep,
thrown over their naked limbs; they breakfast
upon coffee or tea, afterwards dress, and go
about whatever business they may have. Almost
all who have any place or employment must be

at their proper station by eight o'clock, and they remain at work till eleven, or half past. They dine at twelve; take an afternoon's nap till four, and attend to their business till six, or take a ride out of the city in a carriage. At six o'clock they assemble in companies, and play or converse till nine, when they return home: whoever chooses to stay supper is welcome; and eleven o'clock is the usual hour of retiring to rest. Convivial gaiety seems to reign among them, and yet it is mixed with a kind of suspicious reserve, which pervades all stations and all companies, and is the consequence of an arbitrary and jealous government. The least word which may be wrested to an evil meaning, may bring on very serious consequences, if it reach the ears of the person aggrieved, either in fact, or in imagination. Many people assert, that they would not confide in their own brothers in this country.

No women are present at these assemblies; they have their own separate companies.

Married men neither take much concern, nor show much regard, for their wives. They seldom converse with them, at least on useful subjects, or on such as concern society. After having been married for years, the ladies are often, therefore, as ignorant of the world and of manners, as upon their wedding-day. It is not that they have no capacity to learn, but the men have no inclination to teach.

The men generally dress in the Dutch fashion, and often wear black.

As soon as you enter a house, where you intend to stop for an hour or more, you are desired by the master to make yourself comfortable, by taking off some of your clothes, &c. This is done by laying aside the sword, pulling off the coat and wig, for most men wear wigs here, and substituting for the latter a little white night-cap, which is generally carried in the pocket for that purpose.

When they go out on foot, they are attended by a slave, who carries a sun-shade, *sambreel* or *payang*, over their heads; but whoever is lower in rank than a junior merchant may not have a slave behind him, but must carry the *sambreel* himself.

Most of the white women at Batavia are born in the Indies. Those who come from Europe at a marriageable age are very few. They are either the offspring of European mothers, or of oriental female slaves, who having first been mistresses to Europeans, have afterwards been married to them, and been converted to Christianity, or at least have assumed the name of Christians. The children of these marriages may be known to the third and fourth generation, especially by the eyes, which are much smaller than in the unmixed progeny of Europeans.

There are likewise children who are the offspring of Portuguese; but these never become entirely white.

Children born in the Indies are nicknamed *liplaps* by the Europeans, although both parents may have come from Europe.

Girls are commonly marriageable at twelve or thirteen years of age, and sometimes younger. It seldom happens, if they are but tolerably handsome, have any money or expectations, or are related to people in power, that they are unmarried after that age.

As they marry while they are yet children, it may easily be conceived, that they do not possess those requisites which enable a woman to manage a family with propriety. Many of them can neither read nor write, nor possess any ideas of religion, of morality, nor of social intercourse.

Being married so young, they seldom bear many children, and are old women at thirty years of age. Women of fifty, in Europe, look younger and fresher than those of thirty at Batavia. They are in general of a very delicate make, and of an extremely fair complexion; but the tints of vermilion which embellish our northern ladies, are wholly banished their cheeks; the skin of their face and hands is of the most deadly pale white. Beauties must not be sought amongst them; the handsomest would scarcely be thought middling in Europe.

They have very supple joints, and can turn their fingers, hands, and arms, in almost every direction; but this they have in common with the women in the West Indies, and in other tropical climates.

They are commonly of a listless and lazy temper; which is chiefly to be ascribed to their education, and the number of slaves of both sexes they always have to wait upon them.

They rise about half past seven or eight o'clock in the morning; spend the forenoon in playing and toying with their female slaves, who are never absent, and in laughing and talking with them, while a few moments afterwards they will have the poor creatures whipped unmercifully, for the merest trifle. They loll in a loose and airy dress upon a sofa, or sit upon a low stool, or upon the ground, with their legs crossed under them. They chew pinang, or betel, with which custom all the Indian women are infatuated; they likewise masticate the Java tobacco, which makes their spittle of a crimson colour; and when they have done it long they get a black border along their lips, their teeth become

black, and their mouths very disagreeable,
though it is pretended that this custom purifies
the mouth, and is a preservative against the
tooth-ache.

As the Indian women are not deficient in understanding, they would become very useful
members of society, endearing wives, and good
mothers, if they were but kept from familiarity
with the slaves in their infancy, and educated
under the immediate eye of their parents, who
should be assiduous to inculcate in their tender
minds the principles of true morality and polished
manners. But, alas ! the parents are far from
taking such a burdensome task upon themselves.
As soon as the child is born they abandon it to
the care of a female slave, who generally suckles
and rears it till it attains the age of nine or ten
years. These nurses are often but one remove
above a brute, in point of intellect ; and the
little innocents imbibe with their milk all the
prejudices and superstitious notions which dis-
grace the minds of their attendants, and which
are never eradicated during the remainder of
their lives.

They are remarkably fond of bathing and
ablutions, and make use for this purpose of a
large tub, which holds three hogsheads of water,
and in which they immerse their whole body at
least twice a week. Some do this in the morn-

ing in one of the running streams out of the
city.

In common with most of the women in India,
they cherish a most excessive jealousy of their
husbands, and of their female slaves. If they
discover the smallest familiarity between them,
they set no bounds to their thirst of revenge
against these poor bondswomen, who in most
cases have not dared to resist the will of their
masters, from fear of ill treatment.

They torture them in various ways ; they
have them whipped with rods, and beaten with
rattans, till they sink down nearly exhausted :
among other methods of tormenting them, they
make the poor girls sit before them in such a
posture that they can pinch them with their toes
in a certain sensible part, which is the peculiar
object of their vengeance, with such cruel ingenuity that they faint away by excess of pain.

Instances of the most refined cruelty practised
upon these wretched victims of jealousy, by
Indian women, and which have been related by
witnesses worthy of belief, have been recited,
but they are repugnant to every feeling of humanity, and surpass the usual bounds of credibility.

Having thus satiated their anger upon their
slaves, their next object is to take equal revenge

H

upon their husbands, which they do in a manner less cruel and more pleasant to themselves.

The warmth of the climate, which influences strongly upon their constitutions, together with the dissolute lives of the men before marriage, are the causes of much wantonness and dissipation among the women.

Marriages are always made at Batavia on Sundays, yet the bride never goes abroad before the following Wednesday evening, when she attends divine service; to appear sooner in public, would be a violation of the rules of decorum.

As soon as a woman becomes a widow, and the body of her husband is interred, which is generally done the day after his decease, if rich she has immediately a number of suitors; but the laws do not allow a re-marriage till the expiration of three weeks.

Their dress is very light and airy; they have a piece of cotton cloth wrapped round the body, and fastened under the arms, next to the skin; over it is a shift, a jacket, and a chintz petticoat; which is all covered by a long gown or *kabay*, which hangs loose; the sleeves come down to the wrists, where they are fastened close with six or seven little gold or diamond buttons. When they go out in state, or to a company where they expect the presence of a lady of a counsellor of India, they put on a very fine muslin *kabay*, made like the other, but hanging down to the feet, while the first only reaches to the knees. When they invite each other, it is always subject to the condition of coming with the long or the short *kabay*. They all go with their heads uncovered: the hair, which is perfectly black, is worn in a wreath, fastened with gold and diamond hair-pins, called a *condé*: in the front, and on the sides of the head, it is stroked smooth, and rendered shining, by being anointed with cocoanut-oil. They are particularly attentive to this head-dress; and the girl who can dress their hair most to their liking, is their chief favourite among their slaves.

English travellers who have visited Batavia, have all admired the taste of this head-dress, which they think inexpressibly elegant. When the ladies pay their evening visits to each other, the wreath of hair is surrounded by a chaplet of flowers, in which the grateful fragrance of the *nyctanthes sambac*, or Arabian jasmine, unites with the modest sweetness of the *polyanthes tuberosa*, and is beautifully intermixed with the golden stars of the *mimusops elengi*.

On Sundays they sometimes dress in the European style, with stays and other fashionable incumbrances, which however they do not like, being accustomed to a dress so much looser and more pleasant in this torrid clime.

When a lady goes out, she has usually four or more female attendants, one of whom bears her betel-box. They are sumptuously adorned with gold and silver, and this ostentatious luxury the Indian ladies carry to a very great excess.

They seldom mix in company with the men, except at marriage-feasts.

The title of My Lady is given exclusively to the wives of counsellors of India.

The ladies are very fond of riding through the streets of the town in their carriages in the evening. Formerly, when Batavia was more flourishing, they were accompanied by musicians; but this is no more customary at present than rowing through the canals which intersect the town in little pleasure-boats : going upon these parties, which were enlivened by music, was called *orangbayen*.

There was a theatre at Batavia, but it was soon given up.

The coaches are small and light. Glass windows to coaches are alone allowed to the members of the government, who have also the privilege of painting or gilding their carriages agreeably to their own taste.

A slave must run before every wheel-carriage

with a stick in his hand, in order to give notice of its proximity, and prevent all accidents ; for the streets not being paved, the approach of the carriage cannot be easily perceived.

Most people hire a carriage, at the rate of sixty rixdollars a month, of the licensed stable-keepers, by whom the duty is paid. Counsellors of India, and a few others of the Company's upper servants, are exempted from it.

Sedan-chairs are not in use here. The ladies, however, sometimes employ a conveyance some-what like them, called a *norimon*. This is a kind of box, narrower at the top than the bottom, and carried by a thick bamboo pole, fastened over the top. They sit in it with their legs crossed under them, and have then just room enough to sit upright, without being seen.

The carts for the conveyance of goods inland, drawn by buffaloes, are of a very simple and clumsy construction. A long pole, which serves for a beam, goes through an axletree, which turns two wheels, or rather round blocks like quoits, sawn out of the trunk of a thick tree, about four feet in diameter, and having a round hole in the centre, through which the end of the axletree is inserted. At the further end of the beam is a cross piece of wood of four or five feet in length, with four stout pegs, and which is laid upon the shoulders of two buffa-

loes, in the manner of a yoke, so that their
necks fit between the pegs; and this serves both
to bear the weight of the cart and to drag it
along. The carts themselves are small, and
cannot carry a great weight ; they have a covering of leaves, to preserve the load from the rain.

The trade of the Company is managed by the
director-general. The burdensome duty of his
office is greatly alleviated by two assistants, who
are senior merchants of the castle. Their business consists chiefly in superintending the housing
in the Company's warehouses of all goods which
are brought to Batavia by their ships, and the
delivery of them again : all returns on this score
are first made to them. The senior of them has
the superintendence of all the goods which
arrive, and the other over those dispatched.
Deliveries are made on warrants signed by one
of them. All papers relative to trade, which
are received from the out-factories, are examined
by them, and they report their contents to the
director. They are both likewise administrators
of the great treasury, but derive little emolument from it. Their office is one of the most
troublesome of any in the Company's civil service
at Batavia. and is not equally lucrative in comparison with others to which less labour is attached, and whence much greater profits accrue;
yet it is an office of much consideration, as it

gives the precedency over all other senior merchants.

All merchandise is housed in the Company's
repositories, which are situated partly in the city
of Batavia, and partly on the island of Onrust,
under the direction of administrators, or warehouse-keepers, who must render account of the
same.

This branch of business is divided into several
departments, each of which has two administrators, two commissaries, and a book-keeper. Some
of these administratorships are very lucrative,
especially that of the island of Onrust, on account of the large quantities of goods deposited
there. A certain per-centage is allowed to all
the administrators, upon the whole of the goods
which they deliver, for waste, loss in weight, and
damage, when the delivery is effected within a
twelvemonth after the receipt; but when the
goods have lain more than a year in the warehouses, the allowance is greater.

The occupation of the commissaries at the
warehouses, is to take care that the Company
suffers no prejudice at the receipt or delivery of
goods. They are obliged to be present at the
weighing of every thing, and to be attentive to
the accuracy of the weight; an oath of fidelity
in the discharge of their duty is administered to
them annually by the council of justice.

The quantity of goods sent from Europe to India is inconsiderable, in comparison with those which are conveyed from one part of the Indies to another, or to Europe. The chief article of exportation to India is gold and silver, in bullion and coin. The annual exportation of the precious metals to India, by the Dutch East India Company, has been calculated at nearly 550,000*l*.

People well worthy of credit, who have lived forty years and more at Batavia, affirm that there is an inconceivable difference between the actual state of the city, with respect to trade, and its flourishing situation, before the year 1740. Free inhabitants, who had never been in the service of the Company, used then to return to Europe laden with riches, very few instances of which occur at present; hence it may be plainly perceived that there is little chance of making money at Batavia by private trade, and it is well known that it grows worse from day to day; and this, combined with its unhealthiness, may sufficiently account for its deterioration.

Something has been already said of the province of Jaccatra ; namely, that it is a possession of the Company, subdued by their arms, whose natives are their immediate subjects, governed by the council of India, and more particularly under the eye of the governor-general.

A person is appointed by the governor, under the title of commissary of inland affairs, who represents the sovereign in the interior of the country.

He adjusts all differences which arise between the native grandees, with the pre-knowledge of the governor-general, and exacts all penalties and fines laid upon them, the greater part of the profits of which accrue to him. He is feared and respected like a prince, in the interior parts, as the happiness of every individual is almost entirely in his power.

The regents, who are his coadjutors in the administration of the land, are taken from among the natives. The first in rank are the *adapatis*, to whom the government of a large district is intrusted. Then follow the *tommagongs*, who are, however, much lower in rank, having the direction over a proportionately smaller extent of country; although each of them stands alone in his local jurisdiction. These have *inghebées* under them, who are as lieutenants, and before whom disputes of little importance between the inhabitants of their districts are settled; yet the parties may appeal to the commissary.

It is only when very important matters occur, in which the Company have a particular interest, that they are brought to the cognizance of the government at Batavia, and settled by them.

The commissary, who resides without the city, has a guard of natives every night at his house, and twenty or twenty-four armed attendants, who are Javanese, in the pay of the Company.

The chief productions yielded by this province, are sugar, coffee, indigo, and cotton-yarn. The revenues which the Company draw from it, amount annually to full a million of gilders.

The original letters, which are written by the council of India, to the Indian princes, are composed in the Dutch language, and signed by the governor-general, and by the secretary in the name of the government; but translations are always added in the Malay, Javanese, or other language of the prince to whom the letter is addressed. For this purpose, there are several translators at Batavia, who are well paid, and have the rank of merchants.

The letters which are sent by the Indian princes, to the government, are written upon gold or silver flowered paper, and are brought to the council with much ceremony.

All goods which are carried into or out of Batavia, are subject to duties which are levied at the bar, at the entrance of the city. These, as well as the other taxes and imposts, are annually farmed out, generally to Chinese. The whole of them amount together upon an average to

32,000 rixdollars, *f*.76,800 per month, making *f*.921,600 per annum, about 83,800*l*.

Of the several islands which lie before Batavia*, there are no more than four, which are made any use of by the Company ; and of these, Onrust is the principal. This island lies about three leagues N.W. from Batavia ; it is nearly round, rises six or eight feet above the surface of the water, and is of small extent, being about 4800 feet in circumference. In the centre of the island, and within a fort, consisting of four bastions and three curtains, stand the warehouses and other buildings. On these fortifications, and on three small outworks, which are constructed at the water's edge, the walls of all which are whitened with lime, are mounted sixteen pieces of cannon of various sizes. " The fortified island of Onrust," says Captain Parish, who was there in 1793, "is well situated to command the channel that affords the principal passage into the road. The work upon that island was of a pentagonal form ; its bastions were small and low, not more than

---

* They are, in all, fifteen in number, and have the follow- ing names given to them : Onrust, de Kuiper, Purmerend, Engels Onrust, Rotterdam, Schiedam, Middleburgh, Amster- dam, Horn, Harlem, Edam, Enkhuizen, Alkmaar, Leyden, and Vader Smit. The two first are innermost, and are front- ing, and within sight of the city.

twelve feet the highest; and not always connected by curtains. A few batteries were lately
constructed on the outside of this work, that bore
towards the sea. On these, and on the bastions,
about forty guns were mounted in different directions. South of this was another island (this
must be that called de Kuiper), at the distance
of a few hundred yards, on which two batteries,
mounting together twelve guns, had been lately
erected."

In the year 1730 a small church with a steeple
was erected here; where service is performed on
Sundays by a clergyman, who comes hither from
Batavia for that purpose every week.

The Company have here ten or twelve large
warehouses, which are almost always full of
goods; pepper, japan copper, saltpetre, tin, ca-
liatour-wood, sapan-wood, &c. They are under
the direction of two administrators, who, as
before mentioned, have very lucrative places.

On the north side of the island stand two
saw-mills; and on the south side there is a long
pier-head, on which are three large wooden
cranes, erected for the purpose of fixing masts in
ships, or unstepping them. Three ships can lie
here, behind each other, alongside of the pier,
in deep water, to be repaired, or to receive or
discharge their cargoes. There is another pier,
a little more to the westward, called the Japan
pier, where one ship can lie to load or unload.

There is above twenty feet of water against the piers, and it rises and falls about five feet, once in four-and-twenty hours. All the Company's ships which require it are hove down at the wharfs along the piers, and receive every necessary repair with ease and dispatch. " It would be injustice," says Captain Cook, " to the officers and workmen of this yard, not to declare, that, in my opinion, there is not a marine yard in the world, where a ship can be laid down with more convenience, safety, and dispatch, nor repaired with more diligence and skill."

The government of the island, and the direction over the repairs which take place here, are intrusted to a master-carpenter, who has the management of every thing, except what relates to the departments of the administrators of the warehouses. His office is esteemed a very profitable one, and he has the rank of senior merchant. Though the island is but small, the number of people dwelling upon it, is supposed to be near three thousand, among whom are three hundred European workmen.

About sixteen hundred feet from Onrust is the island de Kuiper, or Cooper's Isle, which is one third less in size than the former. The Company have several warehouses upon it, in which coffee is chiefly laid up. There are two pier-heads, where vessels may load and discharge at its south side. There are several large tamarind-trees interspersed over it, which afford an agreeable shade. The workmen who are employed here in the daytime, are fetched away at night to Onrust, and only two men remain behind as a watch, together with a number of dogs, who are remarkably fierce, so that no one dares to set his foot on the island at night.

To the eastward of Onrust, and at twice the distance of Cooper's Isle, is the island Purmerend, which is half as large again as Onrust. It is planted with shady trees; and in the centre is a building which serves for an hospital, or lazaretto, for persons afflicted with the leprosy, and other incurable diseases, who are sent thither from Batavia. It is supported by the alms of Europeans and Javanese, but the latter contribute the largest share.

The island of Edam lies about three leagues N.N.E. from Batavia. It is about half an hour's walk in circumference. It is very woody, and has abundance of large and ancient trees. Among them is one, the trunk of which is so large, that twenty men, with their arms extended, cannot encompass it; its outward branches shoot downwards, and, taking root, as soon as they reach the earth, grow again up into trees; I saw some of them which were already two feet thick; it is the banian-tree, *ficus indica*, or Indian-fig; it is es-

teemed holy by the Javanese, and is much venerated by them. The Company have some
warehouses on this island, for salt; but the
chief use they make of it, is as a place of exile
for criminals, who are employed in making
cordage, and over whom a ship's captain is
placed as commandant.

CHAPTER VI.

*Causes of the Unhealthiness of Batavia.—Mud-banks.
—Morasses.—Familiarity of the Inhabitants with
Disease and Death.—Want of Circulation in the
Canals.—Deserted and untenanted Houses.—
Depreciation in the Value of Houses.—Other
Causes, originating in Europe, applied to explain
the great Mortality at Batavia.—Periods when
the Number of Deaths successively increased.—
Register of Deaths in Hospitals, &c.—Com-
parative Statement of the Number of Men lost by
the Company every Year.*

SOUND reason, and the united experience of
ages, have incontrovertibly demonstrated that
low swampy land, such as has been abandoned,
or thrown up by the waves of the sea, and countries overgrown with trees and underwood, are
all extremely unhealthy, and frequently fatal
to a great proportion of their inhabitants.   And
the insalubrity of the air has been found to
augment or decrease as the habitations of mankind have been placed nearer to or farther from
morasses, or stagnant waters, or woods, which
by their proximity prevent the noxious exhalations from being dissipated by a free circulation
of air.

All these causes of disease and death combine, in a greater or less degree, their baneful influence to render Batavia one of the most unwholesome spots upon the face of the globe.

They make their appearance throughout all the neighbouring foreland; and, from the point of Ontong Java, on one side, to two leagues beyond Ansjol on the other, where the firm sandy beach commences, a dismal succession of stinking mud-banks, filthy bogs, and stagnant pools, announces to more senses than one the poisonous nature of this dreadful climate.

Along this shore the sea throws up all manner of filth, slime, mollusca, dead fish, mud, and weeds, which putrefying with the utmost rapidity by the extreme degree of heat, load and infect the air with their offensive miasmata. This aggregation of mud and putrefaction receives a more peculiar increase during the bad or west monsoon, than at another time; and the constant prolongation of the pier-heads of the river, contributes also a share towards this accretion. The mud-banks thus recently thrown up are soon covered with such bushes and shrubs as are peculiar to morasses, whereby fresh supplies of mud and filth are caught and retained; and the noxious exhalations are augmented and strengthened, while the north-west winds convey the whole of the putrid effluvia to the city.

Near Batavia are likewise several very low
tracts, especially to the west of the city, which
although they lie far enough from the sea not to
be subject to inundation by it, yet by the continual and heavy rains which fall in that season
of the year, often stand under water ; and even
include in their circuit swamps covered with
high trees, which augment the corruption of the
atmosphere by their foulest vapours.

It is not strange that the inhabitants of such a
country should be familiar with disease and death.
Preventive medicines are taken almost as regularly as food, and every person expects the
returns of sickness as we do the seasons of the
year.   In the words of a late intelligent traveller, " the European settlers at Batavia commonly appear wan, weak, and languid; as
if labouring with the ' disease of death.'   Their
place of residence, indeed, is situated in the midst
of swamps and stagnated pools, whence they are
every morning saluted with ' a congregation of
' foul and pestilential vapours,' whenever the sea-
breeze sets in, and blows over this morass.
The meridian sun raises from the shallow and
muddy canals, with which the town is intersected, deleterious miasmata into the air; and
the trees, with which the quays and streets are
crowded, emit noxious exhalations in the night.
There are few examples of strangers remaining

in Batavia long, without being attacked by fever, which is the general denomination in that place for illness of every kind. The disorder at first is commonly a tertian ague, which after two or three paroxysms becomes a double tertian, and then a continued remittent, that frequently carries off the patient in a short time. The Peruvian bark is seldom prescribed in any stage of the disease; or is given in such small quantities as to be productive of little benefit. The chief, or rather the sole medicine administered, is a solution of camphor in spirit of wine. The practitioners of physic at Batavia, where the presence of the most skilful certainly is necessary, not having had the advantages of a medical education, are satisfied as to theory, with considering the nature of the fever as being to rot and corrupt the human frame; and, as to practice, that camphor being the most powerful antiseptic known, it is proper to trust to it, by a rule more simple even than Moliere's, and to exhibit it in every variety and period of the complaint. The intermittent fever does not, however, always prove fatal; but continues, in some instances, even for many years; and the patient becomes so familiarized to it as scarcely to think it a disease, attending, in the intervals of its attack, to his affairs, and mixing in society. A gentleman in that predicament, conversing upon the nature of the climate, observed, that in fact it was fatal to vast numbers of Europeans who came to settle there; that he lost many of his friends every year; but for his part he enjoyed excellent health. Soon after he called for a napkin to wipe his forehead, adding, that this was his fever-day; he had a shocking fit that morning, and still continued to perspire profusely. Upon being reminded of his late assertion of being always healthy, he replied, he was so, with exception of those fits, which did not prevent him from being generally very well; that he was conscious they would destroy him by degrees, were he to remain in the country long, but that he hoped his affairs would enable him to leave it before that event was likely to take place. It is supposed that of the Europeans of all classes who come to settle in Batavia, not always half the number survive the year. The place resembles, in that respect, a field of battle, or a town besieged. The frequency of deaths renders familiar the mention of them, and little signs are shown of emotion and surprise, on hearing that the companion of yesterday is to-day no more." When an acquaintance is said to be dead, the common reply is, " Well, he owed me nothing;" or, " I must get my money of his executors."

The circumstances just noticed would alone be sufficient to render Batavia a most unwholesome place of abode, and the mortality greater here than at any other spot of the Company's possessions; but to these more than adequate causes which occur in the environs and situation of the city, may be added the present interior state of the town itself, whereby the destructive unhealthiness of the climate is carried to the very pinnacle of corruption.

Two principal causes are to be met within the city, and a great part of its insalubrity is to be ascribed to them; namely, the little circulation of water in the canals which intersect it, and the diminution of the number of its inhabitants. The former is occasioned by the river, which formerly conveyed most of its water to the city, being now greatly weakened by the drain which has been dug, called the *Slokhaan*, which receives its water from the high land, and carries it away from the city, so that many of the canals run almost dry in the good monsoon. The stagnant canals, in the dry season, exhale an intolerable stench, and the trees planted along them impede the course of the air, by which in some degree the putrid effluvia would be dissipated. In the wet season the inconvenience is equal; for then these reservoirs of corrupted water overflow their banks in the lower part of the town, and fill the lower stories of the houses, where they leave behind them an inconceivable quantity of slime and filth : yet these canals are sometimes cleaned ; but the cleaning of them is so managed as to become as great a nuisance as the foulness of the water; for the black mud taken from the bottom is suffered to lie upon the banks, in the middle of the street, till it has acquired a sufficient degree of hardness to be made the lading of a boat, and carried away. As this mud consists chiefly of human ordure, which is regularly thrown into the canals every morning, there scarcely being a necessary in the whole town, it poisons the air while it is drying, to a considerable extent. Even the running streams become nuisances in their turn, by the negligence of the people ; for every now and then a dead hog, or a dead horse, is stranded upon the shallow parts, and it being the business of no particular person to remove the nuisance, it is negligently left to time and accident.

The second cause originates in the decay of trade, which was formerly so flourishing in this place, that there used to be scarcely a possibility of procuring a house within the walls of the city ; at present, on the contrary, those houses in which the greatest merchants dwelt, their counting-houses where they carried on their business, and the warehouses which received their immense stocks of merchandise, are now either deserted and untenanted, or changed into stables or coach-houses.   The ruined square, the *Lepel,* or Spoon-street, and other parts of the lower town, afford the most visible testimony of this decay.

The buildings remaining thus uninhabited and uncleansed, speedily contract in this low, warm, and marshy place, an infectious and foul air, and contaminate even the houses adjoining ; and that this both causes and augments the unhealthiness of the place, is evident from the circumstance that the mortality is greater in the lower town, or on the north side, than in the other parts of the city which are more fully inhabited.

The castle, which is now esteemed the most unhealthy part of the whole place, used not to be more so than any other spot around it; but at that time the buildings in it, which are appropriated for the governor general, and for the first servants of the Company, were inhabited by them ; these stand at present empty, are neglected, choked with dirt, and running to decay: the poor office-clerks, who have not the means of procuring another abode, and are compelled therefore to dwell in those buildings erected for them in the castle, are the victims.   The military, who are for the most part quartered in the barracks built for them, and the people belonging to the marine department, who reside upon or

near the admiralty-wharf, which is opposite to the
castle, are no less exposed.

Most people, not satisfied with having left the
lower town in order to go and live higher up,
have abandoned the city altogether, and reside
in gardens without the walls, and as far removed
from the town as their circumstances or the
employments which they have to attend to in the
city will allow them; letting their houses in the
city stand empty, or occupying them only for a
short time of the year, and no longer than is
absolutely necessary. This goes on increasing
from year to year, and will probably, in the
lapse of time, produce the total abandonment
and ruin of Batavia. The amazing depreciation
in the value of houses, is a clear proof of this
assertion.

The Dutch, who are so fond of gardens in
Holland, have transferred that taste, where it can
certainly be cultivated with more success, and
indulge it to a great extent, at their houses a
little way from Batavia; but still within that
fenny district, concerning which an intelligent
gentleman on the spot used the strong expres-
sion, that the air was pestilential and the water
poisonous. Yet the country is every where so
verdant, gay, and fertile; it is interspersed with
such magnificent houses, gardens, avenues,
canals, and drawbridges; and is so formed in

every respect to please the eye, could health be
preserved in it, that a youth coming just from
sea, and enraptured with the beauty of every
object he saw around him, but mindful of the
danger there to life, could not help exclaiming,
" What an excellent habitation it would be for
immortals !"

Although the chief causes of the greater insalubrity of Batavia than any other place under the
same parallels, have been pointed out, it would
be wrong to ascribe solely to these the amazing
mortality among the Europeans who come hither.
There are other causes, which are independent
of Batavia and its climate, which contribute to
this mortality. These may be chiefly considered
as originating in Europe, since it is certain that
the supplies of men arriving in the Indies from
Europe, have not for several years past been
found to bring with them those healthy constitutions which they did half a century ago. The
continual increasing dearness of provisions in
Europe since the year 1740, has, as is naturally
the case, most affected the lowest classes of
society, who have in consequence been obliged
to take up with coarser and less nourishing food,
which must undeniably have a prejudicial effect
upon their animal frame. These, for no other
sort of people, a very few excepted, take service
with the Company, when conveyed on board of

the ships, deteriorate their constitutions, which have been already fundamentally shaken, by the hardships attendant on a sea life, the close and narrow places where they are lodged, and the melancholy with which most of them are attacked, on account of leaving their native country.

Arriving thus at Batavia, the most unwholesome spot which could be selected, with a broken constitution, which has received new shocks from their long voyage, it can scarcely be expected, when to this is added a scanty and insipid diet, consisting of rice and some dried fish, together with the extreme plenty and cheapness of fruit, and the easy access to strong liquors, that they should long survive the fatal moment when they first set foot on this dangerous shore: this regards the soldiery. But it is not only from the military that the muster-rolls of death are swelled: the same mortality likewise takes place among the seafaring part of the Company's servants; yet it is not so much, in every respect, applicable to those who are really seamen, and having from their youth been bred up to the profession, have in general subsisted upon better food, and acquired a more hardy temperament, but with respect to merely nominal sailors, who have never before stood upon a deck, and who constitute the greater number of the mariners in the employ of the Company : these must be looked upon as on an equality with the soldiers.

Thus, when it is said that the mortality is general in the military and marine departments of the Company's establishment, it must be considered, that the greatest number of the individuals engaged in the sea-service, consist of such as differ from the military upon their first coming on board, only in name. Many years ago, a sufficient number of able seamen could be procured, not to be compelled to have recourse to landsmen for filling up a ship's complement; but, ever since the year 1740, the many naval wars, the great increase of trade and navigation, particularly in many countries where formerly these pursuits were little attended to, and the consequent great and continual demands for able seamen, both for ships of war, and for merchantmen, have so considerably diminished their supply, that in our own country, where there formerly used to be a great abundance of mariners, it is now with much difficulty and expense that any vessel can procure a proper number of able hands to navigate her.

Many people who have never visited the countries between the tropics, and are too apt to credit the misrepresentations of travellers, have been led to believe, that excessive heat is the cause of the unhealthiness of Batavia; but the healthiness of many other countries where the same degree of heat prevails, is proof enough of the contrary. At Surat, and in Bengal, which are esteemed the most salubrious parts of India ; more than once the thermometer of Fahrenheit has risen above 100° in the months of March and April, while at Batavia it has seldom been higher than 90°, and generally below that point ; which is a degree of heat not unusual even in our own country : and this is moreover considerably mitigated by the refreshing land and sea breezes, returning alternately at stated hours in regular rotation.

The intermediate calms, however, before these breezes relieve each other, are not wholesome. The stagnation of the atmosphere at those times, and especially in the evening, before the land-wind begins to blow, and when the vapours, exhaled during the heat of the day, hang low over the earth, is hurtful to respiration ; and the evening air is, in consequence, more especially pernicious at Batavia. Yet many of the inhabitants are accustomed to sit out of doors in the evening, because the warmth within exceeds that without.

There may, perhaps, be other causes, besides the various disadvantageous circumstances attending the local situation and actual state of the city above adduced, which may give occasion to the prevailing disorder and great degree of mortality for many years past observed at Batavia, and which are either not yet discovered, or cannot be pointed out with sufficient accuracy of proof; for it is certain, that many of the circumstances here enumerated were in existence at those times when the city was not reckoned a more unhealthy place of abode than any other under the same climate.

An unusual degree of mortality first made its appearance in the year 1733; and in that, and the five following years, the deaths amounted annually to more than two thousand among the free merchants, or burghers, and Company's servants, and full fifteen hundred slaves.

From 1739 to 1743, the mortality was not quite so great; for in those five years, no more than five thousand five hundred and sixty-two of the Company's servants died in the hospitals, whereas the number amounted, in the preceding five years, to eight thousand two hundred and eighty-six; but it afterwards increased again, so that from 1744 to 1771, the deaths in the hospitals alone, into which no others are admitted than such as are in the Company's service, and of these only the common soldiers and sailors, who have not money to provide themselves with better accommodation, are the only persons who claim admittance, amounted to forty-eight thou-

sand and thirty-six. In the year 1769 alone,
there died in and out of the hospitals:

2434   of the Company's servants,
 164   Burghers,
 681   Native Christians,
 833   Mahomedans,
1331   Slaves, and
1003   Chinese.
_____
6446

And of the latter the number may at least be
augmented by one third, as so much may be taken
for the deaths concealed, in order to avoid payment of the tax upon funerals ; and the numbers
mentioned above, are only such as have been
declared.

The dead in the hospitals amounted, from the
beginning of July 1775, to the end of July 1776,
to the number of two thousand five hundred and
ninety-five.

The following is a correct list of the number
of deaths in t he hospitals at Batavia, from the year
1714 to 1776 , viz.

Year.	Dead.	Year.	Dead.	Year.	Dead.
1714	459	1720	750	1726	904
1715	469	1721	614	1727	676
1716	453	1722	730	1728	656
1717	494	1723	657	1729	626
1718	591	1724	769	1730	671
1719	660	1725	925	1731	780

Year.	Dead.	Year.	Dead.	Year.	Dead.
1732	781	1747	1881	1762	1390
1733	1116	1748	1261	1763	1750
1734	1375	1749	1478	1764	1757
1735	1568	1750	2035	1765	1754
1736	1574	1751	1969	1766	2039
1737	1993	1752	1601	1767	2404
1738	1776	1753	1618	1768	1833
1739	998	1754	1517	1769	1742
1740	1124	1755	2109	1770	2434
1741	1075	1756	1487	1771	2480
1742	1082	1757	1441	1772	2066
1743	1283	1758	1638	1773	1187
1744	1595	1759	1337	1774	1957
1745	1604	1760	1317	1775	2788
1746	1565	1761	1000	1776	2877

It was in 1733 that canals were chiefly begun to be dug around Batavia, by which the water was diverted from taking its course through the city, and from that time the number of dead has constantly increased. In 1744, a second hospital was erected, and in order to defray the expenses, the regulation was introduced in both hospitals, that the wages of all the sick who were admitted into them, should be withheld from them while they were under cure, and applied to the benefit of the institutions, whence, it is said, many more patients died from the chagrin this regulation caused them; and we accordingly see that that and the succeeding years are marked with a greater mortality than before. In 1761, they began to stow in the hospital, without the city, more sick people than the two hundred convalescents, who were formerly attended there; and the years immediately following, show another period of increase. In 1775, an hospital-ship was laid up in the road, in consequence of which, as well in that as in the next year, the number of dead was greater than ever.

On making a comparison between the number of deaths, and the remaining servants of the Company at Batavia, and those at the other settlements, it appears, that out of five thousand four hundred and ninety Europeans, who were present at Batavia, according to the annual muster, on the 30th of June 1768, of which number, however, one thousand three hundred and thirty-eight were patients in the hospitals, two thousand four hundred and thirty-four died within the ensuing twelve months : and that the number of the Company's servants, at all the out-settlements, was on the last day of June of the same year, according to muster, fourteen thousand four hundred and seventy Europeans ; of whom, one thousand six hundred and thirty-seven died in the year following: whence it appears, that the proportion of the dead to the living is at Batavia, as twelve to twenty-seven, which is almost one half, and at the out-settlements, as eleven to one hundred, or something less than one ninth. The Company, therefore, lose in general every year one fifth part of their

servants. And they experienced a loss in the
same proportion, during the same period of twelve
months, upon the crews of thirty-seven ships
navigating in India ; and of the crews of twenty-
seven ships that sailed from Europe in 1768-
1769, which all together amounted, by their muster-rolls, to five thousand nine hundred and se-
venty-one hands, the number of dead was nine
hundred and fifty-nine, which is also nearly one
in six.

This comparison may certainly appear in
different lights in different years, yet not so much
so, but that the calculation may in general be
taken for what has for several years past been the
annual result.

CHAPTER VII.

General Review of the Decline in the Company's Affairs.—Recapitulation of the Receipts and Expenditure of each Settlement.—General Statement, &c.—Reflections on the decayed State of the Company.—Receipts and Expenditure.

W ERE the prosperity of the East India Company only in a state of decline, from the circumstances already mentioned, hopes might be entertained of relief and restoration. A fortunate chance of war, or a favourable peace in Europe, might afford sufficient opportunities of engaging men enough to supply, in a very ample manner, the deficiency of people now laboured under.

But many other circumstances concur, if not to render the restoration of the Company's affairs a matter of impossibility, at least to afford the most unfavourble prospects respecting them.

It is not only for a few years past, that the decline of this great body has been manifest, but from much earlier times: " It cannot by any means be denied," says Mr. Van Imhoff, in his Considerations of the year 1742, "that the present state of the East India Company wears a much more disadvantageous aspect, and is not by far in so flourishing a condition as in former times." Mr. Mossel writes to the same effect, in the year 1752 ; and very little reflection is required at present to discover, that in the year 1777, the situation of the Company has, in the last five-and-twenty years, become much worse; and that their affairs threaten a disastrous termination at no very distant period, if more effectual measures of redress are not suggested, and resorted to, than those which have hitherto been employed.

The common course of events, in this world, teaches us, both from ancient and from modern history, that there have been, or are, no empires, states, republics, nor public bodies, but have all, after reaching the summit of their greatness, declined considerably, though the one more than the other, in power and consideration ; although the means which have been resorted to, have ever had the wished-for effect of wholly preventing their ruin ; and it has been fortunate, when, acting as palliatives, they have served to procrastinate the fall. These vicissitudes must be ascribed to the inscrutable designs of Providence ; and it should seem, that by them the Ruler of the universe hath, for the accomplishment of his all-wise purposes, intended to manifest to mankind the utter instability of every thing in this sublunary world.

The primary causes, which sap the foundations of a state or society, whilst in its most flourishing vigour, and pave the way for its decline and fall, are very seldom known. The seemingly unimportant commencements of ruin are nearly undiscernible, and they do not appear till long afterwards, and when the evil is so deeply rooted, and has raised itself to a height visible to all, while it is likewise, in general, too late to remedy it; or if some appearances of the latent source of ruin be discovered, the fatal consequences which may arise from it, are seldom duly appreciated. In this, the body politic resembles the animal frame, and is like a man in the bloom of life, who, enjoying an uninter-rupted state of health, possessed of a firm and unshaken constitution, pays no regard to the first insidious attacks of a slight indisposition, which he presumes will easily be overcome by the natural strength of his constitution; till too late he finds, that with unmarked, but hideous strides, the direful disease has advanced beyond the grasp of medicine, and at length bids bold defiance to every attempt of nature, or of art, to check its fatal progress.

The evil which has its origin in the constitution of the body politic itself, is irresistibly augmented, when accidental extraneous circumstances concur to drag to perdition, the state or institution which thus totters on its base. Both the interior leaven of corruption, and external adventitious evils, have taken place, and still exist, with regard to the Company.

The latter need not be insisted on, they are evident to every eye : with respect to the former, the first germination of those seeds of destruction is to be placed in the period when the conquest of countries, and the increase of territory, were more the objects of the Company's attention, than the prosecution, increase, or improvement of their commerce and navigation ; and this period is to be defined, as having chiefly existed from the year 1660 to 1670, during which time it was that the Company made themselves masters of the Portuguese establishments on the Malabar coast, and of the island of Celebes, both which acquisitions cost them a great expense of blood, and incalculable treasures, and have never been of any other than an imaginary advantage to their interests.

As this chapter is devoted to a general consideration of the affairs of the Company, it may not be amiss to insert here, a recapitulation of the receipts and expenditure of all the establishments of the Dutch East India Company ; the former comprising their territorial revenues, and profits upon the country-trade ; and the latter, all the expenses of each establishment *per*

se, taken from the books of the year 1779, that
s, from the 1st of September 1778, to the 31st
of August 1779 : the order in which the establishments are placed, is that in which they are
arranged in the books of the Company, and
those actually known to be in the hands of the
English, and distinguished by the mark ✝.

	Charges.	Expenditure.
Jaccatra, including Batavia	*f.*1,820,327	*f.*2,384,930
✝ Amboyna	48,747	201,082
✝ Banda	9,350	146,170
Ternate	114,997	229,406
Macasser	63,190	163,137
Timor	13,619	11,712
Banjermassing	—	12,091
Palembang	3,922	49,677
Japan	106,802	96,356
✝ Malacca	162,520	113,235
✝ Padang	74,577	53,675
✝ Bengal	385,159	265,517
✝ Coromandel	427,131	452,133
✝ Ceylon	611,704	1,243,038
✝ Malabar	414,977	489,645
✝ Surat	283,207	—
✝ Cape of Good Hope . . .	195,168	505,269
North-east Coast of Java . .	436,874	281,873
Cheribon	35,761	12,584
Bantam	—	78,262
Landak and Succadana . .	1,764	9,726

Total *f.*5,209,796 *f.*6,799,518
5,209,796

leaving an excedent in the charges of   *f.*1,589,722

or 144,520*l.* 3*s.* 8*d.* sterling. The Indian possessions of the Company were not always a
charge upon them. In 1689, the balance,
drawn in the same manner, was on the other
side, and showed a favourable surplus of
f.937,361. 10. 5 (85,214*l.* 13*s.* 5*d.*) ; and in 1744,
an advance appeared of f.779,056.(70,823*l.* 5*s.* 6*d*).
Mossel, to whom we have so frequently had
occasion to refer, calculated, in his time (1753),
the whole yearly receipts at f.8,791,000, and the
expenditure at f.6,517,500, which would leave
a favourable surplus of f.2,273,500 (about
206,680*l.* sterling), and which is amazingly
different from the later results. The deficiency
is supplied by drafts from India, upon the direction in Holland; and, together with various
other objects, the expenses of equipping twenty-
five or thirty ships annually, the payment
of the wages and premiums to the returning
crews, the salaries of the directors, and
the expenses of the administration at home,
the dividends to the proprietors, &c. form
the general debit of the Company, against the
profits upon the merchandise they dispose of in
Europe. These gains have been calculated upon
an average, at from ten to eleven millions of
gilders, or about one million sterling, per annum;
and this computation appears to be just, from the
following statement of the invoice-prices, and

net proceeds of the cargoes received from India
for the ten years from 1750 to 1759, viz.

Years.	Ships.	Invoices.	Sales.
1750 ·	22 ·	ƒ.7,372,177 ·	ƒ.19,024,209
1751 ·	24 ·	9,630,682 ·	16,670,614
1752 ·	20 ·	7,883,361 ·	23,133,580
1753 ·	22 ·	10,259,866 ·	17,317,037
1754 ·	22 ·	8,859,297 ·	19,840,766
1755 ·	22 ·	9,652,485 ·	19,806,077
1756 ·	25 ·	8,421,419 ·	19,890,066
1757 ·	26 ·	8,935,720 ·	14,829,367
1758 ·	22 ·	6,906,717 ·	18,934,386
1759 ·	28 ·	8,437,469 ·	18,817,328

THE ISLAND OF JAVA.

1774—5.

BOOK II.

CHAPTER I.

Navigation from Batavia to Samarang.—Govern-
ment of Samarang.—Dissension between the Soe-
soehoenam and Manko Boeni.—The latter sup-
ported by the Company —The Empire of Java
parcelled out.—The Sea-coast ceded to the Com-
pany.—They make themselves Masters of Balam-
bouang.—Soera Carta, the Capital of the Soesoe-
hoenam.—D'Jokje Carta, that of the Sultan.—
Residencies of Oelopampang — Sourabaya —
Grisse — Samanap — Rembang — Joana — Ja-
para — Samarang — Pacalonga—Tagal.—Resi-
dents at the Courts of the two Javanese Emperors.
—Establishment, Revenues, &c. of this Govern-
ment.

O<small>N</small> leaving the road of Batavia, navigators
should steer for the island of Edam ; then between that and the island of Leyden, or else
between Leyden and Enkhuizen; and afterwards
round Point Carawang, and so far from the

shore to have offing enough to pass the reef
which runs out from Sedary : the lead is in this
respect the best guide, since you must not suffer
it to shoal more than ten fathoms till this reef is
passed, of which you may be certain in the daytime, when the high trees of Sedary, which are
few, single, and easily to be distinguished on
account of their height, bear s. s. w. ; and in the
night steering to the east, in twelve fathoms
water : it deepens when you are past the reef ;
upon which steer more southerly, keeping however your depth into the bight of Pamanoekan,
till the water shoals to ten and nine fathoms,
when you must steer again more east, in order
not to approach too near the shore of Java ; you
may be sure you will then run clear of the rock
upon which the Castle of Woerden was lost,
although there is sixteen fathoms water close to
it : but the safest is to anchor here during the
night.   Having doubled the point of Pamanoekan, steer for that of Indraymaye, in ten,
eleven, twelve, and thirteen fathoms water ;
upon approaching the last, be sure to keep in
those depths, to avoid falling upon the reef of
Cheribon ; which having passed, steer as much
to the southward of east as to retain nineteen or
twenty fathoms depth ; or in the daytime keeping within sight of the shore till you begin to
near Pamalang, when you must steer so far off

shore as to double the rock which lies N. E. by N. from that place : you will then come in sight of the hills of Tagal, Samarang, and the Two Brothers ; when the last bear due south, steer for the shore, and afterwards along it, till the ensign-staff of Samarang bears s. s. E. and let drop your anchor in five or four and a half fathoms. All along the north coast of Java, the bottom is a soft clay.

This government, which is one of the most lucrative for the Company's servants, was twenty years ago only a commandery ; it was changed into a government upon the considerable acquisition of territory made by the Company along the sea-coast, by cession to them by the Soesoehoenam, at the conclusion of peace, during the government of Mr. Harting, who terminated the war of Java, in which the empire was split into two parts, one remaining under the Soesoehoenam, and the other becoming subject to the present reigning sultan, Manko Boeni.

It is of the utmost importance to the Company that this establishment be well governed, on account of the immediate relation which it has to the two above-mentioned Javanese princes, who nourish the most implacable enmity towards each other. The Company would not wish to see a termination of their mutual hatred, for as long as it remains in force they retain the secure possession of their acquisitions along the sea-coast ; and though not nominally, they are always in reality likewise masters of the inner parts ; for, upon uniting with either of these two princes, they can make the balance lean so much against the other, that they are both constrained to remain quiet.

This was in fact their object in fomenting the dissension which arose between the Soesoehoenam and Manko Boeni, and whence the war of Java had its origin.

The last named, a prince of the imperial family, and a descendant of the former Soesoe-hoenam, wanted to have as an appanage the province of Mataram, which had already been allotted to the hereditary prince Masseyd, son of the Soesoehoenam.

This Masseyd was of a short stature and an excellent disposition; he gloried in the circumstance that he had never killed an European except in battle. Manko Boeni, on the contrary, and his son and heir apparent, more than once caused the captive Europeans to be pounded in their rice-blocks; or he cut off their genitals, and forced them into their mouths. The last-mentioned in particular showed himself an implacable enemy of all Europeans, and of a most cruel and bloodthirsty temper.

As Mataram was an extensive and wealthy

district, which the Company did not wish to remain under the power of the Soesoehoenam, they clandestinely encouraged Manko Boeni to require it at the hands of the Soesoehoenam. The Company did this agreeably to their adopted system of weakening the empire as much as possible, in order to preserve their possessions in Java with greater ease; and they secretly promised Manko Boeni to maintain him in his pretensions.

Immediately hereupon he left the court, and retired to his domains, where he directly rose in arms against the emperor, and began a civil war.

The Company, in order to save appearances, and to render their conduct more defensible than if they had openly espoused the part of Manko Boeni, offered themselves as mediators between these two princes, foreseeing that the Soesoehoenam, who relied upon the superiority of his power, far from conceding, would reject all overtures of peace, and, prosecuting the war with vigour, would endeavour entirely to subdue his opponent.

Exactly as they foresaw, the emperor rejected all offers of conciliation, and entered eagerly into a war which was to end in his discomfiture and disgrace.

There was now the most urgent necessity for

the Company to espouse, in earnest, the quarrel of Manko Boeni, partly in order to persevere in their proposed system, and partly to secure themselves from the ill will which would infallibly, and not unreasonably, be entertained against them by the Soesoehoenam, as he soon became acquainted with their manœuvres to kindle those flames of discord; and, if Manko Boeni were subdued, the power of the Soesoehoenam would thereby be so much augmented, that the Company would, in all probability, have stood in need of the exertion of all their power to resist his attack.

Fortune favoured their arms: and though incalculable sums were expended in the contest, they attained their object—the division and separation of the empire.

A considerable part of the provinces of the empire of Java, among which Mataram was one of the principal, was given to Manko Boeni, under the title of Sultan; the whole of the northeast coast of the island was ceded to the Company, upon condition of their paying a yearly acknowledgment of twenty thousand rixdollars, about 4350*l.* to the Soesoehoenam, who retained possession of the remainder under his former title.

The jurisdiction of this government was further extended by the conquest of the land of Balambouang, situated at the most eastern extremity of Java.

This province, the productions of which can never yield the Company a sufficient compensation for the blood and treasures which it costs, would doubtless have never become an object of their ambition, if the cupidity of one of their servants had not excited in them the desire of possessing it.   Placing no limits to his lust of wealth, he rather, as ordinary methods could not assuage his rapacity, put the interest of his employers to the hazard, than suffer his boundless thirst of gold to remain unsatisfied.

The plausible pretext by which the government in India, and afterwards the direction in Holland, were instigated to disturb the tranquillity of this country, which they had for many years regarded with so much indifference, was the representation that there was reason to fear that the English wanted to take possession of it; nay, that an expedition for that purpose was actually on foot, and was expected, or had arrived at the Straits of Bali; that they had probably already landed, and would consequently establish themselves in time on the island. There was some truth in this report ; but the Company would in all likelihood never have begun that ruinous war, had it not been for these interested instigations; for their competitors would not have found it an easy matter to establish their trade here, notwithstanding this was so much insisted on at Samarang.

In this manner was this empire, once so formidable, split into three parts; and it has thereby, not only become a less dangerous neigh- bour to the Company, but is likewise entirely under their control, by means of their holding the balance between the above-mentioned poten- tates. Even the prince who has the greatest right to the throne is not appointed heir to the crown, without the consent of the Company; and the nomination of the prime ministers of both the princes is likewise vested in the Com- pany.

The capital city of the Soesoehoenam is Soere Carta, commonly called Jolo, and is about two days journey inland, south-east from Samarang. That of the sultan, D'Jokje Carta, lies five days journey south-west from Samarang, at the south side of Java, in the province of Mataram *.

To the government of the north-eastern coast

---

* The resting-places, or stages, on the road from Samarang to D'Jokje Carta, are :

from Samarang	to Onara,	5 (Dutch) miles.
from Onara	to Jambou,	7 ditto.
from Jambou	to Sombou,	7 ditto.
from Sombou	to Surrigenent,	6 ditto.
and from Surrigenent	to D'Jokje Carta,	9 ditto.

of Java, the seat of which is at Samarang, belong all the factories, commonly called residencies, which the Company possess from Oelopampang, as far as the province of Cheribon: which last, in the same manner as Bantam, is under the immediate administration of the government at Batavia.

The sea-coast, thus ceded to the Company, belonging to the government of Samarang, extends from Oelopampang to Tagal, full one hundred German miles in length: the breadth inland is various, running farther into the country at one place than at another *. It is divided into nine residencies.

* Extract from Captain Bligh's Journal, 1789.

" Sunday the 6th. In the afternoon we saw the high land of Cape Sandana, which is the north-east part of Java. The next day we were off the Cape, which is a low point projecting from the high land. It is placed by the Dutch maps in 7° 52′ south; but, according to my observation, and our estimated distance from the land, I make it in 7° 46′.

" We steered to the westward, along the coast of Java, and on the 10th, at noon, we anchored off Passourwang, in two fathoms, distant from the shore half a league; the entrance of the river bearing s. w. The coast hereabouts is so shoal, that large ships are obliged to anchor three or four miles from the land. As soon as we were at anchor, I got in my boat and went on shore. The banks of the river, near the entrance, were mud, on which grew a few mangrove bushes. Among them we saw hogs running, and many were lying dead in the mud, which caused a most intolerable stench, and made

Oelopampang is the first, beginning from the east. This settlement was only established after

---

me heartily repent having come here; but proceeding about a mile up the river, the course of which was serpentine, we found a very pleasant country, and landed at a small and well-constructed fort. The houses at Passourwang are neatly built, and the country appears to be well cultivated. The produce of this settlement is rice, of which they export large quantities. There are but few Dutch here; the Javanese are numerous, and their chief lives with considerable splendour. They have good roads, and posts are established along the coast; and it appears to be a busy and well-regulated settlement. Latitude 7° 36′ south.

" The next day, about noon, we sailed; and on the 12th, in the evening, anchored in Sourabaya road, in seven fathoms: the flagstaff bearing s.¼w. distance from the shore one mile. We found riding here seven square-rigged, and several smaller vessels. Sourabaya is one of the most pleasant places I ever saw. It is situated on the banks of a river, and is a mile and a half distant from the sea-shore, so that only the flagstaff can be seen from the road. The river is navigable up to the town for vessels of 100 tons burden, and the bank on one side is made convenient for tracking. The Chinese carry on a considerable trade here, and have a town on the side of the river opposite to Sourabaya. The country near the town is flat, and the soil light, so that they plough with a single bullock or buffalo. Our latitude observed in Sourabaya road, was 7° 11′ south.

" On the 17th we sailed from Sourabaya. At noon we anchored at Grissee, which is a town, with a small fort, belonging to the Dutch. We remained here about two hours. Latitude of Grissee, 7° 9′ south.

" The navigation through the Straits of Madura is so intricate, that, with the little opportunity I had, I am unable to unthe war of Balambouang, and is under the direction of a junior merchant.

Sourabaya is the next; the chief of which has, at present, the rank of senior merchant, and the title of commander of the eastern district. It mostly yields rice.

Then follows Grissee, where the resident has the rank of merchant, and the chief produce of which is also rice.

Samanap, situate on the island of Madura, is the residence of a junior merchant. It yields

---

dertake a description of it. The next day, September the 18th, having passed the Straits, we bore away to the westward, along the coast of Java. We had regular soundings all the way to Samarang, off which place we anchored on the 22d, in the afternoon; the church bearing s. e. distance from the shore half a league, depth of water two fathoms. The shoalness of the coast here, makes the road of Samarang very inconvenient, both on account of the great distance which large ships (of which there were several in the road) are obliged to lie from the shore, and of the landing, which is in a river that cannot be entered before half-flood. This river resembles the one at Passourwang, the shores being low, with offensive dead animals lying about them. Samarang is surrounded by a wall and ditch. Here is a very good hospital, and a public school, chiefly for teaching the mathematics. They have likewise a theatre. Provisions are remarkably cheap here, beef being at ten doits per pound, and the price of a fowl twelve doits. The latitude of Samarang is 6° 57' south.

" On the 26th, we sailed from Samarang, and on the 1st of October we anchored in Batavia road," no article of trade, and serves only to keep watch over the island in which it lies.

Rembang, where formerly a junior merchant was stationed, but the chief has now the rank of merchant. It yields salt and timber ; and a ship of five hundred tons, and three or four smaller vessels, are annually built here for the service of the Company.

At a little distance from Rembang lies Joana, which is under the control of a junior merchant. It yields rice and timber, also a little indigo and cotton-yarn.

Japara, where the resident has the rank of merchant. Its productions are the same as those of Joana.

Samarang, the residence of the governor of Java. Its chief produce is rice and cotton-yarn.

Farther on is Pacalonga, governed by a junior merchant, and yielding sugar and rice.

Lastly, and most to the westward, Tagal, where a merchant is the resident, which produces rice.

Besides the residents at these places along the coast, those at the courts of the Soesoehoenam, and the sultan, are also subordinate to this government. There are two at each, the first ranking as senior merchant, and the second as merchant ; with the difference, however, that at Soera Carta the former is a captain in the military, while at D'Jokje Carta, they both belong to the corps of *pennists*.

The Company maintain a body of about one hundred and fifty men in the service of each of these princes, nominally as a body-guard in honour of them ; but this number is rarely full, there being a great want of men in this government.

Both these Javanese princes have a number of children by their many concubines, so that the portion of each child is not very brilliant, and some of them are merely common regents at different places : thus I met with one, at the residency of Joana, who was *tommagong*, or regent, of the province of Patti, and at the same time uncle of the reigning Soesoehoenam.

The whole establishment of the Company, in the government of the north-eastern coast of Java, consisted, in 1776-1777, of 234 persons in civil, and 13 in ecclesiastical employments ; 35 surgeons and assistants, 109 belonging to the artillery, 268 seamen and marines employed on shore, 1356 soldiers, and 30 mechanics ; in all 2045 Europeans. The governor has a very lucrative office ; it is estimated to yield from 80 to 100,000 rixdollars, or nearly 20,000*l.* sterling annually. He is generally superseded in two or three years, and must, in his turn, make room for a more unfledged successor, that each may

have his due share of the good things of the
land.   The greater part of this immense revenue
accrues from the trade which the governor is
enabled to carry on.   His ostensible emoluments,
besides his salary, consist in three tenths of an
allowance of five per cent. granted to the Company's servants; the rest being distributed in various proportions to the inferior officers, on all
the import and export duties, and other territorial
sources of revenue of the Company, and in a
yearly contribution levied from the strand-regents,
or native magistrates of the several districts,
amounting together to 1713 Spanish dollars.
Besides the articles mentioned, a large quantity
of lentils, *cadjang*, which are much used for the
consumption of the common people, with some
cardamom, the *amomum compactum*, ginger, *amomum zingiber*, and turmeric, are exported from
this colony.   They are mostly employed in the
country-trade.   Part, however, of its produce
comes to Europe.   In 1778, the following goods,
brought from this part of the coast, were sold in
Holland, viz.

> 20,000 lb. of indigo, at *f.*6 (11*s*. sterling)
>   per lb. which stood the Company in
>   *f.*1 10 (2*s*. 9*d*.)
> 50,000 lb. of turmeric ;

and 65,000 lb. of cotton yarn.

On the other hand, this colony takes opium, to

the amount of f.1,500,000, or about 136,000l. sterling annually, silk clothes, India piece-goods, and European manufactures, on all which large profits accrue both to the Company and to their servants. The statements of Governor Mossel make the yearly receipts of the Company here amount to f.400,000, and the charges to f.380,000 ; but, in 1779, the former were f.436,874, and the latter only f.281,873; leaving a favourable balance of f.155,001, or about 14,000l.

CHAPTER II.

Combats of wild Beasts and Criminals.—The Com-
pany appoint Successors to the Princes of Java—
Likewise Prime Ministers.—Tomogangs, or na-
tive Regents.—Prices paid for the Rice.—Ac-
count of the Depatti of Samarang.—Entertain-
ment at the Governor's House.—River of Sama-
rang.—Tides.—Fortifications.—Chinese Temple.
—Warehouses and Workshops.—Guardhouse.—
Government House.—Suburbs.—Garrison.—View
of Fisher's Island.—Account of Japara.—The
Fort, House of the Resident, &c.—Old Japara.
— Ancient Javanese Tombs. — Old Moorish
Temple.—Character of the present Resident.

THE most favourite diversions of the Javanese
emperors are combats between wild beasts.

When a tiger and a buffalo are to fight for
the amusement of the court, they are brought
upon the field of combat in large cages. The
field is surrounded by a body of Javanese, four
deep, with levelled pikes, in order that, if the
animals endeavour to break through, they may
be killed immediately ; this, however, is not so
easily effected, but many of these poor wretches
are torn in pieces, or dreadfully wounded, by the
enraged animals.

When every thing is in readiness, the cage of
the buffalo is first opened at the top, and his
back is rubbed with certain leaves, which have
the singular quality of occasioning an intolerable
degree of pain, and which, from the use they are
applied to, have been called buffalo-leaves by
our people, but by the Javanese *kamadu*. They
sting like nettles, but much more violently, so
as to cause an inflammation in the skin. On
every vein they have sharp-pointed prickles,
which are transparent, and contain a fluid that
occasions the irritation. Dr. Thunberg says, it
is a species of nettle, before unknown, to which
he gave the name of *urtica stimulans*. The door
of the cage is then opened, and the animal leaps
out, raging with pain, and roaring most dreadfully.

The cage of the tiger is then opened, and fire
is thrown into it, to make the beast quit it,
which he does generally running backwards out
of it.

As soon as the tiger perceives the buffalo, he
springs upon him; his huge opponent stands
expecting him, with his horns upon the ground:
if the buffalo succeed in catching and throwing
him into the air, and the tiger recovers from his
fall, he generally loses every wish of renewing
the combat : and if the tiger avoids this attempt
of the buffalo, he springs upon him, and seizing
him in the neck, or other parts, tears his flesh

from his bones; in most cases, however, the buffalo has the advantage.

The Javanese who must perform the dangerous office of making these animals quit their cages, may not, when they have done, notwithstanding they are in great danger of being torn in pieces by the enraged beasts, leave the open space, before they have saluted the emperor several times, and his majesty has given them a signal to depart; they then retire slowly, for they are not permitted to walk fast, to the circle, and mix with the other Javanese.

The emperors sometimes make criminals, condemned to death, fight with tigers. In such cases, the man is rubbed with *borri*, or turmeric, and has a yellow piece of cloth put round him; a *kris* is then given to him, and he is conducted to the field of combat.

The tiger, who has for a long time been kept fasting, falls upon the man with the greatest fury, and generally strikes him down at once with his paw; but if he be fortunate enough to avoid this, and to wound the animal, so that it quits him, the emperor commands him to attack the tiger; and the man is then generally the victim: even if he ultimately succeed in killing his ferocious antagonist, he must suffer death, by command of the emperor.

An officer in the Company's service, who had

long been stationed at the courts of the Javanese emperors, once witnessed a most extraordinary occurrence of this kind, namely, that a Javanese who had been condemned to be torn in pieces by tigers, and for that purpose had been thrown down from the top into a large cage, in which several tigers were confined, fortunately fell exactly upon the largest and fiercest of them, across whose back he sat astride, without the animal doing him any harm, and even, on the contrary, appeared intimidated; while the others also, awed by the unusual posture and appearance which he made, dared not attempt to destroy him; he could not, however, avoid the punishment of death, to which he had been condemned, for the emperor commanded him to be shot dead in the cage.

According to the stipulations of the last treaty, the Company determine which of the sons of either emperor shall succeed his father, who is then nominated heir to the crown; they equally appoint the *pangorang*, or prince, who has the administration of the empire, and is first *warin*, or prime minister.

The Company's possessions along the coast, are divided into regencies. A Javanese, of somewhat more than common birth, is appointed regent in each, by the Company, under the denomination of *tomagong*, to whom the determination of disputes of small moment, among his subordinate Javanese, is left ; they may even inflict corporal punishment, but not death ; crimes which require the last being only adjudicable by the native council at Samarang.

They must likewise take care that the Javanese inhabitants deliver the produce of their land to the Company, or rather to themselves, in order to convey it afterwards to the several residencies or factories.

A certain contingent, or assessment of produce, is laid upon each of these regents, which they must be attentive to furnish punctually, or they run a risk of being dismissed.

The Company pay a fixed price for every article. That of the rice is ten rixdollars, or twenty-four gilders, for every coyang of 3400 pounds weight, about 1s. 6d. per cwt. ; but when the harvest fails, they sometimes pay five rixdollars more ; or when the wants are very large, as in the year 1773, when the scarcity of this grain at Batavia, occasioned by a certain occurrence respecting the first administrator in the grain-magazine, was very great ; or when several succeeding harvests have failed, orders are then given to the residents to buy the rice immediately from the natives, and the coyang then stands them in fifty rixdollars.

Samarang alone has a *depatti,* who is higher

in rank than the *tommagongs*, and a prince of the blood, or *pangorang*. He has, however, no jurisdiction over the other regents, except those within the district of Samarang itself. He is likewise the chief of the native council.

Stavorinus was once in company with this prince, at the house of the governor of Samarang, who gave an entertainment that evening on the occasion of the birth-day of his little boy. The *depatti* was placed next to the governor, at his right hand; he appeared to be a man of full fifty years of age, rather above the usual stature, thin, and of a brown complexion; he had little beard, a grave deportment, and was very sedate and unaffected in conversation.

He was dressed in a short brown coat, with silver buttons, and silver-edged button-holes; the sleeves sat tight to the arms, below the elbow to the wrists. Under this he wore a chintz *saron*, which reached to the ground. On his feet he had large slippers, square-toed, and turned up. His cap, or head-band, was of white linen, which having been much beat, and prepared with rice-starch, was as transparent as gauze. He was addressed by the governor by the title of *towang depatti*, and treated with great respect. His *dalm*, or dwelling, stands on the Pascébaan, near the house of the governor, whom he is likewise obliged to accompany, when he goes to reside at Boeyang, about half a league farther, where he has also a mansion close to that of the governor.

On the occasion of this festival, two of the elders of the church at Samarang, the fiscal, and the lieutenant of the artillery, danced a reel for the diversion of the company.

The town of Samarang lies on the east side of the river of the same name, which takes its rise about three Dutch miles inland, and falls into the sea, about two hundred roods below the place; at its mouth it is not more than three hundred and thirty, or forty, feet broad. A bridge over it, leads from the town to the usual residence of the governor, which is called the Vryheid, Freedom, and is a large and handsome building. The Chinese and Javanese campons or suburbs are on the same side of the river.

This river, like all others in Java, has a bank lying before its mouth, which is in some places composed of soft mud, and in others of hard sand. At low-water there is scarcely more than one foot water upon it.

Here, as well as all along the coast of Java, the tide rises but once in four-and-twenty hours. In the bad monsoon, or when the west winds blow, it is high-water in the daytime, and low-water at night; and during the good or east monsoon, the contrary takes place. When it is low-water without the banks, the rivers are at the highest; and the moon seems to have no influence, here, upon the tides.

The fortifications of Samarang are in the same state as all those of the Company, most deplorably bad. The walls which surround it, and connect the projections, for they can scarcely be called angles, are low and ruinous.

The most remarkable object at this place was a temple of the Chinese, a middling-large building, with two courts before it; the interior is decorated with the gigantic images of their gods, which are strongly gilt, and make a splendid appearance.

Samarang has a small but neat church; near it is an elegant tomb of Mr. Toutlemond, formerly head administrator and second in command here.

The warehouses and workshops stand in a row, all under one roof, projecting out, and covering a piazza before them, full three hundred feet in length. They are to the south-west of the town, by the river-side.

The guard-house has, besides the place for the privates, two large apartments for the accommodation of the officers upon duty.

The government-house, formerly the residence

of the governor, and where the several offices
are actually held, is near to, and faces the river.
There are three campons, or suburbs—the Chinese, the Javanese, and the Bouginese; of which
the two first are west, and the last eastward of
the river.

When the garrison of Samarang is complete,
it amounts to one hundred and fifty men, besides an independent company of dragoons,
which are under the command of a captain-lieute-
nant; all the other military of the place are
subject to the orders of the captain-commandant
of Samarang.

Visschers, or Fisher's Island, is a small low
island, about two leagues and a half s. w. from
Japara, and particularly distinguishable by two
or three high trees, which grow upon it.

Behind De Nis and a little to the s. e. lies
another island, which is surrounded by very
dangerous shoals, and contracts the extent of the
road of Japara.

From the island De Nis, the water shoals gradually, first, from five to two and a half fathoms; and when in this last depth, you are
abreast of the Foul island: it then lessens by degrees, to six feet, when you are close to a high
rock, called the Walvisch, or Whale, whence
it shoals more and more, with some sunken
rocks, to the mouth of the little river of Japara.

where is two feet water and less, and which is about 140 or 150 feet over. The source of this stream lies no more than a short league up the country.

On entering the rivulet on the north side, is a gentle eminence, about fifty feet high, on the western part of which stands a small triangular fort, with one bastion pointing to the sea, and the other two to the land; in the middle of the curtain which connects the two last is the gate: this fort is mounted with several pieces of cannon of different calibre; it is built of stone, and is kept in good repair: the garrison consists of one serjeant, two corporals, and sixteen privates. The rest of the eminence is used for a burying-ground, in which the ensign-staff is erected.

On the south side of the rivulet are some Javanese hetises and huts, and about sixty roods from its mouth it is crossed by a bridge.

On the north side is the house of the resident, opposite to a large plain, planted with shady trees, and railed round. It has several handsome apartments, furnished neatly and elegantly, in the European style. On the left of it is a pleasant bower, or pavilion, of one hundred feet in length, eighteen in breadth, and ten in height, so closely interwoven with flowering shrubs, that it is impervious to light showers of rain. At the end is a grotto; and when, on an evening, the

M

whole is illuminated, it forms a very charming *coup d'œil.*

About a mile and a half above the settlement the stream turns a saw-mill, which saws the yearly quantity of four or five thousand large logs of timber into planks, termed mill-planks. The water is carried to the mill through a brick channel, and a dam is made across the rivulet, to prevent it from running off, till there is sufficient to turn the mill.

One Dutch mile inland lies the ancient Javanese city of Japara, called Old Japara, formerly the residence of the sovereigns of an empire of that name. The tomb of one of them is still in existence; it contains the body of the emperor, that of his most beloved wife on the right hand, and of two other of his wives on the left, together with several of his children. The shape of these graves is oblong: the approach to them is through a sort of portico, inclosed by a railing, in a large covered apartment. Qver the graves of the emperor and his most beloved wife, a large piece of linen is continually expanded, which covers them both; and they are strewed every Friday with fresh flowers.

Not far from this is an old ruinous Moorish temple, of stone, with such beautiful sculpture of imagery and foliage, that the art and ingenuity of the Javanese of those times excites our admiration. This temple is at least three hundred years old.

At the sea-side, about two miles from Japara, the resident has a wooden summer-house, in a pleasant grove of cocoa-nut-trees, whence there is a very fine prospect out to sea, and of the neighbouring islands.

CHAPTER III.

Mandelique Island.—Account of Joana River.—
Inland Navigation to Samarang.—The Town.—
Chinese Campon.—Fort.—House of the Resident.
—Character, &c. of the present Resident.—His
Emoluments.—Celebration of the New Year.—
Account of the Tommagongs, or native Regents.—
Of the Pattis, or Sub-regents.—Entertainment at
the House of one of the Tommagongs.—Lubok
Island.—Madura.

EARLY on the morning of the 22d of December 1774, we weighed anchor and put to sea, in
order to proceed to Joana.

Mandelique, often called the Duivelsklip,
or Devil's Rock, because, in the east monsoon, ships are detained here a long time by
contrary winds and currents before they can
weather it, is small but of a middling height,
so as to be seen at the distance of five or six
leagues. It lies about half a league from the
coast of Java ; between which and the island
there is a passage, in three and a half or four
fathoms water, but it is too narrow to be safe,
and ships therefore very seldom pass through it.

The river of Joana flows out of a large inland
lake, into which several small streams discharge

themselves. It is called the inland sea, and disembogues its superfluous water mostly through this river, which, after a considerable serpentine course, falls into the sea about four leagues to the westward of Rembang. It is one of the largest and most navigable rivers along the whole north coast of Java, being at the mouth, and a great way up beyond the residency, twenty and more feet deep, and in breadth about two hundred.

In the bad monsoon the afflux is much more violent than in the good monsoon. The water, as is the case with all rapid streams, is turbid; but when it has stood still some time in pots or casks, it becomes very clear and pleasant.

Up this river is a passage along several other rivers to Samarang, and thence farther up the country. This navigation may be performed in boats, termed *permayangs*, in two or three days; and it is especially availed of in the bad monsoon, when the voyage by sea, round the island Mandelique, requires too long a time, and is much too dangerous for small craft.

A broad mud-bank, upon which there is sometimes less than a foot water, lies before the mouth of the Joana river. From its mouth to the residency, which stands full a league up on the west side, it runs between low and swampy grounds, which are uncultivated, and produce nothing but brushwood : they are sometimes inundated when the river rises suddenly after heavy rains.

The town of Joana commences just above the residency. It consists of two rows of houses built along the river, about a quarter of a Dutch mile in length. At the farther end lies the Pascébaan, and not far from it is the dwelling of the *tommagong*.

On the opposite side, upon an island formed by the river of about half a Dutch mile in circumference, stands the Chinese campon.

The *odge*, or fort of Joana, is a redoubt with four demi-bastions, in which are the rice-warehouses, barracks for the soldiery, and some buildings which serve for a kitchen and other offices for the resident. The house of the resident stood formerly within the fort, but it has been pulled down, and a new one has been built without, of freestone, on the east side, and is kept in excellent repair.

This mansion was constructed according to the plan of the engineer Haak. It consists of two pieces opposite to each other, connected by a lofty dome of full twenty-five feet diameter, supported by four columns of the Tuscan order. Both these pieces are, however, but of one story ; they are sixty feet long and twenty-five broad, within the walls. One of them forms a single hall of the same dimensions. The other is divided into three apartments; the middle one, which is twenty-five feet in depth, and about sixteen in breadth, is opposite to the door of the great hall and to the great dome: it is fitted up as a chapel; the entrance to it is through a handsome arch or portico: on each side of it is a large chamber of the same size, making, together with the chapel, the length of the whole building on this side, and the same as that of the great hall. The walls of all these apartments are beautifully stuccoed, adorned with sumptuous gilt cornices; and the roofs are concave, wainscoted, and curiously adorned with carved imagery.

Behind this pile stands a building, constructed entirely of wood, containing three handsome rooms; and above these is one large apartment for the unmarried female slaves, and which might therefore be called the seraglio. From this edifice is a most delightful view backwards over the *paddee* or rice fields, interspersed with small groves, and terminated by the distant and lofty mountains of Japara.

In the front of all stands a handsome saloon, built close to the river-side. It is of an oblong octagon shape, and is stuccoed on the sides and roof, but the cornices are not gilt. A large balcony projects from it towards the river, the only inconvenience of which consists in the swarms of mosquitos which infest it every even-ing.

The emoluments of this residency amount annually to sixteen thousand rixdollars, about 3500*l.* They proceed from the surplus-weight of the rice delivered by the native regents to the Company, and from the cheap rate at which this article is purchased, not to mention what he himself buys up and disposes of to individuals for at least fifty per cent. profit; likewise from the collection of the timber yearly furnished to the Company at a fixed price, and which costs him no more than the labour, which is very cheap, as he has only to send two or three hundred Ja-vanese into the woods to fell the trees, and hew them into logs.

Ship-building also affords considerable gain to the present resident; for both timber and labour cost him little; a Javanese master-shipwright earning no more than about six *dubbeltjes*, or two penny pieces a day, his assistants four, and the common labourers two.

He lately built a snow of one hundred and one feet in length, according to the model of the States' armed snow, the Zephyr, of Rotter-dam, which was handsomely fitted up. It was sold for eighteen thousand rixdollars.

There are also profits attached to the *bhan-*

daary, or farm of the duties, which accrue nominally to the Chinese, but in reality to the resident.

A few days before the new year, every Javanese of the least connexion, either with the
Company or resident, comes to make presents to
him, consisting chiefly of poultry, eggs, sugar,
fruit, &c. Those of a higher order, such as the
Chinese captain, bring rolls of satin.

On the first of January 1775, a salute of one-
and-twenty guns was fired at sun-rise, from
some small pieces of cannon planted before the
saloon. On this occasion an European, a strong
and corpulent man, who acted as gunner, met
with a terrible accident. Passing before the
muzzle of one of the guns, the priming of which
had flashed without discharging the piece, it
went off the instant he was before it, and blew
him upwards of six feet forwards; the loading
had fortunately been rammed down without a
wad, so that he was no otherwise hurt than by
being dreadfully burnt on his side, arm, and
belly.

Two hours afterwards came three Javanese
regents, or *tommagongs*, belonging to the district
of this factory, to congratulate the resident on
the new year, in the following manner : *Salla-
mat taon baro touwang; Alli cassi ou mour panjang;*

that is, " Much joy with the new year; God grant you a long life."

The first of these regents, who was *tommagong* over part of the province of Patti, appeared to be a man of full fifty years old. He had gray hairs and a little beard ; he was esteemed one of the most intelligent of the Javanese, and was even thought so much of, that the Soesoehoenam wanted much to have made him administrator of his empire, but he declined the dignity, pre-ferring to be a common regent in the Company's possessions than a powerful statesman under an arbitrary monarch ; for the ministers of those princes are not only liable to incur a speedy dis-grace, and to be dismissed from their offices, but they are often degraded to the rank of *battari*, which is little different from the condition of a slave, obliged to perform the most menial and most toilsome offices ; while it is very seldom that the Company come to such extremities.

His dress consisted of a short coat, or jacket, of deep red velvet, which came a little below the hips, and was fastened with small silver buttons round the body, under the arms, and round the wrists. The lower part of this jacket, below the buttons, was stiffened out all round. Under it he wore a *saron*, in the country fashion, round his body down to his heels, made of Javanese painted cloth. His *kris* was in a sheath of gold,

beautifully worked, and the handle was made of
cajou pelli, which is reckoned the most costly
wood produced in the Indies ; it is very scarce,
of a grayish colour, with thin black veins running
through it, and of a very hard, close, and fine
texture.   His cap was of purple velvet, bordered
with narrow silver lace.   Like most Javanese of
distinction, he spoke little, and with becoming
gravity.

The next regent was the uncle of the present
Soesoehoenam, and equally regent of the province of Patti.   The simplicity of this man was
as remarkable as the intelligence of the former ;
and the resident was always able to do whatever
he pleased in the province of Patti, as the latter
was very easily persuaded to every thing.

The third regent was the *tommagong* of Joana,
a large comely man, whose good-nature was pic-
tured in his open and friendly countenance : in
understanding, however, he too was not to be
compared to the first.

There was likewise another, who was regent
of Caylam, as well as a native of the place.   The
other Javanese would not acknowledge him, or
any of the Caylammers, to be of their own race, or
true Javanese, saying, that they were produced
from the unnatural connexion of a woman with
a dog.   Indeed, the whole time that they were
together, none of the other regents condescended
to address a single word to him.

Each regent had his *patti*, or sub-regent, with him; but while the former sat upon a chair, the latter was obliged to sit upon the floor, upon his heels, and when called by his superior, to creep along the ground to him, and sit down at his feet, waiting till he was pleased to speak or to issue his commands.

At seven o'clock in the evening these regents came with a number of servants, with musical instruments, &c. to supper to the resident's house. Before supper there was music and dancing in the European style; but after it, several Javanese dancing girls were sent for, with whom each of the regents, and after them their *pattis*, danced, or, as they termed it, *tandacked*, to the sound of their own musical instruments, gomgoms, boudas, and a kind of violins, which continued till late at night, when they all left us for their own houses.

On the 3d of January the resident paid a visit to the *tommagong* of Joana. He received him in state, and during the playing of gomgoms and other instruments. His favourite wife, and the wife of his son, together with his mother, likewise came and drank tea. A large silver plate with confectionary stood upon a table near, and each took what he liked of it.

On the 14th the same regent gave an entertainment on the occasion of the marriage of his daughter, which had been solemnized some time before. The resident had caused, at his desire, the provisions to be dressed by his own people, in the European manner, so that there was little or no Javanese victuals to be seen. After supper some dancing girls were again introduced, with whom the *tommagong* and his sons *tandacked*. Their wives were not present at this; and when, a short time before the company broke up, they came in, care had been taken that the dancing girls were gone before they entered.

Lubok, commonly called the Baviaan or Baboon island, is not large, but extremely populous. Seventy or eighty vessels go continually to and fro, between it and the coasts of Java and Borneo. The inhabitants have no connexion with, and are independent of the Company.

Along the coasts of Java, from Joana, as far as the point of Grissee, where the land turns first to the south, to Sourabaya, and then, behind the island Madura, in an easterly direction to the Straits of Bali, through which it stretches to the south again, as far as the Southern Indian ocean, there is no danger to be avoided. One may sail without apprehension along the shore, at the distance of one or two leagues from the land, only taking care to steer clear of the projecting points.

Many high mountains lie inland ; the foreland is, on the contrary, low, but may be seen at the distance of three and a half or four leagues.

The land of Madura may be seen eight or nine leagues off ; but the eastern part of it, it is said, is visible at fifteen and more leagues' distance.

ON

THE ISLAND OF JAVA.

1775—8.

BOOK III.

CHAPTER I.

Situation of Java.—Face of the Country.—The North Coast.—The South Coast less known.—Weather.— Rivers.—Soil.—Agriculture.—Productions.—Upland and lowland Rice.—Pepper—Quantities furnished to the Company.—Sugar—Chiefly encouraged and manufactured in Jaccatra.—Number of Sugar-mills.—Their estimated annual Income.—Sugar-works, and Method of making Sugar.—Different Qualities of it.—Coffee—Quantities and Prices of it.—Cotton.—Quantities and Prices of Cotton-yarn.— Salt — An Article of Trade to Sumatra.—Timber.—Large Forests.—Indigo—Quantities and Prices.—Other Articles.—Minerals.

THE island of Java may with justice be considered as the most precious jewel in the diadem of the Dutch East India Company: it constitutes, together with Sumatra, Borneo, and Celebes, the Sunda islands, and is the southernmost

of them. According to the most recent and best
observations it is situated between 5° 50′ and
8° 46′ of south latitude, and extends from
120° 5′ to 129° 50′ longitude east of Teneriffe,
full one hundred and eighty Dutch miles in
length ; and at the broadest part, from the point
of Coedoes, near Japara, to the south coast of
the province of Mataram, it is about six-and-
thirty Dutch miles over. Its longest diameter lies
in the direction of w. by N.$\frac{N.}{S.}$N. and E. by s.$\frac{W.}{S.}$s.
To the east it has the island of Bali, from which
it is separated by a strait of the same name : to the
north it has the large island of Borneo, and those
of Billeton and Banca, at the distance of forty or
forty five leagues : to the north-west is Sumatra,
from which it is divided by the Straits of Sunda ;
these are no more than seven leagues over at the
narrowest part, namely, from the Varkens, or Hog-
point, to the opposite land of Bantam, and they
are here still more contracted by the island
Dwars-in-den-weg, or Thwart-the-way, which
lies in the middle of the passage : to the west
and south its shores are washed by the southern
ocean.

A chain of high mountains, commencing to
the east, in the province of Balambouang, and
running through it to the westward, gradually
decreasing in height, divides this island, longitudinally, into two parts, of which the northern

portion is the largest and the best. The north coast has almost every where a low and woody foreland; although it has hills in some places, for instance, a little to the west of Bantam, where the high land stretches down to the sea-coast.

The island has several deep inlets, or bays, on this north side, as those of Bantam, Batavia, Cheribon, Samarang, Joana, and Sourabaya, where there is good anchorage, in little depths. Indeed the whole coast affords both good anchoring-ground and a safe road for the vessels which pass and repass, during the good or south-east monsoon; but in the bad monsoon, when the north-west wind blows hard, and raises a high sea, it is dangerous to anchor near the coast, which is then almost uniformly a lee shore.

The southern coasts of Java are much less known than the northern, for the Company have not hitherto taken much trouble to have them examined; so that the greater part of what is ascertained concerning them, is gathered from the scattered information of the navigators who have accidentally sailed along them *.

* In Valentyn's map of Java, which contains five sheets and a half of large paper, the southern coasts of Java are laid down seemingly with great accuracy; the appearance of the land is every where described, and the track of some navigator who coasted along it at a very short distance, from Prince's Island

In the good monsoon, the sky is almost always clear, though sometimes in the evening a thunder-cloud comes down over the mountains: but this does not frequently happen, except near the time of the breaking up of the monsoon, when many violent thunder-storms rapidly succeed each other.

In the bad monsoon, the prevailing west winds bring with them heavy rains and violent thunder-storms; yet this makes but little alteration in the degrees of heat or cold; in the warmest part of the day, the thermometer generally stands at between 82° and 88°, and is seldom higher.

This degree of heat, if accompanied by a motionless state of the air, would, by continuance, become intolerable; but all-bountiful Nature has afforded her aid to the gasping inhabitants of this torrid clime, by the alternate land and sea breezes, which blow here every day, in regular rotation; and if they do not wholly moderate the excessive heat, yet they render it more supportable, and not very uncomfortable to those who make no considerable stay here.

---

to Balambouang, with his soundings, anchorages, nature of the bottom, &c. is marked down in it; but it does not appear when, or by whom, this voyage was performed, though, from its direction, it appears probable that it was undertaken by the command of the Company, for the express purpose of exploring the south side of Java.

The weight of the air is nearly the same throughout the year; the barometer seldom varies more than two or three lines; but the air does not seem to possess so much elasticity as in the northern regions. Experiments in electricity do not succeed here so well as in Europe.

Java is watered by a great number of rivers, which all descend from the chain of mountains which divides the island; but none of them are navigable for ships, or large vessels, on account of their insignificance, and of the bars before their mouths, and upon most of which there is little more than one foot depth at low-water. The most considerable is that of Joana, and the Sedani or Tangerang.

The soil is almost every where a reddish granulated clay, which, during the dry season, can be little tilled, by reason of its hardness, without a great deal of moistening.

The labour bestowed upon it is very trifling, in comparison with the bountiful fertility of the land in the production of various articles of necessity, luxury, and commercial importance.

Ploughing is performed here, as in most parts of India, with buffaloes, which are numerous. The plough consists of a beam, or pole, eight feet in length, to which, about three feet from the fore-end, is fixed a piece of wood, somewhat crooked and sharp-pointed: this breaks the soil, which is afterwards turned over by a triangular iron of upwards of nine inches in breadth. One or two buffaloes yoked to it, and a Chinese, or Javanese, who guides the plough, leisurely perform the work of tillage.

No manure is used for the land, at least inasmuch as regards the fields employed in more extended purposes of agriculture; garden-grounds, however, are moistened with water in which oilcakes have been soaked; which emits a most horrid excrementitious odour, but renders the soil rich and fat. The only trouble taken with the land, consists in burning upon it all the weeds and rubbish which it produces; and when one piece of ground ceases to yield sufficient crops, another is resorted to, and the first is suffered to lie fallow for several years, after which it becomes again fertile of itself.

The articles produced in the island of Java are far greater in value than those of all the neighbouring countries: they chiefly consist of the following:

In the first place, rice, which, for abundance, excellence, and flavour, excels all other countries; and it not only produces sufficient for the support of its own inhabitants, but also provides the eastern provinces and Ceylon. There are two species of it; one, which, when planted, is set nearly under water, so that the tops just ap-

pear above the surface, as the rice-plants would
otherwise die, or be destroyed; for, being too
weak to stand against the wind by itself, the
plant requires the surrounding water to support
it. The other sort, which is planted in the rainy
season, on high ground, and upon the mountains, receives the necessary moisture solely from
the rains; but it is not so good as the former
sort. The lowland rice is called *sawa*, and is
planted in May; while the upland rice, denominated *tipar*, is planted in November, and
reaped in March; and these two crops bear
some analogy to the winter and summer grain
with us: the upland rice does not yield so great
an increase as the other. These two sorts of rice
are always kept separate, and will not grow together. Mr. Marsden terms the upland rice
laddang, and the lowland *sawoor*. The former,
he says, bears the higher price, being a whiter,
heartier, and better flavoured grain, and having
the advantage in point of keeping. The latter
is much more prolific from the seed, and subject
to less risk in the culture, but is of a watery
substance, produces less increase in boiling, and
is subject to a swifter decay. It is, however, in
more common use than the former. Besides this
general distinction, the rice of each sort, particularly the upland, presents a variety of species.

In general, it may be observed that the larger grained rice is less esteemed than the smaller and whiter. The upland sort is also called *paddee goenong*, or mountain-rice. It was one of the objects of our government in sending Captain Bligh to the South Sea, to procure seeds of this mountain-rice; and notwithstanding his disasters he obtained some from Timor, which were forwarded to His Majesty's botanic garden at St. Vincent, and to other parts of the West Indies, where it is now cultivated with success.

The pepper from Java is an article which, next to the finer spices, yields, perhaps, the greatest proportional advantage to the Company; for though there are more parts where it is produced, and whence it is brought into the Company's warehouses, namely, the coast of Malabar, the west coast of Sumatra, Palembang, and Borneo, yet the greatest quantity of what the Company receive, is produced in the country of Bantam, and its dependent provinces on the opposite coast of Sumatra, as appears from the following list of what pepper was received at Batavia and Onrust, in 1776-1777, viz.

from Bantam and Lampong, -	black pepper	3,714,000 *lb.*
	white ditto	15,000
Borneo, - - -	black ditto	1,117,375
	white ditto	16,250

from Palembang,	-	-	-	black pepper	497,507 *lb.*
West coast of Sumatra,		-	ditto ditto		1,119,436
Province of Jaccatra,		-	ditto ditto		1,900

Sugar is by far the chief produce of the province of Jaccatra ; and although Cheribon, and the north-east coast of Java, annually produce considerable quantities of it, they cannot rival Jaccatra in this respect ; and no wonder, for the culture of it was early cherished by the higher powers in Jaccatra. The cultivators of the sugar-cane enjoy many exemptions of pecuniary imposts, and they have been encouraged by every means, not only by the government of Batavia, but likewise by positive orders from the chamber of seventeen in Holland, under date 20th of June 1710.

On the other hand, the cultivation and manufacture of sugar has never been prosecuted with vigour, nor suitably encouraged, on the north-eastern coast. The various plans of improvement which have been suggested, have never been made any use of ; and the last, which was presented to the governor-general Van der Parra, in the year 1774, by the resident of Japara, Mr. Van der Beke, and which contained many very good things, was never taken any notice of. Nay, so far from any encouragement being held out, the importation of sugar at Batavia, from the north-eastern coast of Java, has been almost

interdicted to private merchants, by a heavy
duty of one rupee per picol, which was solely
laid upon it in order to favour the sugar-mills in
the province of Jaccatra and the Preanger lands;
and thus, the discountenancing of the manufacture of sugar in the other parts of Java, is, probably, the cause why the common Java sugar
has never attained the quality of that of Jaccatra,
the latter being much more substantial and better
granulated.

In the year 1710, there were one hundred
and thirty-one sugar-mills in Jaccatra; their
number, however, decreased considerably before, during, and after the war of Java; so
that at the end of December 1750, there were no
more than seventy-seven, of which only sixty-six
were in a condition to work; these, with seven
in the kingdom of Bantam, eight in that of Cheribon, and thirteen in the province of the north-
eastern coast of Java, made the number of
sugar-mills existing at that time in the whole
island of Java, one hundred and five; but at
present, 1777, they are still more diminished.

Mr. Mossel has made a calculation what profit these seventy-seven sugar-mills, in the province of Jaccatra, might annually yield to their
proprietors, or lessees: he reckoned that a yearly
quantity of ten million pounds weight of sugar

might be produced by them, which he took at
four rixdollars per picol, is . . rixd.   320,000
and an equal quantity of molasses,
from which afterwards, either an inferior sugar is made, or arrack distilled, at one rixdollar per picol, . .   80,000

together, rixdollars   400,0000
upwards of 87,000*l*. sterling, or nearly 1200*l*.
for each sugar-mill.   The whole may be more
amply seen by referring to his " Observations
on the Sugar-works in the Neighbourhood of Batavia, &c." dated the 31st of December 1750.

The sugar-cane, which in general grows here very
luxuriantly, is planted from September to April,
and stands twelve or fifteen months in the field,
according as the land be rich or poor, before it
is cut.   If the soil be good, and adapted to its
cultivation, it can be cut four times; on some
grounds less often, and on others only once.

The sugar-works here, are not so well or so
solidly constructed, as those in the West Indies.
The cane is here bruised between two rollers,
and is therefore twice put through before all the
juice is expressed; the sugar-mills in the West
Indies have three rollers, so that the same quantity of cane can be pressed in half the time taken
for it here : the latter mode, however, requires a
greater degree of strength ; one or two buffaloes

are here sufficient, but at least four horses are required there for turning the mills.

The juice is twice boiled, and afterwards put into pots, upon which a layer of clay, diluted with water, and kneaded into a paste, is laid, and it continues in this state for about twenty days: during this time the clay is once or twice renewed ; and by this operation the sugar acquires a tolerable degree of whiteness ; it is then set in the drying-place, which is a shed, covered with *atap*, where it remains until it is perfectly dry, and the molasses have entirely trickled out of it, through an opening at the bottom.

When a sugar-mill is in good condition, and has no want of work-people, or of buffaloes, about fifteen thousand canes can be bruised every four-and-twenty hours ; these yield from nine to eleven pots, containing each fifty pounds weight of sugar of the first and second qualities, twelve pounds of the third quality, and from sixteen to twenty pounds of molasses.

Mr. Mossel calculated that all the canes which the sixty-seven sugar-mills annually consumed, covered four thousand six hundred *morgen*, 9200 acres, of land, to which adding the same quantity of four thousand six hundred *morgen*, for pasture-ground for the buffaloes, and ten thousand *morgen* for wood for fuel, the whole extent of ground wanted for the prosecution of that manufacture, with that number of mills, would not amount to twenty thousand *morgen*, 40,000 acres, which is but a small part of the province of Jaccatra, north of the mountains.

The first quality of the sugar differs only from the second and third by its greater whiteness. The first sort is that which is alone sent to Europe; the second goes chiefly to the western parts of India; and the third, which is the brownest, to Japan.   There is likewise another sort, which is very brown, and much less dry; it is called *dispens*-sugar, because it is mostly delivered by the *dispensiers*, or purveyors, from the provision-warehouses of the Company, to be used on board of their ships.

Coffee is likewise a product yielding much profit to Java, and great advantage to the Company.   The cultivation of it is performed in the same manner as in the West India islands.   Jaccatra and Cheribon are the two districts where it is most vigorously prosecuted, though the article is equally grown on the north-eastern coast. Java, where it is not indigenous, is indebted for this production to Mr. Zwaardekroon, who was governor-general from the year 1718 to 1725, and who procured the coffee-plant from Mocha, and after paying a very high price for what was first produced, fifteen rixdollars per picol, he continued to encourage the cultivation of it by all the means in his power. His endeavours were so well seconded by his successors, that in the year 1753, 1,200,000 pounds weight of coffee were furnished from Cheribon, at the rate of $2\frac{112}{1000}$ stivers per pound ; and full as much from Jaccatra and the Preanger lands at $\frac{7}{8}$ stivers per pound: and, in the sequel, the quantity produced grew so large, that in the year 1768, the quantity of 4,465,500 pounds weight of coffee, was delivered to the Company from Jaccatra and the Preanger lands, at the reduced rate of four rixdollars per picol of one hundred and twenty-five pounds, 14s. 5d. per cwt.; although the native cultivator must deliver one hundred and sixty pounds for a picol, which excess in the weight is an emolument partly accruing to the commissary of inland affairs, and partly to the administrators in the warehouses.

But the reason why Jaccatra appears to furnish so large a proportion of coffee, is, that a considerable quantity of this produce which is grown in the parts of the province of Cheribon nearest to Jaccatra, come down through the last-mentioned country to Batavia: the income of the commissary for inland affairs is hereby greatly enhanced, and it is pretended, that it is more convenient to the natives.

Cotton is likewise the production of Java. The shrub, *gossypium herbaceum*, which produces it, is cultivated in almost every part of the island by the natives; the kingdom of Bantam, however, excepted, where little of it is found; so that the yarn which is spun of it, in the province of Cheribon, and other parts, yields a considerable degree of gain, on being clandestinely imported into Bantam.

The Company, to whom the greater part of it is delivered, pay for it, according to its qualities, forty-five, thirty-five, twenty-four, and less rix-dollars per picol of one hundred and twenty-five pounds; equal to the respective rates of $17\frac{1}{2}d$. $13\frac{1}{2}d$. and $9\frac{5}{14}d$. sterling per pound.

Jaccatra and the Preanger lands furnished in the year 1753, the quantity of about two hundred picols, or twenty-five thousand pounds of cotton-yarn; and in 1768, no more than 133 picols, or 16,225 pounds. The greater part of the cotton-yarn is sent to Holland; the rest ' employed by the natives in weaving cloths for their own consumption.

Attempts have likewise been made to introduce the manufacture of cotton cloths, as an article of trade for the Company, and to supersede part of their large importations of the article from Hindostan; but hitherto with very little success.

Java also produces salt, though it is not an

article of very extensive commercial importance. Most of it is brought from Rembang, where the Company purchase it at the rate of six rixdollars per five thousand pounds, and they export it to the west coast of Sumatra, where it is disposed of, generally, at the rate of between thirty and thirty-five rixdollars for three thousand pounds weight, which is equal to about 10s. 10d. sterling per ton English, and the selling price from 91s. 8d. to 107s. per ton.

The north-eastern coast, and part of the district of Cheribon, furnish a very large quantity of timber, logs, beams, boards, knees, &c. which is not only sufficient for the consumption of Batavia, for ship-building, houses, and domestic uses, but a very considerable quantity of it is annually exported to several of the out-factories, and, in particular, to the Cape of Good Hope.

The large forests in the above districts, belong to the Company; the natives are obliged to fell and prepare the timber, as a kind of feudal service, so that no other emolument is made by them, on this score, than the hire of the draft-oxen by which it is conveyed to the sea-shore; and this, together with the freight by sea, forms the whole of the purchase-money and charges of the timber. Those forests, however, begin to be considerably diminished.

Next is reckoned indigo, which although not an original production of Java, has been cultivated with tolerable success, since the Company have been established here; insomuch that, whereas formerly that article was obliged to be sent for from the empire of the Great Mogul, and special *firmans* were obtained, with some difficulty, for that purpose, that trade has now been abandoned in Hindostan, and instead of being purchasers, the Company have been able to be sellers of a considerable quantity of the article.

The Company pay for the first quality thirty stivers per pound, and in proportion for the second and third qualities. The indigo is sorted upon its delivery at Batavia, by a person specially appointed for that purpose. In the year 1768, Jaccatra furnished 2875 pounds of indigo, though the inhabitants have been assessed at the quantity of 6125 pounds.

Turmeric, *curcuma*, long-pepper, *piper longum*, and cubebs, *piper cubeba*, are also productions of Java; but the collection and exportation of these articles is not of great importance. The two last are most in demand for Surat.

Of minerals and metals, Java can make boast of none but a little iron-ore and star-stones, *asterias*, called in the Malay tongue, or by the natives, *maasouron*.

CHAPTER II.

Division of Java.—General Population.—Bantam.
— Boundaries. — Government. — Population. —
Dependencies.—Country of Lampoon.—The Com-
pany's Establishment at Bantam.—Expenses.—
Islands in the Straits of Sunda, &c.—Peculiar
Unhealthiness of Bantam.—Jaccatra, and its
Preanger Lands.—Boundaries.—Population.—
Administration.—Rivers.—The Mookervaart.—
Canals and Drains cut by the Dutch.— Produc-
tions.—Cheribon. —Boundaries. — Population.—
Productions. — Establishment. — Expenses and
Profits.—Empire of the Soesoehoenam.—Former
Extent and Grandeur.—Present reduced Situa-
tion.—Dominions of the Sultan —Island of Ma-
dura.—Titles of the reigning Soesoehoenam, and
Sultan.—Political Relations of the Company with
these Princes.

WHEN the Company first established themselves here, Java was divided into three large
empires, namely, Bantam, Jaccatra, and the empire
of the Soesoehoenam, which last was the most
extensive, and comprehended full two thirds of
the whole island, Cheribon being feudatory to
it. Times have now so far altered, that the

island is divided into five states, or empires, which altogether contain one hundred and twenty-three provinces, or governments, amongst which the kingdom of Bantam is considered but as one.

Each province, or government, consists of a certain number of *tjatjars*, or families, the number of which, throughout the whole of Java, including Bantam, amounted, in the year 1777, to 152,014.

These are calculated, upon an average, throughout Java, to consist of two men, two women, and two children, forming, therefore, a population of . . . . souls 912,084 *
But if to this we add the inhabitants
    of the principality of Madura,
    which, though a separate island, is
    always taken together with Java,
    and which contains ten thousand
    families, or . . . . . souls 60,000
                         ————

the whole population of Java and Ma-
    dura will amount to 972,084

---

* Huysers gives the population of Java, exclusive of Madura, as follows, viz.

in the kingdom of Bantam	5,000	tjatjars, or families
in Jaccatra	33,914	ditto
in Cheribon	15,000	ditto
in the Mataram, or empire		
of Java proper . . .	94,200	ditto

in

assuredly a very slender number of inhabitants
for such an extensive island. It was formerly
much more populous; but the long and bloody
wars with which this country has been afflicted,
for nearly a century and a half, before the Company succeeded in establishing themselves in that
firm manner in which their power here is at present rooted, is sufficient to remove our surprise
at the paucity of the inhabitants of this extremely
fertile island. The last war waged against the
empire of the Soesoehoenam seems, in particular, to have produced a great degree of depopulation. According to the statement of the population made in the year 1738, the number of
families in the territories of the Soesoehoenam
alone amounted to 309,700, or souls 1,858,200,
and at present (1777), the same lands,

which were then under the dominion of the Soesoehoenam, part of
which are now, however, taken
from him, contain no more than
118,100 families, or 708,600
                                      ─────────
                                      1,149,600

in all 148,114 families, reckoned at six individuals each, makes
the whole number of inhabitants 888,684; but he adds, in a
note, that, according to more recent accounts, the population
of Java is calculated at one million and a half, or two millions,
of people. These statements, however, do not include the inhabitants of Batavia.

making a difference of more than the half, which
would appear too improbable for belief, were the
statement not made on inspection of authentic
documents *.

The actual five divisions of Java are, Bantam,
Jaccatra, Cheribon, the empire of the Soesoehoenam, and that of the Sultan.

The kingdom of Bantam, which forms the

---

* Valentyn's statement of the population of Java, in his
time, shows a still greater disproportion; his account, in which
he takes every *tjatjar*, or family, at five persons only, gives—

in the kingdom of Ban-
tam, exclusive of the
city of Bantam . . families 5,000, or persons 40,850
in Jaccatra, exclusive of
Batavia . . . . . ditto 19,390, or ditto 96,950
in Cheribon and its de-
pendencies . . . ditto 63,120, or ditto 305,600
in the countries belong-
ing to the emperor of
Mataram, or the Soe-
soehoenam . . . ditto 483,570, or ditto 2,417,850
in the county of Balam-
bouang, a rough cal-
culation, full . . . ditto 50,000, or ditto 300,000
and in the island of Ma-
dura about , . . ditto 30,000, or ditto 150,000

Total 3,311,250

A decrease in this island from upwards of three millions to
ess than one million of people, in about sixty years, is an
amazing instance of the destructive agency of war.

western division of Java, is about one hundred
Dutch miles in circumference, each being of
twelve hundred Rhineland roods. The Indian
ocean washes it on the south; to the north-west
and north it has the straits of Sunda, and their
islands; to the east, it is divided from the empire
of Jaccatra, by a narrow slip of land, called
Grending, lying a little to the westward of the
Sedani, or river of Tangerang, and by a chain
of mountains, known by the name of Goenong
Tjeberum, which terminate to the south in the
bay of Wynkoopsbergen.

Bantam became strictly connected with the
Company, in the year 1680, by means of the
assistance afforded by them against Sultan Agon,
who had formerly abdicated the throne, but who
had resumed the sceptre; his son solicited and
obtained the aid of the Company, toward establishing him in the government. The country
remained, in a manner, independent, and its
trade continued free; but upon this, encroach-
ments were practised from time to time, and it
was sought to draw the bands of connexion with
Bantam closer, by giving assistance, towards re-
ducing the revolted province of Succadana, in
Borneo, which formerly belonged to Bantam,
and is still an appendage of that kingdom. At
last, in 1751, Bantam became wholly a fief of
the Company, occasioned by the fortunate issue

of the commotions there; the king was then privately taken hold of, and continued a prisoner, while a prince of the blood-royal, who had been kept in exile at Ceylon, was exalted to the throne in his stead; and a yearly tribute of one hundred bhars of pepper, amounting to thirty-seven thousand five hundred pounds weight, is now paid to the Company from Bantam.

The rule of succession was, at the desire of the king, regulated by the Company, who choose and appoint the heir apparent to be hereditary prince, as was done in the year 1767: this hereditary prince succeeded to his deceased father in the month of September 1777, and was formally crowned as king of Bantam, by Mr. Breton, the minister plenipotentiary deputed by the Company for that purpose.

Although the sultan, or king, of Bantam, is a vassal of the Company, he is, nevertheless, a sovereign prince, lord and master of life and death, and uncontrolled in his authority over his own subjects; he lays taxes, augments or lightens them, according to his own good pleasure: and has all other regalia, and marks of sovereignty, appertaining to a free monarch, excepting that he is restricted from entering into any alliances or engagements, either with the European or Indian princes; as likewise from selling the productions of his territories to any other than to the Company.

Bantam has the smallest population of all the divisions of Java; its whole extent comprehends no more than five thousand tjatjars, or families, and, consequently, only thirty thousand inhabitants.

The Company keep in Fort Speelwyck, including the guard which is stationed at Fort Diamond, an establishment amounting, when complete, to three hundred men.

In 1776-1777, the establishment of the Dutch Company at Bantam consisted of twenty civil servants, one clergyman, five surgeons and assistants, seventeen belonging to the artillery, thirty seamen, 199 soldiers, and ten mechanics; in all 282 Europeans. On account of its vicinity to Batavia, no revenues, whether territorial or commercial, are drawn from this place; but the charges of the establishment are not heavy: in 1779 they amounted to about 7115*l.* sterling, which is nothing in comparison with the benefit derived from the pepper furnished by Bantam. To the dominion of the king of Bantam belong all the islands in the straits of Sunda, from Prince's Island to Pulo Babi, or Hog Island, close to his capital city. Many of them are inhabited, and produce pepper; others are desert, or the resort of pirates and smugglers, who are dexterous in carrying on an illicit trade in pepper with foreign nations. In November 1769, the Dutch Company's cruising grab Zeeleeuw, the Sea Lion, was attacked, taken, and the crew massacred, in the bay of Lampoon, by these pirates. The Klapper, or Cocoa Islands, which lie on the south coast of Java, near the straits of Sunda, are uninhabited, and are only occasionally resorted to for the sake of the edible birds'-nests which are found there; but they are said to be greatly infested with enormous snakes. Prince's Island is called, in the Malay language, Pulo Selan; and in the language of its inhabitants, Pulo Paneitan. It is woody, and a very small part of it only has been cleared. Valentyn landed on it in 1694, and found it then uninhabited. He adds, that there is good anchorage in the south-west bay, in nine and ten fathoms, and two small fresh-water rivulets running into it. Lieutenant Cook, in the Endeavour, lay ten days on the south-east side, in eighteen fathoms. There is a town upon it, called Samadang, of about four hundred houses, divided into two parts, by a river of brackish water. There is no remarkable hill upon it, yet the English call the highest eminence the Pike. It was formerly much frequented by the India ships of many nations, especially the English, which have, of late, forsaken it, as it is said, because the water

is bad, and touch either at North Island, a small
island that lies on the coast of Sumatra, at the
east entrance of the straits, or at New Bay,
which lies only a few leagues from Prince's
Island, at neither of which places any considerable quantity of other refreshments can be procured. At Prince's Island may be had turtle,
with which the first, the second, and perhaps
the third, ship in the season, may be tolerably
supplied; those bought by the Endeavour's
people cost, upon an average, a halfpenny or
three farthings per pound; large fowls, a dozen
for a Spanish dollar; small deer, not larger than
a rabbit, two-pence apiece; larger deer, about
the size of a sheep, but of which only two were
brought down, a rupee; many kinds of fish,
tolerably cheap; cocoa-nuts, at the rate of a
hundred for a dollar, if picked, or one hundred
and thirty, if taken promiscuously; plantains in
great plenty; some pine-apples, water-melons,
jacks, and pumpkins; besides rice, the greater
part of which is of the mountain kind, yams, and
several other vegetables, at very reasonable rates.
The other islands in the straits of Sunda, appertaining to the dominions of Bantam, are too in-
significant for particular description. They are
mostly level, founded upon beds of coral, and
covered with trees. A few, however, have steep
and naked sides, such as the island Dwars in den

Weg, or Thwart-the-way, and the two very small round ones, called by the Dutch Brabandsch Hoedje, and Toppers Hoedje, and by the English the Cap and Button. The gentlemen accompanying Lord Macartney in the Lion, had occasion to visit the two last mentioned; they were so steep and rugged, that it was difficult to get ashore: at a little distance, they might be taken for the remains of old castles, mouldering into ruins, with tall trees already growing upon the tops; but, upon a nearer view, they betrayed evident marks of a volcanic origin: in the Cap were found two caverns, running horizontally into the side of the rock, in which were a number of those birds'-nests so much prized by the Chinese epicures. The situation of these places was, on that occasion, determined with the greatest nicety, viz.

	South lat.			East long. from London.		
Thwart-the-way	5°	55′	0″	105°	43′	0′
North Island .	5	38	0	105	43	30
Cap	5	58	30	105	48	30
Button . . .	5	49	0	105	48	30

The air is, in general, here very unhealthy, and the mortality considerable. In the year 1768, that is, from the beginning of September to the end of August, out of the complete number of the Company's servants, including pennists, mariners, and military, being three hundred and seventeen, the deaths amounted to sixty, about one in five.

The division which follows next in geographical order, is that of Jaccatra, with its Preanger lands; Preanger lands is the denomination given to those districts which did not originally belong to the kingdom of Jaccatra, but which have been united to the Company's possessions since the year 1677: with respect to their administration, they are divided between Batavia, and the residency of Cheribon.

This division is full one hundred and ten Dutch miles in circumference. To the west it borders upon Bantam, with the districts of Greending, Badak, and Pagadongan; to the south, upon the Southern ocean, for the most part with the district of Jampan, and partly with that of Soekapoura, belonging to the Cheribon Preanger lands; to the east, upon the government of Cheribon itself, with the districts of Timpanganten, Samadang, Pagadeen, and Pamanoekang; to the north, upon the sea, with the districts of Pamanoekang, Tjassen, Crawang, and that of Jaccatra proper, under Batavia.

The country of Jaccatra, with its Preanger lands, comprises, upon the whole, thirty districts, containing together 33,914 *tjatjars*, or families, or 203,484 inhabitants, of which the district of Batavia alone contains 19,469 families, or 116,814 inhabitants; this shows that the other districts are proportionally much less populous, whereby a great extent of capital land remains uncultivated and neglected, and even what is tilled is owing to the industry and perseverance of the Chinese settlers.

The paucity of inhabitants in the country of Jaccatra, cannot, like that in the empire of the Soesoehoenam, be attributed to the ravages of a destructive war; for Jaccatra has, since the last siege of Batavia, in the year 1629, been very little subject to that calamity, except in the insurrection of the Chinese, in the year 1740, when even the Javans of Jaccatra were the least concerned in it; but it may principally be ascribed to the circumstance, that, after the arms of the Company were victorious over the kingdom of Jaccatra, and they had taken the capital, having likewise defeated the army of Bantam, all the inhabitants of the country were carried away into the kingdom of Bantam; whereby Jaccatra remained, for a considerable space of time, nearly uninhabited.

It appears, however, according to Mr. Mossel, that these lands contained only, in the year 1753, the number of one hundred and fifty thousand souls; so that, in opposition to the other parts of Java, the population has here been considerably augmented.

Every district has its regent, who is appointed immediately by the supreme Indian government at Batavia. These regents decide in civil matters of little importance, but affairs of consequence they must lay before the commissary of inland affairs, or the governor-general.

Jaccatra is watered and fertilized by several rivers, most of which, however, are no better than rivulets, in the good or dry season. The largest of these are the Sedani, or the river of Tangerang, and that of Crawang; they descend from the high mountains inland, and flow into the sea, in a northerly direction.

The river of Tangerang runs into the sea, not far from the point of Ontong Java, and near its mouth is a small post of the Company, called the Kwal. Just below that post, the river gives a part of its water to the Mookervaart, a canal cut from that place to Batavia, in order to provide the canals and moats of the city with water; but as, in the rainy season, this river swells very high, and too much would then be conveyed through that cut to the city, a lock was made, in the year 1770, at the upper end of the Mookervaart, which cost full 15,270*l.* whereby no more water than is wanted is suffered to come to Batavia.

It is not the water alone of the river of Tangerang which supplies this canal, but likewise that of the rivers of Ankee, Passangarang, and Grogol; and it is through the Mookervaart that Batavia receives most of its water; for that which comes down by what is called the great river of Jaccatra, is very trifling in comparison with this. The drain, called the Slokhaan (the glutton, or cormorant), which was dug in the year 1746, a little to the eastward of the river of Jaccatra, receives the water from the upper grounds, and thus deprives it of its greatest force. The conformation of the country likewise requires that Batavia should receive its water from the westward, as, on that side, it is more elevated than on the other.

The Dutch seem to have pitched upon Batavia for the convenience of water-carriage; and, in that respect, it is, indeed, a second Holland, and superior to every other place in the world. There are very few streets in the city without a canal of considerable breadth running through, or rather stagnating in them, and continued for several miles beyond the town, intersecting, together with five or six rivers, in almost every direction, the dead flat in which it is situated; nor is this the worst, for the fence of every field and garden is a ditch; and interspersed among the cultivated ground, are many filthy fens, bogs, and morasses, as well fresh as salt : nay, such is the influence of habit, both upon the taste and understanding, that Governor-general Van der Parra, whose country-house was situated upon the only rising ground near Batavia, contrived, at some trouble and expense, to inclose his own garden with a ditch.

The rivers, the Sontar, the Bacassie, and the Tjikarang, fall into the sea to the east of Batavia.

The productions of Jaccatra are principally coffee, sugar, and rice; likewise indigo, cotton-yarn, turmeric, and cadjang, or lentiles, from which last oil is pressed. In 1778 were sold in Holland the following articles, being productions of the colony of Jaccatra:

2,000,000 *lbs.* of sugar, at four stivers.

2,000,000 *lbs.* of coffee, at eleven ditto.

500,000 *lbs.* of pepper, at seventeen ditto.

100 leagers of arrack.

10,000 *lbs.* of candied ginger.

cotton-yarn to the amount of *f.* 20,000, and indigo, to the amount of *f.* 1000.

This may be taken as the annual quantity of what Jaccatra is able to furnish for Europe, and the gain upon these articles is considerable, as none of them cost much; the pepper and coffee scarcely $\frac{1}{2}$, and the sugar $1\frac{1}{2}$ stivers per pound. Of sugar, the Company further dispose every year of full four millions of pounds weight in Japan, Surat, the Malabar, and other establishments, upon which they likewise make considerable profits ; and about the same quantity, four million pounds, is exported in private trade, together with immense quantities of arrack, rice, and other articles. The revenues and expenses of Jaccatra are included in those of Batavia.

The Company possess this empire by right of conquest, having taken it from its king, who was obliged to yield to their arms in the year 1619 ; and Batavia was founded on or near the site of his capital city, Jaccatra.

The third division of Java is Cheribon, which, together with its Preanger lands, may be about half the size of Jaccatra and its dependencies. It borders, to the west, upon Jaccatra, with the districts of Limbangan, Tjauris, Impanagara, and Indramayo; to the south, upon the Southern ocean, with the district of Soekapoura ; to the east, upon the province of Banjoemaas, or Panjoemag, belonging to the sultan, with the district of Soekapoura, upon the country of the Soesoehoenam, with the districts of Octame and Gabang, and upon the strand-regency of Brebes, with the district of Lassary ; and to the north, upon the sea, with the district of Gabang and those of Cheribon proper, and Indramayo.

It comprises in all nine districts, containing full fifteen thousand *tjatjars*, or families, being *sikapo*, or fixed inhabitants, besides the *boedjango*, or unmarried, and strangers.

These lands are divided between two princes, the sultan Anom Soepoe Cheribon, and the Panam Bahan, both of whom are feudatories of the Company. Of the last it is a rule that the children succeed to the father in his dignity, provided they are inclined to do so ; and if they do not choose to be burdened with the cares of authority, they have the right of nominating a deputy to exercise their hereditary power in their stead.

Formerly there were three princes of Cheribon ; but in the year 1769, one of them not treating his subjects well, was exiled by the supreme government to Amboyna, where he still remained in 1775.

These princes are obliged to deliver all the produce of their country for certain fixed prices, exclusively to the Company ; and neither the princes nor their subjects are allowed to have any communication with strangers, much less to carry on trade with foreign nations in any of the articles produced upon their lands. On the part of the Company, as much care is taken as possible to prevent the contravention of these conditions ; and they have a resident here, with a garrison of seventy Europeans, stationed in a small fort in the district of Cheribon, whilst there is also an out-post stationed at Indramayo.

This empire put itself under the protection of

2

the Company in the year 1680. In criminal matters the administration is under the combined authority of the two princes and the Company's resident.

Its productions are coffee, timber, cotton-yarn, areca, indigo, sugar, and also a little pepper: this last article grew formerly here in such abundance, that in the year 1680, the *bhar* of three hundred and seventy-five pounds was paid for at the rate of no more than ten Spanish dollars, about 16s. per cwt. Cheribon contributes many important articles to the consumption of India, and to the European trade. It yields yearly, for the former, at least one thousand lasts of rice, and one million pounds of sugar at $1\frac{1}{2}$ or 2 stivers per pound; and for Europe at least 30,000 *lbs.* of cotton-yarn, of letter A, at 14 stivers (1s. 3d.), 10,000 *lbs.* of indigo, at 30 stivers (2s. 9d.), and 1,200,000 *lbs.* of coffee, at $2\frac{1}{4}$ stivers. Yet in 1778, no more than one million pounds of the Cheribon coffee were sold in Holland at eleven stivers per pound. The intrinsic revenues of this settlement are amply sufficient to defray the charges. In 1779 the last amounted to ƒ. 12,584, and the former to ƒ. 35,761, showing a favourable balance of ƒ. 23,177, or 2107l. sterling. In 1776-7, the establishment of Cheribon consisted of ninety-eight Europeans; namely, fourteen civil servants,

P

one clergyman, three surgeons, two artillery-
men, fifteen seamen, sixty soldiers, and three
mechanics. The resident at Cheribon is said to
make no less than 70,000 rixdollars, upwards of
15,000*l.* sterling per annum.

Before the war of 1740 the Soesoehoenam, or
emperor of Java, as he was called, was sole
proprietor of all the country eastward of the last-
mentioned empire of Cheribon, which was the
western boundary of that of the Soesoehoenam.
This comprised all the rest of the island, and
was inclosed, on the other sides, by the sea and
the narrow straits which separate Java from the
islands of Bali and Madura. It extended in
length, from east to west, one hundred Dutch
miles, and in breadth, upon an average, about
five-and-twenty. It contained fifty-six provinces,
or districts, large and small; and three hundred
and nine thousand seven hundred *tjatjars*, or
families. After that period thirty of those provinces, all situated on the sea-coast, were ceded
to the Company for an equivalent in money;
and seven, amongst which was Mataram, to
the sultan Manko Boeni. This empire, once so
formidable to the Company, is now so reduced
in power and extent, that its monarch can at
present, 1777, enumerate no more than sixteen
provinces under his dominion, containing only
thirty-three thousand two hundred *tjatjars*, or
families.

The dominions which fell to the lot of the sultan Manko Boeni, who is still living, consist of seven provinces, interspersed between those which have remained with the Soesoehoenam; and this intermixture of the territories of these two monarchs, makes them individually much more feeble than if the possessions of each were adjacent, and formed one compact country.

The seven provinces belonging to the sultan contain, together, fifteen thousand eight hundred *tjatjars*, or families; the most extensive and most important is that of Mataram, which is washed by the Southern ocean.

Although the principality of Madura is now solely confined to the island of that name, which lies to the north-east of Java, from which it is separated by a narrow strait of scarcely a league and a half over, it has always been reckoned to belong to the government of the north-eastern coast of Java : the whole island is divided into three districts, and contains thirty thousand *tjatjars*, or families; it is thirty Dutch miles in length, and upon an average scarcely six in breadth.

All these princes possess their dominions as vassals of the Company, whose pretensions to the paramount authority are grounded upon a voluntary cession of all his dominions, alleged to have been made in favour of the Company by

the late deceased Soesoehoenam, upon his death-
bed, in the year 1746 : this, at least, is what is
pretended, for the sake of appearance, as it is
otherwise pretty well understood that the emperor was dead before this pretended cession was
made known to the grandees of the court ; but
this is kept as secret as possible. The empire,
thus weakened and diminished, was afterwards
given as a fief to one of the princes of the
imperial race, to the prejudice of Masseyd ; who,
however, was quieted with a certain appanage,
and the promise, that if the present Soesoehoenam died without issue, his children, in the
right of being the nearest of blood, should succeed to the imperial dignity.

The titles which the reigning Soesoehoenam
has assumed are as follows : *Soesoehoenam*, monarch or sole ruler ; *Pacoeboeana*, axis of the
globe, literally, nail or spike of the earth ; *Senepatty Hiengalaga*, commander in chief of all the
armies ; *Abdul Rachman*, holy priest, literally
slave of the most merciful God ; *Sahiedien*, sovereign king ; *Panatagama*, prince of the faithful :
those of the sultan of Mataram are, *Sultan*,
prince or king ; *Hanim Coeboeana*, regent of the
world ; *Senepatty Hiengalaga*, *Abdul Rachman*,
Sahiedien, *Panatagama*, *Calif*, *Attu lach*, vice-
gerent of the Almighty.

All these princes bound themselves, in the

year 1756, not to deliver any of the products of their respective countries to any other than the Company; and in every case to act both defensively and offensively, in conjunction with the Company, against their enemies.

The provinces have each their regent of their own nation, under the title of *tommagong patti*, who are respectively subordinate to the several residents.

CHAPTER III.

Importance of Java to the Dutch East India Company.—Reflections on the Conduct of the Company towards the native Princes—and their Javanese Subjects.—Necessity of Reform in these Points.

FROM what has preceded, the great importance of the island of Java to the East India Company will have very evidently appeared. It is fertile in productions, which have now, by the progressive increase of luxury in the world, become articles almost of the first necessity, whereby this colony is adequate to bring as much, if not more, wealth into the coffers of the Company than the spice-islands, which have hitherto been considered as the chief means of the prosperity, if not even essential to the existence of that body. But Java can only hope to be equally precious with the spice-islands, by a change of circumstances, by cordial exertions to promote the cultivation of its highly fertile soil with industry and vigour, by ceasing to depress and impoverish the natives by constant injustice and continual extortion, and by avoiding in future every species of war, which, by producing a still greater depopulation, would bring destruction to the Indians and ruin to the Company.

The princes of the country, although sovereign over their own subjects *, are, nevertheless, the one more, and the other less, vassals of the Company; and so far subjected to them, that the mode of succession to their thrones is regulated, and the heirs of their dignity are nominated, by the Company. The dismemberment of the empire of the Soesoehoenam, and the possession of the sea-coasts, render the Company secure from that power once so formidable, and from the consequences of such prejudicial engagements and alliances, as might be entered into by the native princes, with European powers; and although those princes bow with reluctance to the yoke which has been imposed upon them, they are sufficiently wise to consider, that, if they were even fortunate enough to disengage themselves from their present bondage, their power has been so broken by the depopulation of the country, that, freed from the Dutch Company, they would still be obliged to yield to the first foreign nation which should have the inclination and ability to establish itself upon the island, and perhaps be reduced to a more cruel state of servitude than they now experience

* An instance to the contrary occurs in the last chapter, where we are informed that one of the princes of Cheribon was deposed by the Company for misconduct towards his own subjects.

under their actual taskmasters ; of which they have a striking example before them in the Mogul empire.

If, therefore, the government at Batavia were to cherish, protect, and favour as much as possible the several princes of Java, giving them every indulgence in matters of small moment, without suffering any diminution of the power and influence which has been attained over them, those princes would see the sound policy of rather maintaining the Company in their possessions on the island, than allowing them to be transferred to other hands, without opposition on their part.

If it be necessary for the Company to attach these princes to them by the bands of political interest, it is no less an object of importance for their welfare, and perhaps of necessity to their safety, that they equally aim at securing the attachment of their Javanese subjects, by rendering their lives at least supportable, and by opposing and preventing the shameful treatment and crying injustice which these poor people experience at the hands of the governor, residents, and regents. The common Javanese are in an absolute state of slavery: they are no more masters of what little they seem to possess, than an unconditional slave, who, together with all he has, belongs to the master who has purchased him, his labour, and his posterity. The common Javan is not only obliged, at fixed periods, to deliver a certain quantity of the fruits of his industry to the regent placed over him, in behalf of the Company, for whatever price the latter chooses to allow him, and that price, moreover, paid in goods, which are charged to him at ten times their real value; but he likewise cannot consider what may remain as his own property, not being permitted to do with it what he may think fit, nor allowed to sell it to others at a higher or a lower rate; and he is, on the contrary, compelled to part with this also, as well as what was claimed of him in behalf of the Company, to the same petty tyrant, for himself, at an arbitrary and frequently at an infamous price. The regents experience in their turn, though perhaps in a less iniquitous degree, the oppression of the residents; whilst in the country of Jaccatra, the commissary for inland affairs acts the same part, in a no less unjustifiable manner, under the immediate eye of the governor-general, towards the native regents and common Javanese in that province.

The continually decreasing state of the population in Java, which, from the year 1738 to 1777, has diminished more than one half, may be attributed to the natural operation of this abject state of depression and servitude, in which

the common people of Java live, as well as to
the ravages of a war of nearly twenty-five years,
to which it has been the custom solely to ascribe
it ; though this war, and the various civil commotions which have happened besides, have, undoubtedly, greatly contributed to this waste of the
human species.

CHAPTER IV.

*Character of the Javanese.—Their Indolence, not
merely the Result of Climate, but also of the arbi-
trary Government.—Industry of the Chinese.—
Food of the Javanese.—Their Dwellings.—
Household Conveniences.—Usual Period of Life.
—Peculiar Disease.—Religion.—Mosques.—
Mausoleum near Cheribon.—Customs of the
Javanese.—Laws respecting Inheritance.—Their
Appearance, Dress, &c.*

THE Javanese are said to be of an indolent disposition, and to require much pains to excite
them to labour. This is, in general, true of all
the nations who inhabit the torrid zone, and
who live under despotic governments, by which
they are arbitrarily deprived of their property.
But would not this vice, which is represented as
a national blemish in the character of the Javanese, be in a great measure amended—would it
not be removed, if arrangements were made,
that to these miserable people might be left the
property and uncontrolled disposition of only that
portion of the fruits of their labour which might
remain after they have furnished to the Company the quantities and qualities required at their
hands? The inhabitants of Java possess, in

common with all the rest of mankind, a natural
and innate desire of having the free command
and disposal of their own property; and, like
others, they would, to obtain this, submit to
heavy labour, and be more industrious, in proportion as they had the more certain prospect of
earning a property, and of security in the en-
joyment of it.

Deprived of the most distant prospect, and
not encouraged by any hope of bettering their
situation, they sit down sullenly contented, as it
were, with the little left to them by their despotic
and avaricious masters; who, by this unwise,
as well as unfeeling conduct, extinguish every
spark of industry, and plunge their subjects into
the gloom of hopeless inactivity.

The climate, it is alleged, influences their
disposition, and compels them to a life of indolence. But does not the fallacy of this assertion
appear in the Chinese who reside here? These
inhabit the same island, open their variegated
shops next to the dwelling of the Javanese, and
till with laborious industry the neglected soil
around the wretched habitation of the native.
In diligence, perseverance, and manual labour,
they surpass many of the industrious classes of
the community in Europe; but they are com-
paratively unshackled, and are free masters of
what they can earn by trade, or procure by agri-

culture, beyond the pecuniary or other assessments levied upon them by the government. This encourages them readily to undertake the most laborious occupations, and diligently to persevere in them, while they feel a rational hope of obtaining, in proper time, the reward due to their exertions.

The Javanese, possessing no certain property, are satisfied with little. The usual food of those who inhabit the level country is rice, with a little fish; but those who dwell in the high land, and in the mountains, and who plant little or no rice, make use of a certain root called *tallas*, and some salt, which they make out of the ashes of wood.

Their dwellings are little huts, generally constructed of bamboos, plastered with mud, and covered with *atap*, or other similar leaves.

The conveniencies of household furniture are unknown to them. The whole of the apparatus in their wretched hovels consists of a kind of bedstead, two or three feet from the ground, made of bamboos, one or two pots for boiling their victuals, a hollow block to pound their rice in, and a few cocoanut-shells for drinking-vessels.

Generally speaking, their period of life does not much exceed half a century; and few of them are found to attain the age of threescore.

They are subject to a sort of ulcers, which is a disease peculiar to the island and to its inhabitants, and which has thence received from Europeans the denomination of the Java pox. It is a sort of lues, but of a less malignant nature.

Their religion is that of Mahomed, accompanied by many superstitious opinions and observances, retained from the religion of their idolatrous ancestors. In the interior parts they have no abstract ideas of religion, and can indeed form none but such as arise immediately from the gross observation of their senses. The Mahomedan religion was introduced into Java by the Arabians.

In the year 1406, Cheik Ibn Molana, otherwise Ibn Israel, an Arabian, who had contributed to the propagation of the Mahomedan faith at Acheen, Johor, and other places in the East, came to Java, and took up his abode near the place where afterwards the city of Cheribon was built: the Javanese Mahomedans look upon him as the founder of their religion in the island; but it appears from Valentyn, that the kings of Damak and Padjang had been converted to Mahomedanism before the arrival of Cheik Ibn Molana, to whom the king of Damak gave his daughter in marriage, and with her, as a portion, the country of Cheribon: the city of that name was built about the same time, and Cheik Ibn

Molana became both a powerful sovereign and
a venerated apostle of Islamism : both the kings
of Bantam, and the princes of Cheribon, derive
their origin from him ; and Mahomedans, from
all parts of Java, perform pilgrimages to his
tomb as to that of one of their greatest saints.

Their mosques, or places of prayer, are dispersed all over the country. They are mostly
built of wood, and have neither exterior appearance, nor interior ornament, to recommend them
to the curiosity of strangers. Near Cheribon,
however, a very handsome mausoleum was
erected to Cheik Ibn Molana, which, with the
mosque belonging to it, is deserving of particular description. It may rank among the most
curious and magnificent antiquities, not only of
Java, but of the East. It is called *Astana*, or
the palace of the *soesoehoenam goenong djati*, monarch of the mountain of djati-trees. It is a vast
semicircular space, or amphitheatre, seemingly
cut out of a rock, the mountain of the djati-trees,
and divided into five different areas, or courts,
each rising above the other and communicating
by steps. The front is guarded by a row of pa-
lisadoes ; beyond these is a wall of about five
feet high, faced with little white and painted
Chinese tiles, in the middle of which seven steps
lead up to the first court, the largest and broadest
of the five being one hundred feet in front ; on

the wall are ranged nine superb, and inconceivably
large, china vases, with flowers ; and two large
trees grow on the left of this area. Another
wall, exactly similar to the first, divides this from
the second court ; at the foot of this wall stand,
on the right hand, seven, and on the left six
large and beautiful china vases, with flowers ;
the ascent to the second court is by five steps ;
and upon the wall are placed, on each side, four
similar large china vases, and eight trees are planted
in this court, so disposed that each vase stands
between two trees, except on the left side, where
the irregularity is observable of two trees standing together : in this court are two handsome
Javanese houses, intended for the reception of
the princes, or great men, who may come upon a
pilgrimage to this sacred place : four china vases,
with flowers, are also placed in the upper part
of this court, at the foot of the third wall. All
these vases are the gifts of different Mahomedan
princes, the kings of Bantam, Macasser, Palembang, and others, who have at various times
visited the tomb. A neatly paved path leads
quite across the second court to the entrance of
the third, which is through a handsome gate,
and up four steps ; but this court, which is much
smaller than the other two, and is guarded by a
similar wall, has nothing in it. No Christians
are allowed to go higher than this place, although

some of the upper officers of the Company are said to have penetrated as far as the fifth and last court. There is no wall before the fourth, but merely an ascent by five steps cut in the rock; in this is a magnificent Moorish temple, or mosque, with three roofs above each other, all decreasing in size upwards, and the area is planted with trees on each side of the mosque. The ascent from this to the last and smallest of the courts is, probably, likewise by steps, but they are hidden by the mosque and trees in the fourth: this farthest and most elevated area seems to be only eight or nine paces broad on each side, but it runs considerably back, in a semicircular shape; upon it appears only the tomb itself of the holy man: this, by reason of the great height and distance, cannot be accurately described; it seems to be a handsome and lofty structure, with a large arched gate; and some pretend to distinguish a profusion of gilding upon it. It is necessary to observe, that the whole is formed in a sloping direction, and that each court has a considerable acclivity before reaching the entrance of the next, which renders the site of the tomb itself very elevated: these entrances are all closed by small railed gates. The tomb, and the buildings appertaining to it, are kept in very indifferent repair, and are falling fast to decay.

Q.

They do not bury their dead in coffins, as the Europeans or their Chinese neighbours do, but simply wrap them in a piece of white linen, and deposit them in the grave, placing two stones upon it, one at the head, the other at the feet. They believe that these stones are to serve for seats to the two angels, who, after their death, examine into their conduct while in this world.

The laws of Java determine the right of inheritance as follows : when a man dies, leaving a widow, son or daughter, and brother, his substance is divided into eight equal shares; of these the child receives four, the widow one, and the brother three. If the deceased leave two, three, or four widows, then that share which is otherwise given to the one widow is divided, in equal portions, among all the widowed claimants. If the deceased have two, three, or more brothers, the same is done with respect to them, and the three eighths which would have fallen to the share of one, is divided equally among them all, provided they are all sons of the same father.

These laws, however, are sometimes departed from when circumstances afford inducements to favour one of the heirs more than the others.

Thus the high priests of the provinces of Patty and Joana certified to the resident of Joana, that they had fixed the share of the widow of a man who had died there at one third part of the whole inheritance, and had divided the remaining two thirds into eight portions, one of which they likewise adjudged to the widow, four to the daughter of the deceased, and three to his brother; giving as a reason for this departure from the usual mode, that the wife had, by her own diligence and industry, gained the greater part of the property thus left to be divided, and being therefore the occasion of the prosperity of the family, ought to be the greatest sharer in the division of the estate.

The Javanese are, in general, well shaped, of a light brown colour, with black eyes and hair; their eyes are more sunk in the head than is generally observed in the nations south of the line; they have flattish noses and large mouths, are mostly thin, yet muscular; a few corpulent men among them make no exception to this general description. The women, when young, have much softer features than the men; but when they grow old, imagination cannot well conceive more hideous hags.

The dress of the men consists of a pair of linen breeches, which scarcely reach half way down their thighs, and over this a sort of shirt of blue or black coarse cotton cloth, which hangs loose about them below the knees. The hair of the head is bound up in a handkerchief, in the form of a turban.

The dress of the woman consists of a coarse chintz cloth wrapped twice round the body, and fastened under the breasts, hanging down to the calf of the leg, or lower; over this they wear a short jacket, which reaches to the waist: they have no covering to the head, but wear their hair bound in a fillet, and fastened at the back of the head with large pins: they sometimes adorn their hair with chaplets of flowers.

Children, boys and girls, often run about entirely naked till they are eight or nine years of age.

What is mentioned with respect to dress, relates only to the lower classes; the higher orders and rich people wear much more costly garments.

CHAPTER V.

Batavia. — Its Situation.—Harbour. — Canals.—
Walls.—Castle.—Houses, &c.—Inhabitants.—
Revenues and Charges, &c.—Character of the
Inhabitants.—Mode of Living.—Marriages.—
Slaves.—Gaming.

BATAVIA lies, according to the best observations,
in the south latitude of 6° 5′, on the northern shore
of the empire of Jaccatra, in the deepest part of
a bay formed by the points of Ontong Java
and Crawang ; from which points, it lies, namely,
from the former, about four Dutch miles south-
east, and from the latter about five miles south-
west.   Ten or twelve small islands, at the distance of from two to four leagues from the city,
shelter the bay from N. W. to N. by E. from the
swell of the sea ; the road is between a quarter
and half a league from the city.   The ground
upon which the city is built, bears evident marks
of having been left, or thrown up, by the sea ;
as is the case with a great extent of the land on
each side, the shore of which is almost always
soft mud, for a good way up, and which
increases every year.   Above, or to the south of
the city, towards Tanabang and Weltevreeden,
the ground rises by degrees; and the soil be-

comes firmer and drier as you approach the mountains, which lie twelve or more Dutch miles inland.

Batavia receives the greater part of its water by the drain which has been made from the Sedani, or river of Tangerang; but neither is this, nor the water of the other rivers, which, communicating with the Mookervaart, is brought to the city, added to the great river of Jaccatra, which runs through the middle of it, all together nearly adequate to give a proper degree of circulation to the inner and outer canals of the city, whereby most of them have only one or two feet water in the good monsoon, or dry season; and in the cross-canals there is no perceptible current whatsoever.

The form of the city is an oblong square, longitudinally intersected by the great river. Its circumference, including the castle, is about twelve hundred roods, or one Dutch mile; the longest sides, which lie in the direction of s. by E. and N. by w. are about three hundred, and the shortest two hundred roods in length. Besides the city-moats, which run entirely round, each division, on either side of the river, has two canals running parallel with the longest sides, and intersected at right angles by several cross-canals.

The city is surrounded by a wall of coral-

rock, serving as a facing to the rampart behind
it, which occupies but a very narrow space of
ground in many places.   It is defended by
twenty or one-and twenty bastions, if the greater
part of them may be so called, as they are mostly
of a square or semicircular shape, projecting
beyond the curtains, which, with the wall itself,
are built nearly perpendicular, and are in so
ruinous a condition as to threaten to fall down
every day ; for which reason no other cannon are
placed upon them but such as are very light,
and intended only to fire general salutes.

The castle, which formerly lay by the sea-side,
but which is now, by the continual increase of
the mud-banks before it, full one hundred roods
from the sea, stands on the east bank of the
river which divides the town ; it covers about
two hundred roods of ground, and is a regular
square fortress, with four bastions of rock-stone.
For these regions it might be considered as a
tolerably strong fortification, were it not full of
buildings withinside, which must obstruct, if
not render impracticable, its defence. Besides this,
Governor-general Van Imhoff rendered it entirely useless as a citadel, by breaking down the
curtain which formerly connected the two bastions looking towards the city, in order to make
a roomy esplanade before the government-house,
and the other buildings in the castle : indefen-

sible, therefore, on that side, whoever is in possession of the eastern part of the city is equally
master of the castle.

Besides the public buildings, the following
number of houses, of all descriptions, large and
small, are found here according to Valentyn:

In the city 678 large ⎫ Dutch houses.
          564 small ⎭

         997 Chinese ditto.

         203 Dutch ditto, tenanted by Chinese.—In all . . 2442

And out of the city,

	Arrack houses.	Large Dutch do.	Small ditto.	Chinese ditto.	Total
At the New-gate	6	62	181	309	559
At the Diest-gate,	1	7	33	236	277
At the Rotterdam-gate,	5	120	501	106	732
At the Utrecht-gate,	0	27	135	589	751
Coach-houses,	–	–	–	–	9
	12	216	850	1240	2328

                        In all, without the city,   2328

                                   Total   4770

This account appeared to the gentlemen who
were there in 1769, in the Endeavour, to be
greatly exaggerated, especially with respect to
the number of houses within the walls. Huysers
states the number of houses in Batavia to be
3500, but does not add whether he includes the
suburbs. In 1778 there were in the neighbourhood of Batavia sixty brick-kilns, thirty-four
tile kilns, eighteen lime-kilns, seven manufac-
tories of earthen-ware, twenty arrack-distilleries,
and about seventy sugar-mills.

The number of the inhabitants were, in the year 1778, from the statements of Huysers, 468 European burghers, 5582 native Christians, 4873 mardykers, or manumitted slaves of all nations, 23,309 Chinese, 289 Amboynese, 278 Bandanese, 966 Moors, 254 Gentoos, 1852 Malays, 324 Boutonners, 1983 Macassers, 3707 Bouginese, 104 Timorese, 189 Mandharese, 85 Sumbauwers, 13,073 Baliers, 33,408 Javans, and 20,072 slaves; making in all, 110,816, exclusive of women and children, and of the Company's servants. The Company's establishment of Batavia consisted in 1776-1777 of 613 persons in civil, and 35 in ecclesiastical employments, 95 surgeons and assistants, 125 belonging to the artillery, 875 seamen and marines, 1571 soldiers, and 903 mechanics; in all, 4221 Europeans, besides 703 natives in their service.

Among the Europeans are also comprehended the posterity of Europeans born here; of these the most considerable number are females; indeed there are not many women at Batavia who were born in Europe, but the white women, who are by no means scarce, are descendants from European parents, of the third or fourth generation, the gleanings of many families who have successively become extinct, in the male line; for it is certain, that, from whatever cause, this climate is not so fatal to the ladies as to the other sex.

The female Europeans at Batavia seldom expose themselves to the heat of the sun, make frequent use of the cold bath, and live more temperately than the men, which may be the reasons of their suffering less from the insalubrity of the climate.

The important revenues arising from the import and export duties, &c. and the valuable productions which the country around it affords, might induce the supposition, that Batavia, or rather the colony of Jaccatra, for that is the account in the books of the Company, to which all relative to Batavia is carried, were adequate to its own support; yet this is far from being the case. Batavia is the metropolis of the Dutch Indian possessions; it is the seat of their government; a large garrison is constantly maintained in it; most of the Company's ships touch here, both outward and homeward bound; their cargoes are landed and shipped; all recruits are received, maintained, and paid here; in short, almost all the charges of the marine and military establishment of the Company are carried to the account of Batavia; and it cannot, therefore, be but that a considerable balance must appear every year against it. The famous Mossel, it is true, in his Memorial of Economy, maintains, that Batavia might be rendered a source of great revenue to the Company, even after defraying all these charges. Taking as a basis the books of the year 1752, he calculated the profits and revenues of Batavia at $f.$ 3,300,000, and the charges to $f.$ 2,800,000 per annum, leaving a yearly surplus of $f.$ 500,000, about 45,454*l.* sterling. But the books have not been closed so favourably since his time: in 1767, indeed, a favourable balance appeared of $f.$ 233,330, about 21,212*l.*; but in the peaceful year 1779, the collective receipts amounted to $f.$ 1,820,327, and the charges to $f.$ 2,384,930, or $f.$ 564,603, about 51,327*l.* more than the receipts, which is vastly different from the calculations of Mossel.

The various opinions and habits which have been imbibed, by the different modes of education, and manners of life, of so many individuals, from so many different countries, are here all obliterated, or blended into the single passion of amassing riches, which seems to be " their being's end and aim;" and to attain this object, they leave untried no means within their power. With whatever ideas of virtue or honesty they may step on shore, they can scarcely be said to have passed the threshold of their first abode, before those unsuitable notions are dismissed from their minds * : there are very few who resist

* Ovington, a traveller of the last century, relates as a common proverbial saying in his time, that " those who sail from Europe to India, leave their consciences on this side of
the

the temptations which assail them, and who do not deviate from the paths of integrity. Yet there are very few who, although they have sacrificed every consideration, for the sake of the object of their unwearied pursuit, attain the wished-for goal, and acquire sufficient wealth, to satisfy their desire of riches; disappointed, therefore, in their expectations, discontented with their situation, and dissatisfied with themselves, they fall into a state of melancholy and dejection, which, added to the influence of a noxious climate upon their health, and the want of their customary viands, exhausts their animal spirits, and renders them a prey to that death which alone extinguishes their boundless lust of wealth.

Most of the people who live here, and even many of the rich, who, it might be supposed, had attained the summit of their wishes, have something in their countenances expressive of discontent and dejection, and which seems a certain sign, that all is not right within. The climate may, undoubtedly, contribute much to this appearance; the animal spirits do not flow in that free circulation, nor do the powers of the mind possess that strength and elasticity, which

Cape; and in returning thence to Europe, they leave their consciences on the other side of the Cape." So that, except in doubling the Cape, an East Indian was not supposed to have any conscience at all.

animate the human frame, and give energy to the exertions of the soul, in more temperate climes. This is not all; for, after a short residence in this debilitating atmosphere, a state of languor, and love of inactivity, soon overcome all the active powers of the mind, and, occasioning a total neglect of exercise, ruin the constitution, and induce an absolute repugnance to every kind of occupation. The only resource for those who are in this state of listlessness, approaching to torpidity, is, to seek for relief in society, and to endeavour to kill the heavy hours in the most frivolous manner: smoking tobacco, uninteresting and useless conversation, drinking and card-playing, form the sum of their amusements; and having, in this manner, spent the day and part of the night, they rise the next morning, utterly at a loss how to pass the many tedious hours of the day they enter upon; and devoid of all inclination for reading, either for amusement or instruction, they are compelled to go the same dull round, and are only solicitous to make choice of such ways of killing time, as least interfere with their beloved state of motionless repose.

That happy social intercourse, tempered by friendship and softened by love, which is the result of a rational nuptial connexion, is little known here. Most marriages are made with the

4

sordid views of obtaining riches, or securing pre-
ferment; and the few matrimonial engagements
entered into on account of personal qualifications,
afford instances of alienation in a very short
time after the hymeneal knot has been tied:
principally owing to the erroneous education
which parents give to their children, but more
especially to their daughters.

There is another circumstance, which does not
a little contribute to render the domestic lives of
the Batavians disagreeable, or unhappy; this is
the service of slaves; which, as no European
servants can be procured, nor are allowed to be
kept, has become a necessary evil. Every year
full three thousand of both sexes are brought to
Batavia, as well from the coast of Malabar,
Bengal, Sumatra, and other parts, as from Celebes; from which last place, however, the
greatest number are imported. A duty of twelve
rixdollars, about 47s. per head, is paid upon all
slaves who enter Batavia for the first time, excepting upon those brought by the commanders
of vessels, from the places whence the slaves
come, on their own account; and which, with
respect to the ships coming from Celebes or Macasser, is fixed to the number of twelve, who
are permitted to be brought at one time, without
paying any duty.

They are employed in every kind of domestic

and menial service, in which they are instructed
by those who have been longer in the family, or
have had opportunities of improvement; and
they become, in time, good cooks, tailors, coach-
men, &c. and do not yield, in their acquired
qualifications, to the best European servants.
They experience, in general, better usage, at the
hands of their masters, than what the negro
slaves in the West Indies meet with from the
colonists; although instances sometimes occur
here, of barbarity and inhumanity in their treatment: but these are not frequent, and those who
are guilty of such conduct seldom fail to meet
their due reward, and are generally murdered,
or poisoned, by their exasperated slaves; or else
the slaves run away from their masters, who
thereby lose a valuable property, and are pu-
nished in their purses. When the slaves are
well treated, they possess fidelity enough, and
confidence may be reposed in them, provided
they do not carry their passion for gaming, to
which they are extremely addicted, to excess;
for if they have once abandoned themselves to
this infatuating vice, they not only play till they
lose all they may have of their own, but likewise
all they can lay their hands on belonging to their
masters, continually flattering themselves with
the idle hope of retrieving their former losses by
a lucky throw of the dice; in which they are,

generally, miserably deceived ; for the Chinese, who are here accustomed to keep gaming-houses, and, among other games of hazard, have one denominated top-tables, are too great adepts in the art, and much too cunning for the poor slaves, to allow of their regaining what they may have lost.

It cannot easily be conceived why the supreme government does not put a stop to these baneful proceedings, by prohibiting, or destroying, those dangerous haunts of gamesters and sharpers, which are the causes of the seduction and ruin of the larger part of the slaves in the city ; for it is the officers of justice of the municipal go-vernment which fare the best by them, receiving from the keepers of the gaming-houses a monthly consideration for their protection and conniv-ance * ; whence it happens, that these officers will never receive, nor attend to, any complaints which may be made of the seduction of the slaves, on the part of their owners: even the confession of the slave himself, who has lost all his own, and his master's property which he could get at, and the testimony of the master, who has found his slave at the gaming-table, are

* The officers who control the Chinese gaming-houses, are required to pay to the Company, as a consideration for the profits they make by them, a monthly contribution of 3100 rixdollars, or upwards of 8000*l.* sterling per annum.

insufficient to procure the conviction or punishment of the Chinese, if the latter merely persists in swearing that he never saw the slave in his house : " I can do nothing in the business ; the Chinese, you hear, denies it ;" is the only answer, and the only satisfaction, which can, in such cases, be obtained from the executer of the law.

What, however, is the most disagreeable circumstance attending a residence at Batavia, is the insalubrity of the climate, and the great degree of mortality which prevails there, especially among transient visitors, or recent arrivals ; this is apparent to such a degree, that the English, who circumnavigated the globe, 1768-1770, and had experienced almost every vicissitude of climate, declared that Batavia was not only the most unhealthy place they had seen, but that this circumstance was a sufficient defence or preservative against any hostile attempts, as the troops of no nation would be able to withstand, nor would any people in their senses, without absolute necessity, venture to encounter, this pestilential atmosphere.

ON

THE ISLAND OF JAVA.

1804—6.

B O O K   IV.

CHAPTER I.

*Batavia—Its Situation—Government—Commerce.
—General Observations on colonial Produce.—
Relations with Japan.*

Batavia, situate on the northern coast of the
island of Java, in the ancient kingdom of Jacatra, in 6° 10′ s. latitude, and 122° 47′ e. longitude,
is traversed by a great river, which falls into the
sea a short three quarters of a mile from the
town.

This is one of the largest and richest cities of
Asia : all the streets are watered by canals, which
are navigable for good-sized boats. It is the
capital of the Dutch possessions in the East, and
the seat of the head council, which consists of
twelve members, including the governor-general,
who presides. In 1804 it stood as follows :

M. Sibert, Governor-general, President.

M. Wise, Director-general of the Administration.

M. Engelhart, Director-general and Governor
of Java.

Edlers——(Counsellors of the Indies.)

M. Eyseldyck,	M. Waldeck,
M. Bailly,	M. Cantervischer,
M. Holl,	M. Rose, Resident at
M. Rymsdeck,	Tcheribon,
M. Van-Hausen,	M. Sandolhe-Roi, Brigadier.

SECRETARIES.

M. Van-Bram,   M. Mooress.

At the beginning of December, in the same
year, a neutral ship came in with dispatches from
Europe, which made some changes in the government. The governor-general was superseded, which, on account of his age, he had re-
peatedly solicited, and was replaced by Mr. Wise,
who was succeeded by Mr. Eyseldyck.

The council is commonly held on Tuesday and
Friday, from seven o'clock in the morning till noon.
On those days the governor's guard does the same
military honours to each member of the council,
when he passes, as to a general. As soon as two
runners who precede the carriage are seen, the
guard is drawn out, and the drum beats a salute.

The authority of this council is absolute: it
makes and suspends laws, maintains troops, ap-
points kings, declares war, concludes treaties of

peace and alliance with all the Eastern princes,
and places residents at their courts. It takes
cognizance also of all matters, commercial, civil,
and military. The whole authority of the council may be considered as united in the governor-
general, who presides; for he may adopt, on his
own responsibility, any propositions of council
which are rejected contrary to his opinion.

A fiscal is at the head of the police and criminal affairs : he has great authority, and regu-
lates fines and punishments arbitrarily.

A shabendar, agent-general for trade, acts as
consul for all nations, is the medium of every
operation of trade, and introduces foreigners,
whether princes or private individuals, to the
council.

A marine fiscal superintends whatever relates
to the police of the roadstead, river, and navigable canals.

The commerce of Batavia is considerable ; but
it is, properly speaking, merely an exchange
trade, for the export of cash is expressly prohibited : no captain of a merchant-ship, no
trader, who brings piastres, must take any of
them away again ; they must be expended. The
Chinese, who farm the customs, closely examine
whatever is carried on board, and, if they find
any gold or silver coin, it is not only confiscated,
but the owners are also subject to fine and im-

prisonment. When a vessel arrives, the captain incloses his bill of lading to the shabendar, who selects the articles, the exclusive trade in which is reserved to the Company; such as opium, camphor, benzoin, calin, a sort of Indian metal, pewter, iron, saltpetre, gunpowder, guns, &c. and fixes on what is to be given in exchange, and at what price. This arrangement takes place at the house of the director-general: the captain then makes a statement of what remains, and petitions the council, always through the medium of the shabendar, that he may be permitted to sell the remainder to the highest bidder. When he has obtained an answer, which is always favourable in such cases, he affixes his statement to the privileged hotel of the city, and the merchants are then at liberty to treat with him.

It seldom happens that these captains obtain the whole of what they were to have in return, the Company almost always insisting that they shall take a quarter or a third in spices, by which means they secure a consumption equal to their stock on hand.

As this city is the general depôt for all the spices of the Moluccas, and the productions of the island of Java, consisting of rice, coffee, sugar, arrack, and pepper, ships are continually coming from every part of India, America, the African and even European islands; and, notwithstanding the war, and the unhealthiness of Batavia, the road is always full of the flags of all nations, attracted by the profit they are sure to make by it.

Bengal sends drugs, patnas, blue cloths, different kinds of stuffs, and opium, which are exchanged for rice, sugar, coffee, tea, spices, arrack, a small quantity of silks, and china-ware.

The kings of Achem and Natal, in the island of Sumatra, send camphor, the best which is known, benzoin, birds'-nests, calin, and elephants' teeth; and in return have rice. opium, patnas, and frocks, which are made at Java, Macassar, and the Moluccas.

The princes of the isle of Borneo send gold-dust, diamonds, and birds'-nests; and take rice, opium, patnas, frocks, gunpowder, and sometimes small guns, as they say, to defend them against pirates, but rather for their own use as pirates.

The Americans bring kerseymeres, cloths, hats, gold wire, silver, galloon, stationery, wine, beer, Seltzer water, provisions, and piastres, in exchange for spices, sugar, arrack, tea, coffee, rice, rushes, and Chinese silk and porcelain.

The Mascate ships bring piastres and gum-Arabic, in exchange for sugar, tea, pepper, rice, and china.

Those from the Isle of France bring wine,

olive-oil, vinegar, hams, cheese, soap, common trinkets, mercery, and ebony ; and receive back, white sugar-candy, coffee, pepper, arrack, tea, a large quantity of China and Bantam ware, satins and pekins, calin, and rotang.

From the Cape of Good Hope are received kitchen-garden seed, butter, and Madeira and Constantia wine, in exchange for rice, sugar, coffee, tea, and spices.

The Chinese bring an immense quantity of porcelain and silks of every kind, taking in return piastres, opium, ebony, sandal-wood, spices, and birds'-nests, which they esteem great dainties.

These nests are nearly half the size of a woman's hand ; they are made by a very small sea-swallow, and consist of a glutinous substance and froth of the sea interwoven with filaments. They are found on the coasts of all the Sunda islands, in the cavities of steep rocks. The Indian method of procuring them is by fixing a stake on the summit of the precipice, with a rope ladder affixed, whence they descend into the most perilous situations to look for them. These nests are a considerable branch of trade to China. Although they have neither taste nor smell, they have the property of renovating and giving a new tone to a debilitated and worn-out stomach, and restoring all its functions: they are, in short, a most powerful stimulant. They are made into most excellent broth, and are an ingredient in all the ragouts of the princes and governors of India. Their high price prevents the mere colonists from partaking of them, for they fetch from five to six louis a pound : the white nests are most in request. They are prepared by first washing them in three or four changes of lukewarm water; when they have been some time in it they puff up like large vermicelli *.

* These nests, so highly thought of, particularly in China, are the production of a kind of swallow, the salangana, *hirundo esculenta*, of a blackish grey colour, a little inclining to green, with a shade of mouse-grey on the back and under the belly; the middle toe, including the claw, is longer than the foot; the nail of this toe is very long, sharp, and crooked; the bird uses it in fastening itself to the rocks; the tail is longer than the body, neck, and head together; it is also rather forked.   This swallow nearly resembles, in shape, the bank-swallow, but it is so light and delicate, that ten of this species weigh only about two ounces and a half.

The salangana prepares its nest with its dung, and is two months in completing it.   In form it is a half oval elongated, and intersected at right angles by the centre of its little axis. In two of the nests which I inspected, feathers were introduced into their semi-transparent substance.   The nearer white the nests are, the more they are valued.   The Chinese hold them in the highest estimation, and serve them up, prepared in various ways, at opulent tables, not only as a delicious dish, but as a restorative and most powerful stimulant.   The European palate discovers nothing more in this singular dish than an insipid jelly, nearly resembling vermicelli.—*Sonnini.*

The Dutch being the only Europeans who keep up a communication with Japan, the governor-general of the Indies sends a ship of 1200 to 1500 tons from Batavia every year, in the month of July, laden with kerseymeres, fine cloths, clock-work, and spices : these are almost wholly exchanged for bars of copper, which is made into a very clumsy kind of coin for paying the Indian and European troops, as well as the people employed in the counting-houses of Java and the Moluccas. These ingots are of the finest red copper, and as thick as a finger ; they are cut into two, four, six, and eight sous pieces of Holland ; the value is inscribed on them : this coin is termed, in the Malay language, *batou*, which signifies stone. The Company also takes camphor from Japan, but it is far inferior in quality to that of Sumatra.

These voyages are very advantageous to the captains of the ships sent out. As they are allowed several tons, independently of the cabin and deck, they bring, on their own account, different sorts of furniture, fans, various articles of copper, and sabres, the temper of the blades of which equals the best workmanship of Turkey. These sabres are contraband, and are sold at Batavia from four to eight louis apiece.

The cargo always contains a present for the emperor of that vast territory, and he, in return, sends one to the governor-general of the Dutch possessions in India. It consists mostly of desks, drawers, and close-stools, of valuable inlaid wood, covered with a varnish peculiar to the country, and incrustated with flowers, or other designs, in mother-o'-pearl of different colours.

The mode of dealing at Japan is wholly private, since the missionary Jesuits were driven out of it for wishing to sow dissensions, by propagating their doctrine. The India Company has a permanent commissioner in a small island, Naugazacki, a short distance from the main land. When the Batavian ship is a little way off, the emperor's agent hails it, to demand whether the captain is a Christian ; he answers that he is Dutch, when a signal is made for him to approach : from that moment he is surrounded by innumerable armed boats. He is first boarded, to see that he has neither women nor books ; for the law is very severe against the introduction of either into the island. A Dutchman, who was to announce that he had either, would be immediately sent back, without being allowed any anchorage ; and such an occurrence would be sufficient to break off all commercial intercourse. This visit concluded, the merchandise is all put ashore, the ship is disarmed and unrigged, without the aid of the captain or crew, and the whole is carried on shore ; the captain transmits the bill of lading to the emperor's agent, with a note of what he desires in exchange, and waits quietly for the merchandise he is to have in return. A sufficiency of provisions and women for him and his crew are sent to the island without delay, their laws permitting an intercourse with the females of the country. During this interval the captain transacts his own business and his private exchange. When the whole is finished, the return merchandise ready on the beach, and the emperor having notified what he chooses for the ensuing year, the Japanese again load the vessel themselves, replace its rigging, and restore all the arms, papers, and effects which they secured on its arrival. There is no instance of any thing being lost : in fact, honesty is carried to so great a pitch in this country, that the merchants mostly leave their shops and storehouses without either guards or clerks. If a Japanese wants any thing, he goes into the shop where it is sold, and if he finds no one at home, he takes it, lays down the value which is marked upon it, and goes out.

All the streets of the towns are closed at night by iron gates ; each Japanese is responsible for his neighbour, so that they are all interested in no harm happening to each other : besides, when a theft or other crime is committed in any quarter, and the author cannot be

discovered, the crier, who is a kind of police-
agent, the commissary of police intrusted with
the watch, the judge of the division, and the
neighbours, would be forced to make good the
loss, and be subject to severe corporal punishment : the family of the two latter would be put
to death.

This people is very strict in the observance of
its laws, customs, and civil and domestic manners. The Dutch, in their embassies, have been,
and still are, necessitated to submit to humiliating conditions to keep up their communication
with Japan. The ambassadors and their suite
have no knowledge of the interior of the country, being conveyed to the capital in palanquins
well inclosed with fixed lattice-work, and nothing could induce the bearers to indulge them
with a view of the country they pass through to
make any local observation, so that what is known
of the interior is very little and uncertain. The
seas which lave the shores of Japan, are very dangerous, and not much known ; nor is there any
good chart ; therefore the officers, sent with the
merchant-ship from Batavia, are almost always
selected for their great experience.

CHAPTER II.

*Defence of Batavia.—Banks.—Troops.—Popula-
tion.—Walks.—Unhealthiness.—Productions.*

THE line of defence of Batavia, which is the
depôt for the whole wealth of Holland in India,
extends from the mouth of the river Antijol to
that of the river Ancka.

Besides the walls of the city, composed of well-
built bastions, inclosed by a wet ditch, very deep
and wide, there is also a good citadel with four
bastions, also of stone. This citadel commands
the city, and defends the entrance of the river
Jacatra, called the Great River, which, running
through Batavia, fills its dikes and those of the
citadel. On the extremity of the left bank, at
the mouth of this river, is a fort, named Water-
castel, which is washed by the sea. Its platform is of stone, and the parapets are well covered
with turf; it mounts thirty sixteen and twenty-
four pounders, and contains barracks, built of
bamboo, for about one hundred men, some officers'
rooms, and a well, all in good repair. The fort
is flanked by capital batteries, raised on the right
and left bank, in front of the citadel and fortifications.

The left wing is defended by four works, viz. a

redoubt, called the Flute, somewhat above the mouth of the Ancka, which it commands, as boats might come up there, and a very fine causeway which communicates with it, extending to the city walls.

Along the coast are the Beschekerme and Middel batteries : the latter is between that and the Water-castel. A redoubt, named the Siberg, is just erected, to flank the Beschekerme and defend the grand causeway of the Ancka. The right wing is also defended by four works, three of which are on the coast : the Castor, near the mouth of Emerald river, which contains three, four, and five feet water; the Bottelier, whose flanks have been recently rounded, also situated near a small river, but where a landing of any moment would be found very difficult ; the Zelucht, at the mouth, and on the left bank of the river Antijol, which has lately been constructed in lieu of an isolated battery which was on Stingerland Point ; and lastly, the Tolbruck, a strong battery placed near and above the great wooden bridge over the Antijol, to defend the passage and communication with the great causeway from Tijelenking by Tanijong-Priock. The Tolbruck was also to replace a work traversed by the causeway from Tijelenking to Batavia, which was covered on one side by the river Antijol, near a Chinese temple, and, on the other, by marshes which line the coast.

The little fort of Antijol is very old, built of brick ; its parapets are scarcely four inches thick, and it could, at the utmost, merely serve as a defence against the natives. It may be said to be relinquished. In a second line on the great causeway from Batavia to Tolbruck, is a good battery which communicates with, and flanks it. All these works are of earth lined with turf, and contain barracks made of bamboo for about one hundred men.

An European artillery officer is always resident at the Tolbruck, Bottelier, and Water-castel ; in the others Sepoy serjeants, who command detachments of fifteen to twenty Chinese and Malays, who mount guard armed with sabres and spears.

The whole left wing is so unwholesome, owing to the marshes of which it consists, and whence arise pestilential exhalations, that those who are on this station often fall victims to it within four or five hours after they arrive at their posts ; they must, in part, be daily recruited, and those who can bear it drag on a languishing existence, although born in the country.

The two sides of the causeway, which extends from the Flute redoubt to the city dikes, were formerly enriched with pretty country-houses and pleasure-gardens, of which some vestiges are still visible; but they have been all deserted, from the unhealthiness of the air.

All the plain which forms this defence is composed of muddy and impracticable morasses, which extend beyond the city, and are intersected by canals. In times of extreme drought, the top of the great mud-bank, which is at the mouth of the Jacatra, is perceptible at low water : vessels are obliged to weather its east side to get in. When they have proceeded up the river to the mole called the Jacpatte, they find horses which drag them up to the custom-house, where they unload.

At the mouth of the Ancka, by the natives called Caimans river, because it abounds in those reptiles, the bottom is mud and sand, as is the bank, which has accumulated at the mouth within four or five years ; but at Stingerland Point the bottom begins, on the coast, to be a mixture of sand and coral, with occasionally small shells, almost to Tijelenking.

The coast from Stingerland Point, to the great village of Tijelenking, is less unhealthy : we therefore see pretty country-houses, tolerably sized villages, and hamlets.

An enemy making an attack upon Batavia, could, at the worst, only run the ships on shore ; and might then perhaps, by means of its small craft, exposing itself to the fire of the batteries, burn a few, as the British squadron did when it block- aded the road : but supposing him to obtain posses- sion of Batavia, in spite of its defences, natural and artificial, he would still be very far from master of the Dutch possessions in the island of Java, and it would, moreover, be impossible for him to maintain himself there ; for the environs of the town cannot nearly produce the provisions necessary for the immense population, native and Chinese, which it contains; he would further have to guard against the king of Bantam, a neighbouring prince and faithful ally of the Hollanders, whose country is very populous ; and the council of India retiring to Samarang, on the northern coast, the governor-general would derive great resources from the emperor of Mataram, and the sultan of Joucki, who would readily furnish 25 or 30,000 brave and well- armed men, independently of Europeans, and Madurans and Sammanapps, regimented and commanded by their native princes.

Samarang receives the produce of all the northern and eastern coast, and of the interior principalities; and from this depôt, the maga- zines of Batavia are supplied.

The European and Indian troops entrusted

with the defence of Batavia and its out posts, consist of

	Men.
French auxiliary troops of the 12th battalion, about .	240
23d Dutch battalion	600
National troops three battalions	2400
Of the above, 200, including officers, subalterns, and grenadiers, are Europeans; the remainder Madurans and Sammanapps.	
1 Battalion infantry chasseurs, Madurans and Sammanapps	400
Foot artillery (mostly recruits), Madurans	600
1 Company of light artillery, Madurans	100
European cavalry	200
	4540

There is also a corps of military engineers, mostly Europeans. Among them are two French officers, Col. Barbier, director of fortifications, and a captain: the others are German and Dutch.

The commandant of these troops is a Swiss; he has the rank of brigadier, and is a counsellor of the Indies. The second in command, M. Vaugine, a Frenchman, regimental colonel of the national troops, is invested with the details of the service and administration. The artillery is under the command of a Frenchman, who has resided here forty years: his name is D'Ormancey d'Hormois : he comes from Dijon.

All these troops are quartered in the environs, on account of the unhealthiness of the city and coast ; the third battalion only remains in the city, to take the duty of the castle and gates, with some Indian artillery in the batteries on the coast. It must be admitted, notwithstanding the courage and a kind of ferocity natural to the Malays, that, even if they were backed, supported, and commanded by Europeans, directed also by princes of their own, it would be difficult to make them stand a sharp action. There is reason to apprehend they would give way, and that nothing could rally them afterwards. The recruits, which daily come in, desert forty to sixty at a time. Their princes, who reside at Batavia, and for whom they have great veneration and love, must be the pretext for subjecting and rallying them; but they must also be promptly embodied before they can get on board the canoes, which are always upon the coast, and by which means they easily make the island of Madura, their own country; or they take refuge in the kingdom of Bantam, which is the common resort of deserters and robbers, both Malay and Chinese. This kingdom, wherein all malcontents readily meet assistance, although the king is allied and almost tributary to the Dutch Company, has its frontier at Tangarang, two leagues from Batavia.

To this inconvenience must be added that of the misunderstanding which continually prevails among a great part of the superior officers, owing to a want of confidence in the brigadier, who, from his particular character and principles, has never succeeded in obtaining it from any of them. Besides, no real military spirit and union can exist in a mercantile government, where the lowest clerk has a high rank, and in which every new-comer may be indiscriminately received as an officer, may soon attain the most elevated rank, and whose sole object is to make a fortune by every means which this colony, so abundant in resources, presents. It is, however, indebted to these strangers for its numerous European population, without which it would be reduced to the few colonists who are fixed there. It will be easily perceived, that, without the natural defence of this island, the mildness of its government and its adroit policy in keeping up a constant division of the most powerful princes, who govern under the title of allies, tributaries and protegées of the Company, and who are really under its dominion; but for these concurrent circumstances, the Dutch, unless they had a far greater European force, would have considerable difficulty in preserving their establishments in the island of Java. We may add, that the Company has a great ascendancy over the princes of the other Sunda islands, so that all the petty kings round about, although they have no commercial relations with Batavia, do not feel their

power secure, until they have obtained the appro-
bation of the governor-general, which they send
ambassadors to solicit.

The population of Batavia, including the
suburbs, is estimated at about 160,000 inhabitants.

The Chinese alone are 100,000, and in a
great measure occupy the principal suburbs: the
others live in the city. The natives, Armenians,
Persians, Arabs, and Europeans, make up the
population. The latter are scarcely 12 to 1500,
in the service of the Company and private merchants. Few of them sleep in the town where
are their store-houses, to which they go at six
o'clock in the morning, transact business till ten or
eleven, and then return to the country, on account
of the unwholesomeness of the city, and the extreme heat, which compels the most inconsiderable private person to keep a carriage ; the heat
is too great, and it would be attended with too
much danger, to go on foot. If some Europeans
do occasionally remain in the town, it is only
from a desire of gain, which induces them to
risk death or a state of languor, that they may
have a better chance of doing business with the
captains or supercargoes of the vessels which
daily arrive.

Noon is the general dinner-hour, and one
o'clock that of the siesta. The climate renders

this life indispensable; and, until five or six in the
evening, no one is to be seen on business, which
is almost wholly transacted in the morning.

After siesta the Dutch get into their carriages,
and take a ride round the ancient kingdom of
Jacatra, crossing the grand Chinese cemetery,
which is nearly in the centre. In this burial-
place are immense quantities of tombs, with
inscriptions, specifying the time of the death,
age, name, good qualities, and virtues of those
within. These tombs are environed by cypress
and many other small trees, and ornamented
with more or less elegance, according to the
means of the surviving relatives. They consist of a cut stone three feet long by the same
width; at the head is another stone of an elliptical form, set perpendicularly to a mass of
earth, which slopes down behind; on this stone is
the inscription; at the two sides are long benches
of turf or stone, as seats for the relations to
repose on, under the shade of the cypress, when
they come to perform their funereal duties.

This ride is one of the finest imaginable; all
the ways which communicate with it are adorned
with magnificent palaces, occupied by the counsellors of the Indies, the principal persons in the
Company's service, and the richest merchants.
In front of these palaces, parallel to the causeway, is a navigable canal, crossed by bridges

very ingeniously constructed of bamboo, con-
necting the opposite bank, which is covered with
Indian villages, many of the huts of which are
scarcely visible through the cocoa, banana, papaya, and other bushy shrubs which conceal
them, and with which every hut is surrounded.

Going straight from the city to Jacatra, before
we come to the Chinese burial-place, and near
one of the lodges of Freemasons, is the ancient fortress, whither the unhappy prince of
this kingdom withdrew when the Dutch had
conquered it for the purpose of establishing themselves there, and in which he died gloriously in
the last engagement.

The cause of the insalubrity of Batavia may,
in a great measure, be attributed to the large
bank of mud which has accumulated opposite
the mouth and across the river of Jacatra; to
the canals of stagnant water which are in the
different quarters, into which all the filth and
carcasses are thrown, retaining and spreading
infectious effluvia in so hot a climate; and lastly,
to the nature of the soil, composed of wet marshes
full of miasmata, which incessantly exhale and
produce the putrid diseases so fatal to Europeans,
and even to the Chinese and natives.

The most hale and robust man, without having
been guilty of any excess, is momentarily subject to be attacked by a disease and carried

off in a few hours, owing to the rapid progress which putridity makes in the viscera. A person should expose himself as little as possible to the night-air, eat and drink very moderately, and take much exercise on horseback—these are the most certain means of preserving health.

The camp of Welte-Freden and Jacatra, which are a league and a league and a half from the city, and where the Europeans in general reside, as the most healthy spots, are not exempt from disease. The body is in a continual perspiration, the pores always open, and, if at that time we experience a little cool air, which is common in the morning and evening, from the land and sea breezes, the pores are instantly closed, and a slight attack of the ague shortly follows. You no sooner go to bed than it increases, and if its progress is not quickly checked, the senses are gone in five or six hours afterwards. Before twelve hours have elapsed, putridity has already commenced its ravages, and death ensues before the friends with whom the previous evening was probably spent, know of the illness ; consequently there is no country in which the news of a death creates so little surprise, whatever may be the interest taken in the life of the victim.

When an European marries, the attorney who draws up the contract, at the same time makes the will of the couple. The unmarried who have natural or adopted children, which is very common in this colony, or who wish to benefit their friends, make theirs in like manner *. This precaution is necessary on account of a law, whereby government is authorized to take possession of all succession-property, the heirs to which are not ascertained either by will or marriage-contract †. It is evident that the object of government, in making this law, was to prevent the disadvantageous consequences to which families would be liable from the sudden mortalities of the climate.

The only method of rendering Batavia more healthy, would be to remove the banks which are at the mouths of the rivers of Antijol, Jacatra, and Aneka, and to make such a declivity in all the canals, that the water cannot stagnate, but have an uninterrupted and sufficiently rapid current to carry off the filth which they are always filled with; to build good sluices to clear them somewhat above their mouths, particularly at Jacatra, so that a considerable body of water falling, with great force, might carry off

* The expense of a will is fixed at ten rixdollars, which is equal to five piastres, whatever may be its contents, and without any reference to the value of the legacy.

† Independently of those portions pointed out by law, a will is requisite to give the heirs a right to the residuary part of a succession.

whatever had subsided at the entrance of the river, and prevent the reaccumulation of the mud forming another bank. The bank of Jacatra is always infested by a prodigious quantity of sharks and monstrous caïmans, a kind of alligator, on the watch to devour the carcasses which float down the river.

The marshes also should be drained and brought into cultivation. This work has indeed already been commenced. On the plain of Batavia is delineated, on the left bank of the river of Jacatra, between the town and the coast, a large flat which they have been at work upon, but it is a slovenly performance; part only has been drained, and it is always marshy, wet, and impenetrable. The policy of the Dutch may possibly too have some effect in the continuance of this unwholesomeness. In the first place, these marshes are a natural defence, and the British squadron, when it blockaded Batavia in 1804, only relinquished it from the mortality which prevailed in the squadron, neither officers nor men being free from it. They in fact lost so many men in this road, that when they wanted to weigh anchor they were necessitated to call in the remnant of the crews of two or three frigates to accomplish it. When one frigate was got under way, the same was done for the others. Another motive seems also to afford a justification of their neglect to render the country healthy: the insalubrity tends to keep away many foreign fortune-hunters who would swarm the colony too much. The governors and European merchants there, are used to the climate, and their constant residence in the country protects them against the bad effects of the unwholesomeness of the city air, fatal only to those who reside in it, or to strangers who settle there for commercial purposes.

The environs of Batavia produce only a little corn, maize, and rice. The fruit-trees are the cocoa, areca, different species of the banana, the papaya, white and red shaddock, mangostan, rambootang, an enormous quantity of ananas, much betel, a creeping plant, whose aromatic leaf is chewed by all the Indians. They spread over this green leaf a little slaked lime, and at one end, a small piece of areca nut and cardamom; they then roll it together and masticate it continually. They retain this composition in their mouths for hours together, which blackens their teeth and reddens their lips and gums; but the Chinese and Malays consider teeth, black as jet, very beautiful. Many of the Malays affix a little curled tobacco, which always hangs out of the mouth, to one end of the roll of betel.

At Batavia is collected saffron, and every kind of allspice, which is much used in whatever they eat, particularly in rice, which is the principal food, as being a tonic, necessary in a hot climate, where the stomach is so easily disordered.

Food is cheap in this country; poultry, particularly Manilla ducks, are very plentiful: ten large fowls are sold for five francs, and other articles in proportion. Wine alone is dear; in one part of 1805 it fetched ten francs a bottle; but from neutral and French ships coming in from the Isle of France, it was reduced to two shillings, which is generally its lowest price.

CHAPTER III.

The Chinese.—Ceremonies at their Feast of the Dead. — Peculiarities. — Industry. — Domestic Virtues.

O<small>N</small> the 5th of April, according to annual custom, from sunrise, an endless multitude of Chinese, of both sexes and all ages, some on foot, others on horseback or in carriages, repaired to Jacatra, near the site of the capital of that ancient kingdom, where are all the tombs of their countrymen. These tombs were previously ornamented with bands of paper, or silk, of different colours, and three red wax tapers were burning on each. Every Chinese brought, or sent his slaves with, various provisions, which were placed as offerings on the tombs. The opulent were easily distinguished from the rest by the luxuriousness of their meats; there were dishes spread with all which the most splendid Oriental table could suggest, of viands, fish, fruit, sweetmeats, and drink. After having left these various provisions for some hours on the tombs, they ate part, offered some to the spectators, and carried the rest away. Several, however, left behind them roasted poultry, which they had kept whole on purpose.

Women wept over the graves of their hus-bands; children deplored the loss of the authors of their days; and the old sighed for their faith-ful companions, appearing to regret having sur-vived them.

Moveable theatres are constructed at the side, and temples on the plain. These temples are large saloons, ornamented with grotesque and antique statues, especially those representing Josi in the midst of his family.

Josi, a disciple of Confucius, to whom he had been servant, and afterwards his most intimate and confidential friend, who became the greatest legislator of that ancient nation, was of the low-est and most degraded class of the people. After the death of Confucius, the emperor disgraced and banished him. He retired into the bosom of his family, and was reduced to his primitive sta-tion, where he said that he found the happiness which he had lost during the whole time he had directed the affairs of the empire. To him, and to his laws, the Chinese are indebted for the pre-servation of their manners, customs, and dress. It is in his retirement, surrounded by his rela-tives, that he is represented and adored in the temples; a proof that the Chinese felt the extent of their loss in the change of administration,

and that they were sensible of the mildness and
wisdom of the laws of Josi. Opposite to each
of these Gothic idols were red wax tapers of
different sizes burning, and small matches of
incense, which diffused an agreeable perfume.
Before, and in the midst of, these statues is a
kind of altar, covered with the greatest dainties;
in a room behind this altar is another altar back-
ing the former, and surmounted by a statue of
Josi and other figures. An old bonze, of venerable aspect, with a long white beard, stood up,
reciting some prayers in a low voice; he was covered, and continually balanced his body with
great regularity; he had a piece of wood, like a
ruler, in his hand, which he now and then let
fall, and as often picked up again : at the end of
half an hour he withdrew. Under the vestibule
of one of the temples two victims, as burnt-of-
ferings, were killed, and placed on a prop ; they
were skinned, and their entrails taken out and
set in front of them. One was a hog, the other a
goat with the horns left on. The selection of
these animals for sacrifice originated with Josi,
who justified the preference, inasmuch as these
animals, eating and destroying whatever might
serve as food for man, could not but be an ac-
ceptable offering.

The interior of the temple was filled with
tables, where they ate sweetmeats and preserved

fruits, drank tea, and smoked. This seemed, however, to be only permitted to the bonzes and wealthy; for the multitude remained without, not daring to approach. Preparation was now made for the ceremonial. A kind of vestry-room contained the ornaments and dresses for worship; in this the bonzes dressed and made every thing ready : behind it was a kitchen, pro-bably for preparing the offerings.

The dress of the bonzes consists of a tunic of violet silk, transparent as crape, thrown over their ordinary clothes; they then gird themselves with a girdle of twisted silk, ornamented with gilding, to which are attached the ornaments and instruments required for the ceremony; over this is a robe, whose long sleeves, embroidered in gold, turn up at the wrists. These robes are also violet, but of a kind of Pekin work, very strong and fine; they are close all round, and are put on over the head. On the breast and back are two plates of gold embroidery, very rich and beautifully wrought. These pieces of embroi-dery represent a bird almost like an eagle. They have ornaments on their arms, also embroidered, and which closely resemble the amice. In their hand is a large fan, the case of which is sus-pended from their girdle like a knife-sheath. Their head-dress is a white straw or rush hat, in the shape of a cone, at the point of which is a

T

little ball of gold or crystal, and behind a small tuft of red silk which covers half the hat. Their slippers are square at the toe, and embroidered with gold ; their legs are naked.

Many bonzesses were in the vestry-room. They also had violet silk robes, but neither gilt nor embroidered. These robes were open before, and covered the whole body. Their hair, twisted and turned up behind, formed a round tuft, fastened with two pins, of which the heads were diamonds. These tufts were surrounded, in the Malay manner, with other very rich pins or aigrettes, forming the beams of a most brilliant sun. Their slippers were like those of the bonzes. They bore no part in the exterior ceremonies, as would be supposed from their dress, but remained in the vestry.

The time of the ceremonies having arrived, the bonzes, fifteen in number, left the vestry, to the sound of shrill noisy music, insipid to an European ear. They took their stations before the altar, where they made many genuflexions and gestures ; they then presented to the high-priest, the chief of the bonzes, who had no distinguishing mark, many meats which were on the altar ; he made different signs, pronouncing some words in a whining tone of lamentation. After having made various libations with several liquors, which he mixed and spread over the offerings, the other bonzes replaced them on the altar. One of them then took a card, containing some characters which he sung. The words seemed to have little analogy to the day and ceremony, judging from the loud laughs of part of the auditory. Every bonze held in his hand a box, or small case, filled with incense-matches, and which he lighted as often as they were extinguished. After a repetition of this ceremony, during which the music was never discontinued, they entered the side-room, to take refreshment. After drinking tea there, they went, in procession, to a second temple, where the same ceremony was gone through. Thence they repaired to the theatre, when they had reached the foot of which they halted: the chief bonze mounted it alone, made many gestures and violent exclamations, and the performers began the spectacle.

During all these ceremonies and scenes, the gates of the temples and both sides of the theatre were filled with Chinese, especially children, playing different games of chance, the ruling passion of this people. Such are the ceremonies of this day, which the Chinese consecrate to the memory of their ancestors and friends.

A great part of the roasted poultry was left all night on the tombs. The common people imagine that, in the night of this ceremony, the

dead assemble and regale themselves. The unhappy strew along the graves of their ancestors,
whom they most regard, amulets, to induce
them to interest themselves in their misfortunes.
These amulets are pieces of silk paper, on which
is spread a sheet of leaf-silver: it is considered
to be paper-money, which passes current among
the dead.

The Chinese are so numerous at Batavia, and
so easily stirred up, that the policy of the Dutch
is always careful to give them some kind of
amusement. To accomplish this, their chief,
who has the title of captain, is obliged to maintain, at his own cost, a troop of public Malay
girls, termed *rouguins*, and on the Malabar and
Coromandel coasts *bayaders*. These girls, every
day without exception, from nine o'clock at
night till daybreak, act a play in the middle of
the street, on a kind of theatre built in the
Chinese campong. It is difficult to give an idea
of the performance, which always seems to represent the wars of the Tartars against the Chinese. It appears as though various chiefs, dif-
ferently dressed, their faces smeared black and
white, or masked, came to announce a new war,
in which they anticipate great success: they harangue the soldiers with variety of gestures and
grimaces: then comes a general or high-priest,
by his dress, who, after talking, exclaims

and gesticulates some time, gets up and seats himself on a bamboo-seat, raised on a small table of the same, placed to remain at the back of the centre of the theatre. After he has made a kind of speech, the combatants appear. The Chinese have each a different head-dress and costume; they are armed with lances, or rather iron-shod sticks, seven or eight feet long, which serve both for offence and defence They twist them about their bodies, and make use of them in parrying blows. The Tartars are in uniforms, short coats, large trowsers, and hats or caps like a callotte; they are armed with a sabre and great shield, which covers the head and half the body. These combats end with more speeches by the chiefs and high-priest, on the courage of the soldiers.

The roaring music of gomgoms, which sound equal to striking four or five great kettles, never stops during the performance. The *rouguins* enact every character. They always have a great number of Chinese, and some Europeans, strangers from Batavia, as spectators.

About the theatre, and along the principal street of the Chinese campong, in the midst of which it is built, are immense numbers of gaming and eating tables, all Chinese. The seats as well as tables are made of bamboo; many strangers take a walk and sup there : they eat with little sticks, which serve as forks; the spoons are of common china, with a short crooked handle. In their eating-places is an endless variety of victuals; each portion is served up on a small plate like a saucer. The eatables consist of jelly, mince, or soup, and are almost always cold: their drinks, on the contrary, are always hot; one kind, called *touyou,* is made of arrack, sugar, and hot water.

One of their favourite dishes is a dog, which they eat with every kind of sauce. They have a particular species with a smooth skin, which they fatten, and are very partial to, as well as to pig; of which no nation eats so much as the Chinese. The hundred thousand Chinese at Batavia may be reckoned to feed from three to four hundred thousand pigs: there is not a family which does not keep many, and which contributes, in no small degree, to promote the bad air and filthiness prevalent in their campong, and about their houses.

Independently of the playhouse, in the streets of the campong, are processions of men with masked or painted faces, kettle-drums, gomgoms, and tambarines; many are dressed as devils, who are carried in triumph on poles, and others in hampers, ornamented with paper, ribands, and little bells, seated on monsters, like our representation of sea-horses.

The reason they give for these feasts to the devil is, that the God of heaven and of earth being infinitely good, it is not necessary to implore him; that, on the contrary, the devil must be feasted and intreated, to amuse him, and prevent him, by this means, from temptations, and making tours fatal to the nation: consequently there is not a Chinese house which has not in the shop and chamber a great fat figure, painted on paper or on the wall, representing Confucius, their first lawgiver, whom they designate as a monstrous Chinese, and the devil at his side tempting him. On each side are pots of flowers, and tapers of red wax gilt, which are lighted on certain days, together with a little lamp in front, as in small Romish chapels.

The Chinese girls are always shut up and employed in sewing and embroidery: they are never seen in public, and are only known to be in the house by an earthen vase as long as a common flower-pot, placed on the roof, and which is broken on the day of their marriage, to signify that those who were there are no longer to be disposed of. The marriages are made between the parents, without the couple ever holding communication till their celebration. Once married, the women are equally shut up in the interior of their family, being only permitted to see their relations; the poorer sort alone let them work and serve in their shops, but they are closely watched there. Notwithstanding the life of severity and slavery which the Chinese women lead, no people has more domestic virtues. The Chinese is a good son, a good father, good husband, and good friend ; he carries gratitude almost to an extreme : it is natural to them, and they have been frequently known to offer and divide their fortune, or what little they had, with Europeans who had assisted or served them, and had become in turn necessitous. Many of the Chinese, however, are very depraved in their manners; so avaricious are some, that they let out the persons of their nieces, and even daughters, when they are under their care.

Batavia affords many examples of Chinese, who, not having the means of making good their engagements, nor extending their trade, have made over their daughters to Europeans, as a security for money advanced. The wretched victims of this infamous traffic are slaves until the parents choose to redeem them by paying the loan : it is true that they transfer widows in preference.

Little need be said on the commercial genius and industry of the Chinese, whose disposition in that respect is well known. There are in and round Batavia some who carry on every art and trade, engross all the house and ship building, and transact every kind of retail business. They are very active and ingenious, and particularly intelligent. They will execute any plan, however difficult; but they think extremely well of themselves, and are so excessively conceited of their own talents, that, in their opinion, no people can equal them. If a comparison is drawn between two similar objects, one made in their own, the other in another country, however inferior the former might be, they would give it the preference.

They are ill adapted to military science; but, although cowardly and effeminate, are inclined to revolt. Their immense population renders them very restless, but their insurrections never break out until they are fully assured that they are three or four times the number of their opponents, and the same in their private disputes.

In the villages of Java is always a Chinese chief, who is called a captain; in towns two, the second a lieutenant. These chiefs superintend their laws, religion, and private police. In serious matters, and in disputes with the Europeans and natives, reference is made to the fiscal.

The Chinese pay enormous annual duties on their industry and trade, which are collected by the Company. They pay a duty for being allowed to let their nails grow very long, especially those on their little fingers. This is considered a great luxury amongst them, as it is an unequivocal proof that they do not work for their living.

The twisted tail, which they wear extremely long, sometimes down to their knees, pays in proportion to its length; which is regulated and measured every year at a fixed time.

Their dress consists of large trowsers, and round coats which reach to the middle of the thighs; they are always of black, or very bright sky-blue. They use white for mourning, which, for very near relations, is designated by a rent in the collar.

They have the dangerous custom of keeping corpses in the house for seven entire days, though, from the heat of the climate, they become putrid in a few hours; a custom pernicious not only to the immediate family, but to the neighbourhood. A Chinese house, where a death has happened, is known by a white cloth hung in lieu of the door.

CHAPTER IV.

*Environs of Batavia.—Welte-Freden.—Tanabang.
—Mester-Cornelis.—Isles of Cambusa and Onrus.
—Description of Tijelenking—Its false Bay.—
Sacred Trees.—Tombs·of the Kramates.—Vege-
table Poisons.—Bohon Upas, or Antiars, &c.
Their Antidote—Andira.*

THE camp where all the troops are, in bamboo
barracks, situated near the city, being in a low
and unhealthy situation, and the high regency
of Batavia having, in 1799, received the 12th
French battalion as an auxiliary troop, a new
camp was established in a woody plain, a league
and a half up the country, upon an airy site, the
land of which is dry and the vicinage little
marshy. It is called Welte-Freden, and French
Camp. The road to it is the fine causeway,
which is part of the ride from Jacatra. On one
side it is dotted with country-houses belonging
to the counsellors of the Indies, and which are
so many palaces; and, on the other, a navigable
canal, on the right bank of which are Indian
hamlets. Quitting the city on the left, is a work
called the Water-platz, in which are some guns
of a middling calibre, and a barrack and guard-
house for the Madurans and Sammanapps. Three

quarters of a mile on this side the camp is a barrack and post for cavalry entirely Europeans.
In front of the military hospital is a fine
sluice, placed on the great river, to preserve the
water, which would otherwise be lost in a
branch which there falls into it, and to supply
all the navigable canals, and inundate the
environs, in case military operations should render it necessary.

After passing the sluice, leaving on the left
the avenue which leads into the midst of the
Chinese tombs, the camp appears in the shape
of a long square, about half a league in circumference; on the two near fronts are the officers'
houses; those of the field-officers are isolated;
the other form two rows of buildings, in
which each has his particular room, according to
his rank. The barracks, which are built of
wood and stone, occupy a third of the ground,
on the side opposite the entrance; the remaining space is appropriated for exercising. The
engineers' camp has accommodation for four
officers; it is isolated, and within two gun-shots
behind the extremity of the right front of the
grand camp, in a small plain formed by a creek
in the great river. Their residence occupies two
fronts of the creek; the intermediate ground is
planted with cocoa and different very large trees,
which always supply shade, air, and a pleasant

walk : the situation is altogether picturesque. As
this place is very lonely, and the natives thievish
and cruel, particularly after smoking opium, an
European sentinel is placed there every night.
At the extremity of the little attached gardens
runs the river with a small Malay village, and
the hospital burial-ground, planted with trees
of different kinds in front. An avenue, forming
the left front of Welte-Freden, leads to a large
Chinese village only separated from the barracks
by a ditch, over which is a bridge. A large general market is held there daily.

The road from Mester-Cornelis joins the
bridge; opposite the officers' dwelling, which
occupies the right front of the camp, runs the
great road, which leads to a pretty country-house
of M. Siberg, the late governor. One end of
the house joins the camp ; another is fronted by
a Chinese village, and the great river runs behind it. The gardens, which are open to the
public, are magnificent.

Between the military hospital and horse barracks already mentioned, is Tanabang causeway,
to the right of which is the grand cemetery of
Batavia, surrounded by a wall seven feet high.

Tanabang is a large Malay village, in which
are several Chinese families; a great market is
held there the year through. This village is on
a height, two leagues and a half from the city;

there is also a very pretty country-house belonging to counsellor Rymsdeck. On the same causeway, a little beyond the cemetery of Batavia, and
on the same side, is an immense plain, where
the grand reviews and manœuvring of troops
take place.

Mester-Cornelis is a small fort, a full league
from Welte-Freden; the road to it is very pleasant and even, passing, from the camp, directly
opposite M. Siberg's front gate. A gun-shot
farther, on the right, is a considerable Indian
town; a little nearer, on the other side, a Chinese
village, and afterwards, at various distances, many
other Malay towns, as large as the first, separated
by meadows: on the right is an immense plain
of maize, in which is another large Malay and
Chinese village, and beyond it an avenue leading to a country-house, commanding a fine view
of the plain.

On this road are several *varous*, or Indian
huts, where are sold boiled rice and roasted
maize, to which the Chinese and Malays are very
partial, as well as fruit and betel.

The ground rises insensibly to Mester-Cornelis, which is discovered about half a mile off.
This fort lies in a hollow, on the bank of the
great river, and is commanded by a small height :
on the right and left of the road are bamboo barracks for the Maduran artillery, of which this is

the depôt : the recruits in daily training are six hundred.

The fort is built of stone, but is not strong; the demi-bastions are scarcely two feet thick, and four high: it has some moderately sized guns, and is surrounded by a dry ditch, partly filled up. The entrance is by a stone bridge ; within is a guardhouse, occupied by M. Phils, a native of France, who, from major in the Dutch artillery, was promoted to the rank of lieutenant-colonel commandant of the place. He was one of the expedition sent in search of La Pérouse, under the command of D'Entrecasteaux.

At the side of this is another house occupied by European artillery. The fort is quitted by another bridge, on the opposite side, communicating with a range of wooden barracks, in which are the artillery officers, and the companies which are formed and trained there.

A Malay prince has been many years confined in a small room behind the guardhouse: he is the eldest son of the last king of Bantam but one. On his father's death he wished to enjoy his right of inheritance ; but the India Company thinking it more politic to give the crown to his uncle, this prince made a considerable party in the country, and declared war against his uncle for the recovery of his throne ; but he was vanquished, made prisoner, and shut up in

Mester-Cornelis, under the responsibility of the commandant of artillery.

This prince goes without shoes, and in no other costume than that of the common Malays; his food is only rice, pimento, and fish; with betel occasionally. He is attended by a Javan, and is allowed to walk in the fort-yard. He still expresses a hope of resuming his throne. He was so glad of a glass of arrack, which the European officers sometimes gave him, that he promised to reward them when he should be king; but the sentinels were shortly afterwards desired not to let him hold any communication with them.

In going to Batavia, through the Straits of Sunda, are several small islands; among them that of the Great Cambusa, which is not large enough to be inhabited; but always has a small guard of artillery with one gun, as a signal to ships entering the Strait. Next to this, on the right is the isle of Onrus; it is fortified with several pieces of cannon, fifty European infantry and some artillery-men, the whole under the command of a lieutenant. The post is very unpleasant, from the unwholesomeness of the island; it has been observed that no detachment ever returned from it complete; some always drop off, and the survivors are in a very languid state. It is, notwithstanding, the only place where the Company can build and refit vessels.   The timber-yards are very good.

About five leagues E. of Batavia is the great Malay village of Tijelenking; it is intersected by a river which unites with the Antijol, and the mouth of which is at the extremity of a kind of small bay, containing no where more than six or eight inches depth of water on an oyster-bottom.   In the middle is a serpentine channel, which goes to the mouth: it is twelve to fifteen feet wide, and two to four feet deep: it is only navigable for small country boats and large canoes, of which the river is always full, as far as a large wooden bridge which crosses it, and communicates to a considerable bazar, which the Chinese hold all the year, for the sale of every kind of eatable and stuffs used in India· At Tijelenking all the roofs of the houses are made of the leaves of the cocoa-tree, and which are adopted in the environs of Batavia.   From this place is derived most of the salted and fresh fish for the consumption of the city and the neighbouring country.   Much salt is also made here.

At the end of the bazar is a fine house belonging to an European merchant.

Along the coast and near the point which forms the false bay is ten feet water on a sandy bottom.   Going out of the bay is ten feet water, at the mouth of the channel, and then gradually six, eight, and ten.

A short distance from the village, on the right bank of the river, above the bridge, are two roads which cross the country to the back of Batavia. On the left bank, at the end of the bridge, is a great road leading to the sea-coast at Tanijong-Priock Point, and thence, by Tolbruck, to the city. From the end of this bridge, where the great road begins, is a direct communication with the coast by a very narrow mound raised in the marshes, beyond a small wood which must be traversed to get to it. Half a league from Tijelenking, upon the coast, and on the causeway of Batavia, is a pretty seat of M. Van Basel, a Dutch merchant. It is surrounded by a Malay village; the inhabitants subsist on fish and on the produce of the cocoa-trees, with which the coast and environs abound. The oil which they extract from the cocoa, when fresh, is as good as olive-oil; but in a few days it is only fit for burning and tanning; the Indians, however, use it in frying.

A little further, on the same side, is the great village of Coijack, half the inhabitants of which are Chinese; the houses occupy the space of three quarters of a mile from the coast. Fish and cocoa-trees are also a principal part of their resources. The Chinese have several yards on the coast for building and repairing large canoes. Almost all the houses of this village are built of bamboo, and raised on large piles ten feet above the ground, especially those on the sea-shore. This precaution is necessary to secure them from the tigers and serpents. One room serves the whole family; the floors are made of rotang with holes in it, that the air may circulate freely; the beds consist of a single mat, as is the case with all those of the natives of the Sunda islands.

Next to this, still following the coast, is the point of Tanijong-Priock; the name of a large fine stone house belonging to counsellor Rymsdeck. It is entirely isolated on the sea-shore, and has no other protection than that of some Indian huts. Tanijong-Priock Point is conspicuous, from the many trees which surround a kramate's tomb.

The kramates are Malay priests, who, having made a journey to Mecca, are considered as saints after their death. Those who survive, to make the situation of their graves respected, plant a tree, resembling the tamarind, which they call sacred and poisoned; a very corrosive gum oozes from it. They plant in addition, at the foot of each tree, a creeper, which soon entwines the trunk and branches, and emits a liquor which is a very subtle poison. It is not improbable that this creeper gave rise to the fable of the bohon-upas, a tree "whose smell," says a Dutch doctor, "is so powerful and poisonous, that no plant can grow within a league and a half of it, and all the birds which come within that distance of it instantly die *."

The island of Java contains every kind of serpent. The most dangerous, whose bite is mortal, are the smallest; they are scarcely thicker than a common candle, and from two to three feet long : their colours are various ; some are grey, spotted with white; others green, with bright red spots and white streaks. They are common in the plain of Welte-Freden and about the engineers' camp ; attention is therefore paid to examine the rooms occasionally, for these reptiles often insinuate themselves under the table, and beds. M. Tombe killed one which was pursued by a brother-officer. He gave it two cuts with his sabre, and thought it dead; but an hour afterwards wondered to see it move. It lived fifteen days, which was not considered a matter of surprise, as it was of the species slowest of digestion. It measured sixteen feet in length, colour iron-grey with white spots, and of a most dangerous kind.

Colonel Legrevisse, a native of France, born at Givet, who had been twenty-five years in the Company's service, had, at his house, a live serpent which all the Europeans went to see. It was

* See on Vegetable Poisons, page 330.—*Editor.*

of the thickness of a man's arm, and nearly twenty feet long. It would swallow a fowl as we swallow an oyster; but it was not dangerous. The colonel has another, stuffed, as thick as a man, and fifteen feet long. These large kinds are most commonly found in the Chinese and Malay cemeteries.

The salamander is a lizard as thick as an arm, and about two feet long. This creature avoids man, but destroys poultry, and the Indians therefore call it fowl-eater. It is amphibious, and may be found in the morning on the river sides *.

But one of the greatest inconveniences which M. Tombe experienced, particularly in the rainy season, was the clouds of great winged ants, as large as honey-bees, which so annoyed him with their buzzing, that he was obliged, in the middle of the night, to get out of bed, and walk into the yard till they had all entered; for they fell the instant after in every direction, particularly about his chamber-lamp. In the morning they lay upon the ground dead or crawling; and such as could not get quickly enough into holes to hide themselves, were eaten or drawn away by a lesser

---

* I can scarcely think the reptile here spoken of, is the salamander. It seems more likely to be a species of the iguana (Iguana Amboinensis), which is very common in the islands of Java and Amboyna: its flesh is very delicate and savoury.— *Sonnini.*

kind of black ant, nests of which are found in all parts of the house, in spite of every precaution to the contrary. To keep provisions, the feet of whatever they are placed in, are put into jugs or holes of water, which must be always kept full.

There is likewise the building-ant, which is the most destructive. In a single night these ants make subterraneous passages, whence they get about and into every kind of furniture, and gnaw a trunk of linen, books, and papers, so as to render them useless. If the servants once omit to destroy these kind of galleries, the contents of the house would almost be in danger. They are called carias, and are so destructive that they eat away the wood, little by little, so that houses have at last been abandoned, because they were in danger of falling, the timber was so full of them *.

The moutouke is an animal less troublesome, but equally voracious. It is a thick white maggot, which lives in the wood, and so eats it away, that the backs of chairs, and feet of drawers, although apparently sound, are frequently rotten within, and fall into dust when it is least suspected. This creature may sometimes be heard at work. It is as big as a silk-worm and

* These white ants are the TERMES.—*Sonnini.*

very white, a mere lump of fat. Thirty are roasted together threaded on a little stick, and are delicate eating. They are commonly found on the feet of old bamboos *.

ON VEGETABLE POISONS.

THE existence of the bohon-upas in the island of Java can scarcely be a matter of doubt; and if M. Tombe has not met with it, it must be from his not having traversed those districts in which, unhappily for mankind, this dangerous tree grows. The following passage from " The Monthly Repertory †" gives some particulars of the tree in question. The writer is an Englishman, and only signs his initials C. H.

" In the year 1774 I was stationed at Batavia, as a surgeon, in the service of the Dutch East India Company. During my residence there,

---

* It is the larva of some large beetle.—*Sonnini.*

† It is very singular, that a man of science and literature, for such M. Sonnini certainly is, should have made a reference, so incorrectly, that the article which he refers to cannot be discovered by it. Such is the case with the present reference. But far more extraordinary is it, that a gentleman so studied in natural history should, at this time, not know that such an account is the notorious fabrication which first acquired celebrity in this country, by Dr. Darwin's introduction of it into his " Botanic Garden, or Loves of the Plants," from the London Magazine, into which it was translated from the publication of M. Foerch; for a high character of the veracity of whom, see page 330. I have retained the narrative, which the reader will probably peruse if he has not already met with it, and is in a disposition for romance-reading. It is a great pity, however, to deprive C. H. of such flourishing laurels, in whatever periodical work he may have planted them.—*Editor.*

I received several different accounts of the bohon-upas, and the violent effects of its poison. They all then seemed incredible to me, but raised my curiosity in so high a degree, that I resolved to investigate this subject thoroughly, and to trust only to my own observations. In consequence of this resolution, I applied to the governor-general, M. Petrus Albertus van der Parra, for a pass to travel through the country : my request was granted, and, having procured every informa-tion, I set out on my expedition. I had pro-cured a recommendation from an old Malayan priest to another priest, who lives on the nearest habitable spot to the tree, which is about fifteen or sixteen miles distant. The letter proved of great service to me in my undertaking, as that priest is appointed by the emperor to reside there, in order to prepare for eternity, the souls of those who, for different crimes, are sentenced to ap-proach the tree to procure the poison.

" The bohon-upas is situated in the island of Java, about twenty-seven leagues from Batavia, fourteen from Soura-charta, the seat of the em-peror, and between eighteen and twenty leagues from Tinkoe, the present residence of the sultan of Java. It is surrounded, on all sides, by a circle of high hills and mountains ; and the country round it, to the distance of ten or twelve miles from the tree, is entirely barren. Not a tree nor a shrub, nor even the least plant or grass, is to be seen. I have made the tour all around this dangerous spot, at about eighteen miles distance from the centre, and I found the aspect of the country on all sides equally dreary. The easiest ascent of the hills is from that part where the old ecclesiastic dwells. From his

house the criminals are sent for the poison, into
which the points of all warlike instruments are
dipped. It is of high value, and produces a
considerable revenue to the emperor.

" The poison which is procured from this tree is
a gum that issues out between the bark and the
tree itself, like the camphor. Malefactors who,
for their crimes, are sentenced to die, are the
only persons who fetch the poison; and this is
the only chance they have of saving their lives.
After sentence is pronounced upon them by the
judge, they are asked in court, whether they will
die by the hands of the executioner, or whether
they will go to the upas-tree for a box of poison?
They commonly prefer the latter proposal, as
there is not only some chance of preserving their
lives, but also a certainty, in case of their safe
return, that a provision will be made for them
in future by the emperor. They are also permitted to ask a favour from the emperor, which
is generally of a trifling nature, and commonly
granted. They are then provided with a silver
or tortoiseshell box, into which they are to put
the poisonous gum, and are properly instructed
how to proceed while they are upon their dangerous expedition. Among other particulars, they
are always told to attend to the direction of the
winds; as they are to go towards the tree, before
the wind, so that the effluvium from the tree is
always blown from them. They are told likewise, to travel with the utmost dispatch, as that
is the only method of insuring a safe return.
They are afterwards sent to the house of the old
priest, to which place they are commonly attended by their friends and relations. Here they
generally remain some days, in expectation of a

favourable breeze. During that time the ecele-
siastic prepares them for their future fate by
prayers and admonitions. When the hour of
their departure arrives, the priest puts them on
a long leather cap, with two glasses before their
eyes, which comes down as far as their breast,
and also provides them with a pair of leather
gloves. They are then conducted by the priest,
and their friends and relations, about two miles
on their journey : here the priest repeats his in-
structions, and tells them where they are to look
for the tree. He shows them a hill, which they
are told to ascend, and that, on the other side,
they will find a rivulet, which they are to follow,
and which will conduct them directly to the
upas. They now take leave of each other ; and
amidst prayers for their success, the delinquents
hasten away. The worthy old ecclesiastic has
assured me, that during his residence there, for
upwards of thirty years, he had dismissed above
seven hundred criminals in the manner which I
have described, and that scarcely two out of twenty
returned. He showed me a catalogue of all the
unhappy sufferers, with the date of their departure from his house annexed, and a list of the
offences for which they had been condemned;
to which was added, a list of those who had returned in safety. I afterwards saw another list
of these culprits, at the jail-keeper's at Soura-
charta, and found that they perfectly corresponded
with each other, and with the different informa-
tions which I afterwards obtained. I was present
at some of these melancholy ceremonies, and
desired different delinquents to bring with them
some pieces of the wood, or a small branch, or
some leaves of this wonderful tree. I have also

given them silk cords, desiring them to measure
its thickness. I never could procure more than
two dry leaves, that were picked up by one of
them on his return; and all I could learn from
him, concerning the tree itself, was, that it stood
on the border of a rivulet, as described by the
old priest; that it was of a middling size; that
five or six young trees of the same kind stood
close by it; but that no other shrub or plant
could be seen near it; and that the ground was
of a brownish sand, full of stones, almost impracticable for travelling, and covered with dead
bodies. After many conversations with the old
Malayan priest, I questioned him about the first
discovery, and asked his opinion of this dangerous tree; upon which he gave me the following answer:—' We are told in our new Alcoran,
that, above an hundred years ago, the country
around the tree was inhabited by a people
strongly addicted to the sins of Sodom and Go-
morrah; when the great prophet Mahomet determined not to suffer them to lead such detestable
lives any longer, he applied to God to punish
them: upon which God caused to grow out of
the earth this tree, which destroyed them all,
and rendered the country ever uninhabitable.'

" Such was the Malayan opinion. I shall not
attempt a comment; but must observe, that all
the Malayans consider this tree as an holy instrument of the great prophet to punish the sins
of mankind; and, therefore, to die of the poison
of the upas, is generally considered among them
as an honourable death. For that reason I also
observed, that the delinquents who were going
to the tree, were generally dressed in their best
apparel. This however is certain, though it may

appear incredible, that, from fifteen to eighteen
miles round this tree, not only no human creature can exist, but that, in that space of ground,
no living animal of any kind has ever been discovered. I have also been assured, by several
persons of veracity, that there are no fish in the
waters, nor has any rat, mouse, or any other
vermin, been seen there; and when any birds
fly so near this tree that the effluvium reaches
them, they fall a sacrifice to the effects of the
poison. This circumstance has been ascertained
by many delinquents, who, in their return, have
seen the birds drop down, and have picked them
up dead, and brought them to the old ecclesiastic. I will here mention an instance, which
proves the fact beyond all doubt, and which
happened during my stay at Java.

"In 1775 a rebellion broke out among the subjects of the Massay, a sovereign prince, whose
dignity is nearly equal to that of the emperor.
They refused to pay a duty, imposed upon them
by their sovereign, whom they openly opposed.
The Massay sent a body of a thousand troops to
disperse the rebels, and to drive them, with their
families, out of his dominions. Thus four hundred families, consisting of above six hundred
souls, were obliged to leave their native country.
Neither the emperor nor the sultan would give
them protection, not only because they were
rebels, but also through fear of displeasing their
neighbour the Massay. In this distressful situation they had no other resource than to repair to
the uncultivated parts round the upas, and requested permission of the emperor to settle there.
Their request was granted, on condition of their
fixing their abode not more than twelve or four-

teen miles from the tree, in order not to deprive
the inhabitants, already settled there at a greater
distance, of their lands. With this they were
obliged to comply; but the consequence was,
that, in less than two months, their number was
reduced to about three hundred. The chief of
those who remained returned to the Massay, informed him of their losses, and entreated his
pardon, which induced him to receive them
again as subjects, thinking them sufficiently pu-
nished for their misconduct. I have seen and
conversed with several of those who survived,
soon after their return. They all had the appearance of persons tainted with an infectious
disorder; they looked pale and weak, and, from
the account which they gave of the loss of their
comrades, and of the symptoms and circumstances
which attended their dissolution, such as convulsions, and other signs of a violent death, I
was fully convinced they fell victims to the poison. This violent effect of the poison, at so
great a distance from the tree, certainly appears
surprising, and almost incredible; and especially
when we consider that it is possible for delinquents, who approach the tree, to return alive.
My wonder, however, in a great measure ceased,
after I had made the following observation : I
have said before, that malefactors are instructed
to go to the tree with the wind, and to return
against the wind. When the wind continues to
blow from the same quarter, while the delin-
quent travels thirty, or six-and-thirty miles, if
he be of a good constitution, he certainly sur-
vives. But what proves the most destructive is,
that there is no dependence on the wind in that
part of the world for any length of time. There

are no regular land-winds; and the sea-wind is
not perceived there at all, the situation of the
tree being at too great a distance, and surrounded
by high mountains and uncultivated forests. Besides, the wind there never blows a fresh regular
gale, but is commonly merely a current of light
soft breezes, which pass through the different
openings of the adjoining mountains. It is also
frequently difficult to determine from what part
of the globe the wind really comes, as it is divided by various obstructions in its passage, which
easily change the direction of the wind, and often
totally destroy its effects. I, therefore, impute
the distant effects of the poison, in a great measure, to the constant gentle winds in those parts,
which have not power enough to disperse the
poisonous particles. If high winds were more
frequent and durable there, they would certainly
weaken very much, and even destroy, the ob-
noxious effluvia of the poison; but without them
the air remains infected and pregnant with these
poisonous vapours. I am the more convinced of
this, as the worthy ecclesiastic assured me, that
a dead calm is always attended with the greatest
danger, as there is a continual perspiration is-
suing from the tree, which is seen to rise and
spread in the air like the putrid steam of a
marshy cavern.

"In the year 1776, in the month of February,
I was present at the execution of thirteen of the
emperor's concubines, at Soura-charta, who were
convicted of infidelity to the emperor's bed. It
was in the forenoon, about eleven o'clock, when
the fair criminals were led into an open space
within the walls of the emperor's palace. There
the judge passed sentence on them, by which

they were doomed to suffer death by a lancet, poisoned with upas. After this the Alcoran was presented to them, and they were, according to the law of their great prophet Mahomet, to acknowledge, and to affirm by oath, that the charges brought against them, together with the sentence and their punishment, were fair and equitable. This they did by laying their right hand upon the Alcoran, their left hand upon their breast, and their eyes lifted towards heaven; the judge then held the Alcoran to their lips, and they kissed it. These ceremonies over, the executioner proceeded on his business in the following manner: Thirteen posts, each about five feet high, had been previously erected. To these the delinquents were fastened, and their breasts stripped naked. In this situation they remained a short time in continual prayer, attended by several priests, until a signal was given, by the judge, to the executioner; on which the latter produced an instrument, much like the spring-lancet used by farriers for bleeding horses. With this instrument, it being poisoned by the gum of the upas, the unhappy wretches were lanced in the middle of their breasts, and the operation was performed upon them all in less than two minutes. My astonishment was raised to the highest degree, when I beheld the sudden effects of that poison, for, in about five minutes after they were lanced, they were taken with a tremor attended with a *subsultus tendinum,* after which they died in the greatest agonies, crying out to God and Mahomet for mercy. In sixteen minutes, by my watch, which I held in my hand, all the criminals were no more. Some hours after their death, I observed their bodies full of livid spots, much like those of the *petechiæ*, their faces swelled, their colour changed to a kind of blue, their eyes looked yellow, &c. &c.

" About a fortnight after this, I had an opportunity of seeing such another execution at Samarang. Seven Malayans were executed there with the same instrument, and in the same manner; and I found the operation of the poison, and the spots in their bodies, exactly the same.

" These circumstances made me desirous to try an experiment with some animals, in order to be convinced of the real effects of this poison; and as I had then two young puppies, I thought them the fittest objects for my purpose. I accordingly procured, with great difficulty, some grains of upas. I dissolved half a grain of that gum in a small quantity of arrack, and dipped a lancet into it. With this poisoned instrument I made an incision in the lower muscular part of the belly, in one of the puppies. Three minutes after it received the wound, the animal began to cry out most piteously, and ran as fast as possible from one corner of the room to the other. So it continued during six minutes, when all its strength being exhausted, it fell upon the ground, was taken with convulsions, and died in the eleventh minute. I repeated this experiment with two other puppies, with a cat, and with a fowl, and found the operations of the poisons in all of them the same: none of these animals survived above thirteen minutes.

" I thought it necessary to try also the effect of the poison given inwardly, which I did in the following manner: I dissolved a quarter of a grain of the gum in half an ounce of arrack, and made a dog, of seven months old, drink it. In

seven minutes after, a retching ensued, and I
observed, at the same time, that the animal was
delirious, as it ran up and down the room, fell
on the ground, and tumbled about; then it rose
again, cried out very loud, and about half an
hour after was seized with convulsions, and died.
I opened the body, and found the stomach very
much inflamed, as the intestines were, in some
parts, but not so much as the stomach.   There
was a small quantity of coagulated blood in the
stomach; but I could discover no orifice from
which it could have issued; and therefore supposed it to have been squeezed out of the lungs,
by the animal's straining while it was vomiting.
From these experiments I have been convinced,
that the gum of the upas is the most dangerous
and most violent of all vegetable poisons; and
I am apt to believe that it greatly contributes to
the unhealthiness of that island.   Nor is this the
only evil attending it: hundreds of the natives of
Java, as well as Europeans, are yearly destroyed,
and treacherously murdered, by that poison,
either internally or externally.   Every man of
quality or fashion has his dagger or other arms
poisoned with it; and, in times of war, the Malayans poison the springs and other waters with
it: by this treacherous practice the Dutch suffered greatly during the last war, as it occasioned
the loss of half their army.   For this reason they
have ever since kept fish in the springs of which
they drink the water, and sentinels are placed
near them, who inspect the waters every hour,
to see whether the fish are alive.   If they march
with an army, or body of troops, into an enemy's country, they always carry live fish with
them, which they throw into the water some

x

hours before they venture to drink it ; by which means they have been able to prevent their total destruction."

Other travellers have given nearly similar accounts of the bohon-upas, but they rather incline to the marvellous.   A scientific gentleman, who accompanied D'Entrecasteaux in his expedition in search of La Pérouse, M. Deschamps, a physician, asserts, that the bohon-upas certainly exists in Java, but that the stories with which it abounds only arise from mistake.   The following notes on the subject of this tree were communicated by M. Deschamps to M. Malte-Brun, who has published them in his French edition of the Voyage to Cochin-China, &c. by Barrow, vol. ii. p. 267, &c.

"The bohon-upas is common in the province of Balembouang.   It looks like an elm ; and grows to the height of about thirty or forty feet.   The leaves are alternate, oval, and rough to the touch.   The flowers are diœcial and axillary. The male, formed of a round receptacle, sprinkled with stamina, resembles that of a doorstania: the female has two pistils.   The fruit is round, and contains a kernel.   On breaking a branch of the tree, a milky juice runs from it, and immediately condenses itself: it is the famous poison.   Mixed with the blood, it kills almost instantaneously.   The Javans eat the animals killed by means of this poison, without feeling any ill effects from it.

"The fiction which has gone abroad of the very atmosphere of the tree being mortal, is unfounded, as I have myself cut branches from it ; but originates in the following circumstance :

"The sovereigns of Java, who are much em-'

barrassed by the great number of brothers which the custom of polygamy produces, get rid of them, by banishing them, with other state-criminals, to very marshy and unhealthy islands, situate on the southern coast of the great island. As the greater part of these exiles perish there, the people have the idea that they are killed by the exhalations of the bohon-upas."—*Sonnini.*

Memoir on the Strychnos-tieute, Antiaris-toxicaria, and Andira Harsfieldii, of the Island of Java. By M. Leschenault, Naturalist travelling at the Expense of Government.—Taken from Annales du Muséum d'Histoire Naturelle, Cap. XI. XII. p. 457, &c. in which are engravings of the three plants.—Editor.

In the equatorial regions, the juices of plants, incessantly at work, from the effect of continual vegetation, have a degree of intensity far beyond that in temperate countries ; plants, whether salutary or the reverse, have greater power. This fact is proved by the great number of valuable products which the arts and physic are obliged to procure from hot climates, at a heavy expense. If some of these products can be substituted by analogous plants in our own climate, they are very inferior in quality and in efficacy.

There undoubtedly are no plants more noxious than those which supply the inhabitants of the place where they grow with the poison which they put on to the points of their arrows : these poisons are secreted under different forms in vegetables, whence they are extracted by various means. Man, always ready to lay hold on whatever can add to his strength, seems every

where to have discovered this fatal secret of
nature; and to have added thereto, to his utmost,
either by a mixture to increase the activity of
these poisons, or by his mode of making use of
them.

The use of poisoned arrows is of remote an-
tiquity: the Gauls employed them, but merely
in hunting; the Scythians and Brachmans as-
sailed the Macedonians with poisoned arrows.
It is prevalent in the hot countries of both hemi-
spheres; but European travellers, either misled
by the natives, who seem, universally, to make
a secret, to foreigners, of these dreadful preparations, or not having made the necessary researches, have hitherto given but very vague and
indefinite accounts of the effects of these poisons,
and of the plants which produce them. The
savages of Surinam are known to poison their
arrows with the juice of a large tree, but the
species of tree is not known; the ahouaiguacu,
piane or curara, and the woorara, which grows on
the banks of the Amazons River, are plants
which the natives of America use for poisoning
their weapons, but we have no description of
these plants. Salt, sea-water, or sugar, taken
in a great quantity, are said to oppose their action. M. de la Condamine, in the account of
his voyage, gives some detail of the poison prepared from the Ticunas : he says, that more than
thirty species of herbs or roots, and particularly certain creeping plants, are in the composition which is in common use in the Amazons
River; but he describes none of the vegetables of
which it is composed. According to his account
there is no danger in eating the game killed with
arrows dipped in this poison; the natives assured

him that sugar was a certain antidote to it. M.
de la Condamine procured several of these poisoned arrows, and, above a year afterwards, made
experiments with them at Cayenne. Animals
struck with these arrows died in terrible convulsions; a fowl pierced, but instantly made to
swallow sugar, survived : other experiments were
afterwards made by him at Leyden, where the
sugar given to the wounded animals succeeded
but indifferently ; a hen which swallowed a considerable quantity seemed merely to live somewhat longer than the rest.

The celebrated travellers, Baron Humbolt
and Bompland, have, however, ascertained the
mode of preparing the poison used on the Amazons River, and the creeper curara which supplies it : they happened neither to find it in
blossom nor in fruit; but Messrs. de Jussieu and
Wildenow, after examining its branches, are of
opinion that it belongs to the genus *coriaria*.
Subjoined is an extract of a letter from M. Humbolt, on the poisons of South America, and a
note, communicated by M. Bosc, on the plant
which the North American savages use for poisoning their arrows :

" On the Oroonoko, from the cataracts of
Atures to the sources of the river (east of Mount
Duida), the natives distinguish two vegetable
poisons by the names of curara of roots, and
curara of the stem, of a creeper. The Indians
who inhabit the village Mandavaca, situate on
the banks of the Casiquare and Esmeralda, are
famous for preparing these poisons, which are
equally in use in war and in the chase: they form
a very considerable branch of trade. Half a pound
of curara, preserved in the fruit of the crescentia,

costs the missionaries of St. Francis from six to seven francs, about the price of eight to ten days labour. Thousands of Indians make daily use of arrows poisoned with the curara, without knowing the plant whence it is derived : its preparation is the secret and monopoly of some old men, termed Masters of Poison. In crossing from Riotemi to Punich, in the forests of Javita, while our canoe was got over the carrying-place of Rio Negro, our guide was an Indian, who was acquainted with the creeper, the root and stem of which supplied the raiz curara. The name of this creeper is mavacura : it has the appearance of a phyllanthus, but the leaves are contrary, oval, pointed at the top, and have three cavities.

" In going up the Casiquare, the arm of the Oroonoko which connects that river with the Guiania, or Rio Negro, we undertook the dangerous course of the Esmeralda, for the sake of seeing the poison prepared. The creeper which is used comes from the distant mountains of Guanaya and Jumariquin : it is also called mavacura ; but it seemed, both to M. Bompland and myself, to be a rubiacea, from its *stipulæ* and opposite leaves. From the same place is procured the juvia, described by the name of *Bertholettia excelsa*, in our equinoctial plants, and a grass or reed, the joints of which are nearly six metres in length.

" To prepare the curara of Esmeralda, they scrape the rind and sap of the stems of the mavacura, throw cold water upon it, filter the infusion, which is yellowish, and concentrate it by fire. It is absolutely false that blood, poison of vipers, and other ingredients, as father Gumilla mentions, are mixed with it.

" As the venomous juice is not sufficiently thickened by the fire, to give consistency to the poison, the glutinous juice of the keraca-guero-tree is put to it : it is this juice principally which gives the curara the carbonic and olive tint, which makes it resemble opium. As the manufacture does not always succeed equally well, poisons of very different strength are found on the Oroonoko. They catch the small monkeys, which they sell to the white people, by wounding them with arrows, the point of which is touched with weak curara, and put common salt into the sore, to prevent the operation of the poison. Throughout the whole district of the Oroonoko, the muriate of salt-wort is looked upon as the most active counter-poison : unhappily salt is very scarce south of the Cataracts.

" In 1802, when M. Bompland and I were on the banks of the Amazons River, we were not so fortunate as to procure the flowers of the creepers, which yield the famous Ticunas poison, and that which is made at Mojobamba. We kept up a correspondence for a year after with the governor of the province of Jaën de Bracamoros, to obtain from him the blossoms and fruit ; we only got the latter, and, from their insertion in a common receptacle, we supposed the plant to belong to the ménispermis family.

" Those so experienced in travel as you are, know the obstacles which impede botanical research : plants, even under the equator, flourish only in particular seasons. It is fortunate to procure the leaves or the fruit ; but leaves, fruit, and blossom together, are more than can be

hoped for. You, my friend, were more fortunate in the forests of Java: your discoveries
respecting the boa-upas are the more important,
as all naturalists had conspired to confuse the
object so worthy the attention of the literati.

" All the poisons of South America are con-
centrated juices, thickened by evaporation; the
ebullition makes the poison more active, while it
decomposes the venomous principle of the jatro-
pha manihot. The curara is known in Guiana
as a remedy which strengthens the stomach; it is
always tasted by a purchaser, being active in
proportion to its bitterness, and acts as poison
only when it comes in contact with the blood.

" HUMBOLT.
" Paris, 22 November 1810."

" The cynanque of Carolina, of which there
is a drawing by Jacquin, termed vincetoxicon
gonocarpos by Walter, and gonolobus macro-
phyllus by Michaux, passes, in the country, for
the plant which the savages use for poisoning
their arrows. For this purpose they mix its juice
with little balls of white clay, which they then
place in cavities made on purpose, somewhat
above the point of the arrow; this clay, being
moistened by the blood, remains in the wound.
The savages are said to have retained to this
plant the name which formerly designated its use.
I brought some seeds from America with me, but
they have not grown."—Bosc.

Bruce gives some details of the vegetable
poisons with which the natives of southern Africa
poison their arrows. The plants whence these
poisons are extracted are the Amaryllis disthica,
euphorbia caput Medusæ, and a species of rhus.

A young negro, named Bognam-nonen-derega, of the Macpas tribe, on the western coast of Africa, in the service of the celebrated traveller Michaux, the elder, told me that, in his country, arrows were poisoned by steeping them in the juice of a plant combined with the venom of an animal, which, from his description, I conceive to be a large species of scolopendra. Thunberg says, that the Hottentots employ a poison prepared with the juice of a kind of lignum vitæ (sideroxilum toxiferum, denominated by M. Deleuze, in a note on Darwin, cestrum), and the venom of a serpent, but he enters into no particulars of its preparation or effects.

The famous poison which the Indians of the archipelago of the Moluccas and the Sunda Isles make use of, known by the name of ipo and upas (words which in those islands mean vegetable poison), has excited the curiosity of Europeans beyond every other, because the accounts given of it have been exaggerated, and accompanied by the marvellous with which the people of India like to adorn their narratives. These popular stories have been collected and confidently repeated by travellers, in other respects of value, from their excellent observation and long labours. In the Ephémérides des Curieux de la Nature, décurie 2, year 3 (1684), obs. 45 and 54, are the accounts, of André Cleyerus and Speilman, of the poison of Macassar, as an antidote to which they administer human excrement, taken internally, which acts as an emetic.

The laborious Rumphius calls the tree which produces the ipo, *arbor toxicaria*. He repeats what he was told by the natives, and gives an incomplete description and print of the tree, from

a branch and fruit, which were sent to him. I
have reason to think that he was deceived, at
least in the fruit, which certainly does not belong
to the tree which furnishes the poison. Thunberg and Acymelœus, according to the Dutch
travellers above cited, have written a dissertation
on the ipo of Macassar. The inestimable translator of Darwin, M. Deleuze, gives an extract
from the dissertation, in a note, with a caution
against believing the circumstances which it contains. The whole of these travellers have
merely repeated what they were told : they may
be accused of too great credulity, but not of wilful
misrepresentation. It is not so with one Foerch,
a Dutch physician, who has endeavoured to mis-
lead Europe with a degree of impudence scarcely
to be believed or forgiven. After having made
a collection of the most absurd stories, to which
he has added his own inventions, he, on his return to Europe, gave, as an eye-witness, a narrative *, accompanied by all those minute and
circumstantial details, which are generally the
seal of truth, and which prevent a man being
accused of falsehood, unless he is held in the
most profound contempt. This ridiculous fable
has been long properly appreciated, and has
been satisfactorily refuted by M. Charles Coque-
bert in the Bulletin des Sciences de la Société
Philomatique. The naturalists and literati of
Europe, without having any faith in these fables,
wished to know the precise nature of these poisons.
Inquiry was made at Java, but it was productive
of little satisfaction, owing to the secrecy observed
by the natives. They gave the lie to the fictions

* See page 311.—*Editor.*

which had been spread abroad, but they did not
ascertain the fact as to what really was in existence.

While Labillardiere was at Java he never
heard mention of it. Lord Macartney, on his
way to Batavia, made some inquiries, the result
of which went to treat, as fabulous, the accounts
brought to Europe, but gave no further satisfaction ; the same answer was also given to the
directors of the Dutch India Company, who
wrote to India for information.

When I set out upon a voyage of discovery to
the southern hemisphere, the respectable and
learned M. de Jussieu recommended me, in
the event of my landing at Java, to make every
possible inquiry on the subject. I was very desirous to resolve the question, to which fortunate
chance and some perseverance of research, have
now enabled us to speak with certainty.

I procured not only the two species of poisons,
or upas, which are collected and prepared at
Java, but also those of the islands of Borneo and
Macassar : I brought to Europe a great quantity
of them, with which M. Delille, physician and
botanist to the Egyptian expedition, and M.
Magendie, have made an infinity of interesting
experiments, which show the activity and mode
of action of these poisons on the animal economy.
These experiments, managed with equal skill and
care, have been the subject of two memoirs read
at the Institute, and of a dissertation delivered
before the Faculty of Medicine at Paris, by M.
Delille.

I shall now give the history of these poisons,
how they are prepared, and a description of the
plants they are extracted from.

I procured the poison, which, in the island of Borneo, is called ipo, at Sumanap in the isle of Madura. A boat coming from that country, had on board one of those men who inhabit the interior of the mountains, and are denominated orang-daias; they are easily recognised by their arms, which are tatowed with a blue substance which I suppose to be indigo. They are the only people of the island who are in possession of the secret of the plants which furnish the ipo, and who know how to prepare it ; they keep it carefully rolled up in palm-leaves. The orang-daias, to check curiosity, or for some other reasons, talk much of the danger attendant on collecting the ipo ; he whom I saw had a kind of pointed tube like a pea-shooter, and a small quiver full of poisoned arrows ; they are the weapons most in use among the islanders both in hunting and in war : I bought them of him as well as three rolls of ipo, on the gathering and preparing of which, not a word which he said was reasonable. The only positive fact I got from him, and which I afterwards verified, was, that the poison was prepared from very large creepers.

The orang-daias make their arrows with bits of slit bamboo ; they are very thin, and about eight inches long ; at the upper end is a bit of pith very like that of the elder-tree, which serves to force the arrow from the tube by the breath, as from a pea-shooter. The arrows, used in the chase, are headed with sharp iron, and coated with ipo ; those intended for war have a small shark's tooth or copper blade, which, slightly inserted in the shaft of the arrow, is only fastened by the resinous gum of the ipo ; the warmth of the blood dissolving it instantly, the point remains fixed in the wound, after the arrow is withdrawn ; and the great quantity of poison it is plastered with, mixes in the blood, and causes speedy death. I made many experiments with small arrows coated with this ipo, on fowls, and on a dog : the fowls died in one, two, and three minutes, according as I suffered the poison to dissolve in the wounds; the dog died in eight minutes; I struck the arrow into the fore part of the thigh, about half an inch, and let it remain in till he died. All the animals died in violent tetanous convulsions, which threw them backwards, and were intermittent.

The orang-daia showed me how to soften the ipo and lay it on to the arrows. He took the root of a species of ménispermis, by the Malays called touba; from which he expressed the juice, and mixed it with the ipo; he then put some of this root into a pot, over the fire, with that of the dioscorea triphylla, in Malay, gadon ; he added a small quantity of water; shut the pot with a lid, in the upper part of which he made a little hole for the steam to pass through, and, with the steam, he softened the ipo, and spread it on the arrows; he said that this was the method of his country, and that it revived, and gave a new strength to the poison.

The poison of Macassar, also called ipo, was given to me by M. Carrega, captain of a ship in the Dutch service, on his return from a voyage to that country. He learnt that it was a resinous gum from a large tree, mixed with the juice of the root of the amomum zerumbet, by the Malays termed lampouiang ; he gave me no more particulars, but I found that it was the same as one of those of Java of which I shall now treat.

There are two kinds, known by the name of upas, which the inhabitants, principally of the eastern part, lay on small bamboo arrows, which they blow through tubes and employ in the chase; they also mix the upas with rice or fruit; with this mixture they make a bait which soon destroys the animals which take it; the flesh of the animals so killed, or of those wounded with the poisoned arrows, retains no noxious quality; it is only requisite to cut out the parts, in immediate contact with the poison. The plants which produce them will only grow in the province of Bagnia-vaugni; one of these poisons is the upas antiar; the other, upas ticute; the latter is the strongest and least known, because it appears that the natives, even amongst themselves, make a secret of the preparation, which is much more complicated than that of the upas antiar.

During the first part of my stay at Java, my researches were useless; at Batavia and Samarang I learnt absolutely nothing; I was only told some absurd stories not worthy repetition, nearly similar to those which Foerch relates. At Soura-carta, the residence of the Sousounan, or emperor of Java, I was told that the upas existed in the province of Bagnia-vaugni, which I visited towards the end of July 1805. It was a Javan whom I took into my service, and who killed me some birds with arrows tipped with the upas antiar, who pointed out to me the tree which yields the poison, and taught me the pre-paration by making it in my presence. Ob-serving that I attached some value to the knowledge, he told me, that there were, in the

mountains, some men who knew of another
species of upas which was still more violent;
that, for his own part, he was ignorant respecting it, except that he was told it was fetched a
long way off, and from places very difficult and
dangerous of access. I immediately desired him
to bring me one of the men, to whom I gave
some money, with a promise of more if he would
give me information. He told me that, in fact,
he had some of the poison, but that the man
who gave it to him had died long since, without
telling him whence he got it; at the same time
he offered to sell me some. I told him, that I
did not want the upas, but only to discover the
place it came from, and the plants which supplied it; that if he could and would have informed me, I should have given him the sum he
asked, at the same time showing some piastres,
which excited his cupidity. He then confessed
that it was extracted from a creeper named tieute,
which grows in the circumjacent woods, and was
prepared from the rind of the root; that those
who were in possession of the secret never made
the preparation without concealing themselves in
the depth of the woods. He then conducted me
about a league and a half from the Dutch fort,
into a place where I saw several of these creepers.
They had neither flower nor fruit. I took many
specimens of the plant, while the Javan uncovered and took up great pieces of the root.
When I got home, he grated it carefully, paying
great attention not to mix bits of wood with the
rind, which he kept together, and part of which
he put into a copper pot of water; when the
rind had boiled some time, he poured off the de-
coction, and added a further portion of rind;

this he repeated three times, when he suffered the extract to reduce itself to the consistency of treacle: when the preparation was on the point of being completed, he threw into it two onions, a clove of garlick, a good pinch of pepper, two pieces of the root of the Kæmpheria galenga, which the Malays call konkior; three small bits of ginger, in Malay djiaha, and a single grain of capsicum fructicosum, or pimento. This mixture being made, he left it a very short time on the fire ; he cleaned it, turning his head away, to avoid inhaling the steam of the kettle: about three pounds of rind gave nearly four ounces of extract.

I instantly laid some on two pieces of bamboo, and, by the Javan's advice, let them dry before I used them: I then pricked a middling-sized fowl in the belly; it died in violent convulsions in the space of about a minute: another full-grown strong fowl died in the same way in two minutes, from a wound at the bottom of the leg ; a very strong wild cock, pierced in the thigh with a small arrow touched with this upas, after it had been exposed to the air for three days, died in four minutes ; two dogs, slightly pricked in the buttock with the same arrows, died in half an hour. I only particularize these experiments, which are uninteresting after those made by Messrs. Delille and Magendie with the same substance, to show that this poison lost nothing of its strength at the end of four years, the result of the experiments, in both cases, being nearly similar.

The repeated experiments, so carefully made by Delille and Magendie, which leave nothing to be sought for as to all the organs of the animal economy, show that the poison acts " by the way of the absorbent and sanguiferous vessels, on the marrow of the spine," and, by its irritation, causes *tetanus*, *asphyxia*, and death.

The upas antiar is prepared from the resinous gum which issues from a very large tree, from notches made in the trunk. This poison is prepared cold in an earthen vessel; with the resinous gum are mixed grains of the capsicum fructicosum, pepper, garlick, roots of the Kæmpheria galenga, maranta Malaccensis, by the Malays called banglá, and those of the costus Arabicus, named koutjià: each of these substances is pounded and mixed slowly, except the corns of the capsicum fructicosum, which are rapidly thrown, one by one, to the bottom of the vessel, by means of a small wooden peg; each grain occasions a slight fermentation, and rises to the surface, whence it is taken and another thrown in, to the number of ten; the preparation is then finished.

The effect of the upas antiar on the animal economy is less immediate than that of the upas tieute, and its operation is different. A small water-hen, which I pricked in the thigh, with an arrow, recently prepared, died in three minutes; at the moment of its death it had a strong convulsion, and at the same time threw up the food which was in its stomach. An azurin, in Malay ponglor, a bird as large as a thrush, also pricked in the thigh, died in the same space of time, and with the same symptoms. The upas antiar occasioned every animal which was wounded strong evacuations both ways, generally frothy and tinged with green. M. Delille, to whom I sent a considerable quantity of this

poison, made a variety of experiments, the results of which were pretty nearly the same.

From these various observations it may be in-
ferred, that the upas antiar acts first as a purga-
tive and emetic; it then presses on the brain,
the functions of which it disturbs, and causes
death, accompanied by tetanic convulsions. The
ipo of Macassar acts in the same way; and, from
the accounts given to M. Carrega, proceeds from
a large tree, and is obtained by incision. This
similarity of circumstances, and of climate, affords
a reasonable supposition that it is the same as the
upas antiar. The same reasoning applies to the
ipo of Borneo, which is the juice of great creepers,
and acts in the same way as the upas tieute,
which it also resembles in its excessively
bitter taste; I therefore think that this substance
is the same, but the preparation is different.
At Java this prepared poison resembles thick and
very brown treacle, which is kept in small bamboo tubes, similar to what I brought. That of
Borneo, on the contrary, is concrete, and is kept
in palm-leaves; to give it this dry consistency,
it seems to be mixed and beaten up with a kind
of earth. I dissolved some ipo of Borneo in
water: a sediment took place of a brown and
brittle substance, which, after being washed in
a great deal of water, and dried, retained little
of its bitterness.

The arrows of the Javans differ from those of
the inhabitants of Borneo. The head, instead
of terminating with sharp iron, is shaped like a
very fine long awl, so that it is very brittle, and
remains fixed in the wound; and, as M. Delille
has well observed, the smaller the wound the
greater the danger: when the aperture is larg

it frequently occasions a considerable hemorrhage, and the blood, which flows abundantly, carries with it the poison, as fast as it dissolves, and weakens, or even destroys, its effect.

The Javans say that the remedy for this poison is sea-salt, taken in large quantities. From my own and M. Delille's experiments it appears that this remedy is of very little or no efficacy, and seems to me only to torment, without giving relief to the victim.

I have observed, and M. Delille confirms the observation, that the liquid poison, introduced into a wound, is less violent than when it has dried on the instrument which gives the wound. It appears that, in a fluid state, it mixes with the blood, and runs out with what escapes; which is not so in the other case, where absorption takes place, in proportion as the poison dissolves. In the serous cavities and digestive channels the absorption goes on very well, although the upas be extended by much water, or mixed, as a liquid, with the aliments.

The antiar is a monœcias tree, of a new species, which I shall call *antiaris toxicaria*; it is very large. I have always found it in fertile places, and, owing to such fertility, surrounded by a great number of vegetables, to which its proximity is in no respect detrimental. Its trunk is straight, with protuberances at its base, like those of the common canarium. Its rind is whitish and smooth; the wood white: the leaves fall before it flowers, and do not put forth again till after the fall of the male flowers, when the buds are impregnated; they are oval, coriaceous, generally curled; of a pale green colour, dry consistency, unpleasant to the touch, covered with short rough hair. The leaves of very young antiars are different from those of the full-grown plant; they are about six inches long, almost sessiles, shaped something like a spatula, a little indented at the edges, and not so rough as those of the old trees. The juice of this tree is very viscous and bitter; that which comes from the young branches is white, and from the trunk yellowish: it flows plentifully on a notch being cut in the bark.

The emanations from this juice, like those which come from the sumacs and euphorbias, or from the mancenillier of America, are dangerous, particularly to those the texture of whose skin, or whose constitutions are more disposed to absorb these emanations; while others are not at all affected by them, as the following circumstance proves.

The tree which furnished me with the specimens of the plant and upas which I brought home, was above a hundred feet high, and the base of its trunk about eighteen feet in circumference. A Javan, whom I employed to get me some branches of the tree in flower, was obliged to climb up and cut them. He had scarcely climbed twenty-five feet when he found himself so indisposed that he was forced to come down. He swelled, and was ill several days, experiencing vertigo, nausea, and vomiting; while another Javan, who went to the very top, and brought me exactly what I desired, was not in the least incommoded. Having afterwards felled one of the trees, which was four feet round, I walked in the midst of the broken branches, had my hands and face besmeared all over with the gum which issued from it, and felt

no inconvenience : it is true, I took the precaution
of washing myself immediately. The approach
to the antiar is, in no respect, noxious to animals; I have seen lizards and insects on its
trunk, and birds perching on its boughs.

The antiar* belongs to the nettle family, and
nearly approximates to the brosimum.

The tieute † is a new species; it is a very
large creeper, which I found in fertile places.
Like the antiar, it is noxious neither to animals
nor to vegetables ; it reaches to the tops of the
highest trees. No juice runs from its stem. Its
root strikes about two feet into the earth, and
then extends several fathoms horizontally ; the
root is as thick as a man's arm, ligneous, and
covered with a fine reddish brown rind, bitter
to the palate. This bark furnishes the gum
with which the upas is prepared; it does not
run from it, but is obtained solely by ebullition. When the root is cut fresh, it emits a
great quantity of tasteless innoxious water. The
wood is of a yellowish white, moderately hard,
of a spungy appearance : its smell is not strong,
but rather nauseous; the bark of the stem is

* Antiaris toxicaria: arbor monoica.
Flores masculi, axillares, plures, super receptaculum commune impositi: receptaculum pileiforme, longe-pedunculatum,
convexum, irregulare, subtus squamulatum squamulis imbri-
catis raris, supra squamosum squamis rectis, antheras subsessiles
duo-loculares, distinguentibus et apice curvo obtegentibus.
Flores feminei solitarii axillares subsessiles; squamulæ decem vel duodecim imbricatim circum ‚positæ, appressæ cali-
cem supplentes ; germen unum ; superium styli duo longi, di-
varicati; stigmata duo acuta ; semen unum, calice persistente,
drupaceo tectum ; drupa pruniformis, obliqua, vestigia squa-
mularum evanida.
† Strychnos tieute: inermis ; caule sarmentoso excelso ;
foliis ellipticis, apicibus acutis; cyrrhis simplicibus incrassatis.

reddish, that of the young sprouts green and smooth; the axillary branches are slender and very divergent; the leaves are opposite on a short petal; they have three cavities, of which the two lateral ones do not extend quite to the top, are elliptical and sharp, full, smooth, and of a deep green; the very young leaves are reddish; the young boughs have tendrils in shape like fish-hooks; these tendrils are few, opposite to the leaves, inflated towards the top, with a very little stipula at the base, which is perhaps merely the remnant of the leaf, of which this assumes the place.

Although M. Delille, who has made endless experiments on many kinds of vegetable and mineral poisons, has told me that he found none so violent as those extracted from the two plants, the subject of this memoir, the natives, and from them travellers, have gratified themselves with exaggerating their activity *; but I think I can now assert that the different substances known in the Moluccas and Sunda islands, by the names of ipo and upas, and perhaps too the poison used by the Philippine † islanders, all refer to

* The Javans who live where the upas is collected, cannot impose respecting its powers; but at Bragnia-vangni they say, that the antiars formerly yielded a more active poison than they do now, and that there still is at Bali a king or gousti, in whose states is an antiar, the upas of which is so violent, that death is the consequence of respiring its emanations. I got a letter written to this petty king, who is also king of Karan-assam, to procure me this pretended poison; but my request was ineffectual.

† According to M. de Sainte-Croix, the inhabitants of the peninsula of Camarines in the isle of Lucon employ a very active poison, which the uncivilized Indians supply the Spanish alcaides with, for the defence of the coasts against pirates.   M.

those extracted from the strychnos tieute and antiaris toxicaria, and that the only difference consists in the mode of preparing it, which can in no instance augment their malignity to the pitch of producing the phenomenon, which some travellers pretend. I moreover am of opinion that the greater part of the preparations, which are adopted and transmitted by prejudice, are of no effect ; the substances made use of for that purpose in Java, all pungent and aromatic, have never been supposed hurtful, and the unprepared upas, with which I have made some experiments, seemed no less violent than the other.

After having described the two plants supposed to be the most noxious in Java, I shall mention one, which, among the inhabitants, has a contrary reputation.

This plant is a new species of the andira. It is very rare, and is found in the Tingar mountains in the district of Passourouang. The natives term it prono-djivo, which signifies giving strength to the soul. The Javans look upon the fruit of this plant, reduced to powder and mixed with food, as a preventive against a multitude of diseases, giving power to the stomach and arresting the effect of poisons. They also use it as a specific against the bite of venomous beasts ; in this case they mix it with lemon-juice, and apply it to the wound. The berries are bitter. I named this plant Harsfieldii, from Mr. Harsfield, an American physician and botanist, who is principa lly engaged, at Java, in in-

de Sainte-Croix has not seen the plants which yield a poison killing with violent convulsions; he told me that the inhabitants keep the preparation secret.

vestigating the vegetable productions of that island which may be of service in the medical art, in the number of which, according to the natives, this holds the first rank.

Each fruit of the andira Harsfieldii * commonly sells in the country for about two pence half-penny to five pence, a large sum for the Javans; and which is a proof of their confidence in its virtue.

" † *Experiments with the Upas Antiar ‡, by B. C. Brodie, Esq. F. R. S.—Read at the Royal Society, 21st February* 1811."

" *Experiment* 21.—About two grains of this poison were made into a thin paste of water, and inserted into a wound in the thigh of a dog. Twelve minutes afterwards he became languid ; at the end of fifteen minutes, the heart was found to beat very irregularly and with frequent inter-missions ; after this he had a slight rigor. At the end of twenty minutes, the heart beat very feebly and irregularly ; he was languid ; was sick, and vomited ; but the respirations were as frequent and as full as under natural circumstances, and he was perfectly sensible. At the end of

---

* Andira Harsfieldii: flores papillionacei; calix urceolatus, basi gibbosus, limbus quinque-dentatus subæqualis; vexillum arctum alis, æquale; carina duo petala; stamina decem diadel-pha; stamen superum liberum; antheræ parvæ; germen oblongum stipitatum; stylus unicus brævis; legumen siccum, non dehiscens olivæ-forme nitidum violaceum; unum-sper-mum semen, membranulâ, vestitum.

† Philosophical Transactions, Part I. 1811.—*Editor.*

‡ We are informed, that the island of Java produces two powerful vegetable poisons, to one of which the natives give the name of upas tieutè, and to the other that of upas antiar. I was supplied with a quantity of the latter through the kind-ness of Mr. Marsden, who had some of it in his possession.

twenty minutes he suddenly fell on one side, and was apparently dead. I immediately opened into the thorax, and found the heart distended with blood in a very remarkable degree, and to have entirely ceased contracting. There was one distinct and full inspiration after I had begun making the incision into the thorax. The cavities of the left side of the heart contained scarlet blood; and those of the right side contained dark-coloured blood, as in the living animal."

" *Exp.* 22.—A small quantity of upas antiar, prepared as before, was inserted into a wound in the thigh of a young cat. She appeared languid in two minutes after the poison was inserted. The symptoms which took place did not essentially differ from those which occurred in the last experiment, except that there were some convulsive motions of the limbs."

" At eight minutes after the poison was inserted she lay on one side, motionless and insensible : the heart could not be felt; but the respiration had not entirely ceased. On opening into the thorax, I found the heart to have ceased contracting. It was much distended with blood, and the blood of the left cavities was of a scarlet colour. There were two full inspirations after the incision of the thorax was begun. On irritating the heart with the point of the scalpel, slight contractions took place in the fibres of the appendices of the auricles, but none in any other part."

" *Exp.* 23.—The experiment was repeated on a rabbit. The symptoms produced were similar to those in the last experiment; but the animal did not vomit, and the convulsive motions were in a less degree: he died eleven minutes after the poison was inserted. On opening the chest, the heart was found to have entirely ceased contracting: it was much distended with blood, and the blood in the cavities of the left side was of a scarlet colour. On irritating the heart with the point of the scalpel, the ventricles contracted, but not sufficiently to restore the circulation."

" *Exp.* 24.—About a grain of the upas antiar was inserted into a wound in the side of a rabbit. He was affected with symptoms similar to those before described, and died in ten minutes after the poison was applied. On opening the thorax, immediately after death, the heart was found to have ceased contracting, and the blood in the cavities in the left side was of a scarlet colour."

" *Exp.* 25.—It appears from these experiments that the upas antiar, when inserted into a wound, produces death (as infusion of tobacco does when injected into the intestine), by rendering the heart insensible to the stimulus of the blood, and stopping its circulation. The heart beats feebly and regularly before either the functions of the mind or the respiration appear to be affected. Respiration is performed even after the circulation has ceased; and the left side of the heart is found, after death, to contain scarlet blood, which never can be the case where the cause of death is the cessation of the functions of the brain or lungs. The convulsions which occur when the circulation has nearly ceased, probably arise from the diminution of the supply of blood to the brain, resembling those which take place in a person who is dying with hæmorrhage."

CHAPTER V.

Assassination of the King of Bantam.—Coronation
of his Successor.—Sketch of the Kingdom.—Views
of the Dutch on the Lampons Country.—Factories
of the Islands of Borneo, Timor, and Bymon.

On the night of the 18th or 19th of March
1804, the king of Bantam was murdered in his
bed by one of his grand-nephews, a young prince,
son of him confined in Mester-Cornelis fort.
This prince, to carry his intention into effect,
disguised himself as a female, that he might
obtain admission into his uncle's seraglio, and
get to his bed-room. He concealed himself under
the bed, and waited the return of the king, who
was gone to dine on board the ship of the Dutch
admiral Hartzing, whose division was moored in
the road.

This event was said to be the result of a popular conspiracy against the king, who was pretended not to be the legitimate sovereign, being
only brother to the king last deceased, as has
been already stated.

The murderer, instead of saving himself, or
running to attack whoever was near him or in
his way, as the Malays generally do in their

rage, confessed his guilt, and delivered himself to the Dutch resident, saying, that he had just revenged the injustice done to his father, the legitimate sovereign of the country, who was their prisoner.

Agreeably to the law of retaliation, which prevails among the Indians of this part of Asia, the assassin was immediately put to death in the same way which he had himself adopted; and the high regency held an extraordinary sitting to proceed to the appointment of a successor.

M. Eyseldyck, counsellor of India, and then director-general, was fixed on by the high regency to elect and crown the new king in the Company's name. He set off on the 27th of March for Bantam, in a ship armed on purpose, accompanied by four of the first merchants as commissioners. He had also a guard of honour, consisting of a lieutenant, sergeant, two corporals, eighteen grenadiers of the 12th battalion, and as many Dutch : this guard was commanded by lieutenant-colonel, then major, Legrevisse. The counsellor, on his arrival at Bantam, assembled all the princes, patys, and mandores, before the people; addressed them on the duties they had to fulfil towards their sovereign, and announced the prince whom the high regency had appointed to rule over them. A large pair of scales was set up before the palace gate;

young girls brought fruit, flowers, and every kind of herb which the country produces, in baskets; placing them in one scale. The appointed prince being placed in the opposite scale, and having weighed down all these productions, which were to represent those of the earth, he was acknowledged and proclaimed king: the counsellor at the same time placing the crown upon his head and embracing him; all the princes, his brothers, and even his father, prostrated themselves at his feet, to evince their respect for him. The king then promised to be a faithful ally to the Company, and ratified the engagements of his predecessor, relative to assistance of what men might be needful in case of war, and to the delivery of all the productions of his territory, at the price and on the conditions which were established of old.

The ceremony took place under a discharge of the palace and fort guns, and was terminated by feasting, which continued fifteen days. During this time the king was installed, and examined into the situation of his kingdom. The new king made every one a present of money, from the counsellor down to the private soldier: this present was taken from the treasury.

These ceremonies of Bantam always prove fatal to those who are sent upon them, for the air is still more pestilential there than at Batavia; all the grenadiers and European subalterns died either during their stay, or after their return; only two or three of the French and officers were saved. The secretary Schmith likewise fell a victim to it. M. Eyseldyck, his wife who had followed him, and major Legrevisse, together with the four merchants, all experienced putrid disorders, which brought them almost to the grave.

The kingdom of Bantam was formerly the greatest, and its sovereigns the most powerful, of the whole island of Java; but it has been much reduced since the Dutch have interrupted its communication with the other parts of Java, by taking possession of the kingdom of Jacatra. It includes, notwithstanding, a great extent of territory, from the river Tangarang, two leagues from Batavia, and which serves as its boundary, to the western extremity of the island. Its population is considerable, and is much increased by the Maduran deserters, slaves, Chinese bank-rupts, and even murderers, who take refuge there; for, besides its proximity, they are at-tracted thither by the certainty of finding an asylum, because, the natives not being subjects of the Company, the country is privileged, and the Dutch police can neither pursue nor arrest any of those who fly to it, although the sovereigns are under the dominion of the high regency.

The capital, built wholly of bamboo, is situated on the sea-shore, near the mouth of a great river, which empties itself into the bay. The king resides there in a kind of palace, built, in the European style, within an old ruinous fort, with eighty pieces of brass cannon of all sizes, partly without carriages, and altogether unserviceable.

The Dutch, on the contrary, have, at the side of it, a fort in a very good state, which commands that of the king as well as the city. They have a commandant, four artillery officers, and fifty Europeans, who encamp without the city on account of its unhealthiness. The king of Bantam assumes the European costume on great public days; he has a scarlet or other coloured coat embroidered with gold, with boots, spurs, a hat, sword, and poniards. On other occasions he dresses in the Malay manner, but very rich, and always carries two poniards. The natives of his kingdom are generally distinguished from those of Java : the former have their hair loose, with a small cap, or narrow round hat without a brim ; their eyes and features also appear more ferocious than those of the Javans.

The seraglio contains from three to four hundred women.

The kingdom produces an immense quantity of rice and pepper, with some small portion of tin and calin. From Bantam to Batavia, by land, is ninety miles.

The Lampons country in the island of Sumatra, though larger than the kingdom of Bantam, is dependent upon it. The king derived much more advantage from it a few years since, but the Lampons having risen and given shelter to some pirates, with whom they make common cause, his authority is almost at an end, and the calin-mines are not worked.

The Batavian government has long had in serious contemplation to establish a factory in the island of Sumatra, which is only separated from that of Java by the Straits of Sunda, and would open various lucrative branches of commerce; its camphor being the best which is known, and producing large quantities of benzoin, pepper, rice, and calin. Its attention was therefore directed to Lampons Bay, which is spacious, deep, with good anchorage, and situated at the entrance of the Straits of Sunda, near the southern point of the island, almost opposite to Bantam; but this bay being the resort of vast numbers of pirates who infest those seas, they were prevented forming an establishment

by the almost utter impossibility of rooting them
out, or rather by the inadequate means employed
to effect it. Armed ships were often sent to
burn the villages of the pirates; but being confined to this object, they always returned when it
was accomplished. The whole country is entirely a habitation for Indian vagabonds and
thieves, and is, in a great measure, in a state of
insurrection against its sovereign, the king of
Bantam.

In the last expedition which the high regency
fitted out against it, M. Brandels, an able
officer, was sent to fix upon a favourable situation for a fort, barracks, and storehouses; but
this ended, like the former, in burning a few
huts, the Indians sheltering themselves in the
interior; and the officer reported that he could
discover no place suitable for such an establishment, having seen nothing but impenetrable
marshes the whole length of the coast, and some
distance up the country.

The Hollanders were not discouraged by the
ill success of these endeavours.

The Batavian government, for the better accomplishment of its purpose, made it a matter
of interest to the king of Bantam, who was afterwards assassinated, and who, on coming to his
throne, engaged to supply government with a
considerable quantity of rice and pepper at a

shamefully low price, which, being unable to deliver to the extent, as he was forced to collect the greater part from the Lampons, his richest possession, which their rebellion and the number of pirates prevented, he felt himself interested in supporting the regency. He consequently undertook to subject and reduce the rebels to obedience at any rate, provided the high regency would be at the expense of, and furnish him with, three hundred European troops. His proposal was accepted, and the three hundred men were sent, with major Legrevisse at their head. These troops repaired to Bantam, where they remained at the king's disposal, expecting that every thing was ready for their embarkation; but, in the interval, news having been brought to Batavia, by an American, that war had actually taken place, the government lost no time in recalling the troops, and the project was again deferred to a more favourable opportunity.

It is very clear, that if the Dutch obtained a respectable footing in the Lampons country, with a fort, garrisoned by three or four hundred Europeans, some Maduran companies, and a resident, they might easily hold a communication with the sultan of Palimbang; in like manner form alliances with the different kings and petty princes within the line which bounds the kingdom of Achem, whose sovereign is the most powerful of the whole island; destroy, and ultimately, by degrees, annihilate the English factory at Bencoolen; by their alliances effect a balance of power against Achem, and secure nearly all the produce of the whole island of Sumatra, which is very great, both for fertility and extent.

The 30th May is the anniversary of the conquest of Jacatra and founding of Batavia. A salute of artillery from all the forts and batteries of the line of defence announces this fête in the morning. The governor-general and the whole council repair, in full dress, at seven o'clock, to the hall of audience in the castle. The edler-bailli, president of the city magistracy, leaves them, takes a coat and black cloak, and, at the head of all the sheriffs, in similar costume, renews, to the council, their oath of fidelity to the noble Company, high regency, and the Batavian republic; after which the governor delivers an appropriate speech, and they withdraw in the same order. The edler-bailli then resumes his seat amidst his colleagues, and a grand council is held till one o'clock. In the evening the governor has a party extraordinary at his house; and thus the day concludes.

CHAPTER VI.

Palankang.—Balembouang.— Bagnouwangie Bay.
—Indian Prince and Dutch Commandant.

Palankang is a village a league and a half up
the country, to the right of the mouth of Balembouang Bay. It is intersected by a small river,
whose entrance is opposite to it. On the 13th
February 1805, general Tombe and his company
were visited by the Joudo-Nogoro, prime minister
of the country. He came on horseback with his
escort to Palankang, where he got into a canoe.
Scarcely had he reached the side of the bay when
the Malays did him homage, by seating themselves cross-legged on the ground behind him.
His business was to announce the Dutch commandant, who arrived at three o'clock in a
beautiful barge with an awning, on which the
Dutch pendant was hoisted. They returned in
the same style.

The landing at Balembouang is difficult, and
the coast dangerous, particularly at the north of
the river, where is a sand-bank. The commandant, a German, Baron Wikermann, had
formerly been one of the guard of honour to the
emperor of Mataran, when he married a Malay

lady, and on this, the eldest son's birth-day, he gave a great entertainment.

Extending at the bottom of a grand saloon, was a transparent curtain, for a Malay comedy, which opened with noisy music, disgusting to the ears of an European. The musicians all sate cross-legged; a dozen of them beat gomgoms, a kind of copper, and very sonorous, cymbals, of different sizes for variety in sound. The director of the band played the principal instrument in use among the Indians; it is a two-stringed fiddle, the handle about a foot and a half long, and flat. The body is made of a very large, scarce, and dear cocoa-nut, which the Malay princes procure at an exorbitant price. This species is only found in the islands of Madura and Baly. The nut is fastened to the handle, almost at the end; the fiddle-stick is a bent *rotang*, and the strings of horse-hair. The instrument is placed perpendicularly on the ground, like a violoncello, and the sound is not unlike what is produced from that instrument when the bow is drawn over the strings behind the bridge. The musician sometimes stops to sing, which he does most wretchedly, and always in one tone.

The music played during breakfast, which consisted of tea, coffee, and fruit; the ladies afterwards withdrew to the saloon, where the music was, and, seating themselves on one side

on great mats spread on the ground, began play
ing cards.

At noon dinner was served, and as the company
were of three very different nations, it was in the
European, Chinese, and Malay style, so that each
might choose. Toasts were drank in Bourdeaux
wine, of which the commandant had received a
few bottles as a present.

Tea followed, and betel was handed to the
tomogon, to his ministers, the prime mandore
of the Malay army, and the chief of the Chinese;
card-playing and smoking then continued till
nine o'clock, when supper was served. The
next day the fête was repeated as from Madame
Wikermann, to whom the visitors paid their
respects accordingly. After dinner the party
took a ride, in carriages, to a pepper and coffee
plantation, which the commandant had first
established on the India Company's account, in
New Land, a mile from the village; and then
on to an old plantation, named Socoradija, also
under his direction, a league further up the
country than the former.

During a ten days stay here M. Tombe and
his friends visited a prince, who is also
high - priest, and a chief of the Chinese.
They were well received by both, state chairs
and music being prepared on their entering the

palaces, where they took tea, coffee, and preserved fruits, and smoked pipes. These chiefs
had probably been informed of the intended
visits by Baron Wikermann, as the company
found that they were expected, by similar preparations being made at both places.

Bagnouwangie is the only Dutch post on the
eastern part of the island of Java; it is situated
five leagues from the mouth of Balembouang
Bay, in the Straits of Baly, and seven from the
coast; a small river, also named Balembouang,
runs through it. It has a little earth fort lined
with turf, surrounded by a ditch full of water,
over which are two drawbridges. The garrison
consists of—1st, a lieutenant, who has the
command of and lives in the fort, where are
three capital residences with out-offices, besides
a guard-house—2d, a company of Madurans
intermixed with about ten Europeans and some
Sammanapp artillery, with a Dutch second-
lieutenant and sergeant.

Opposite to, and at the side of, the mouth
of the river are a bank and several reefs;
but there is anchorage notwithstanding. Two
pilots, who reside in the village, precede the
ships which pass the Strait, to point out anchorage to such as want to take in provisions
and water.

The commandant has the management of two fine plantations of pepper and coffee, as already mentioned, and an indigo manufactory adjoining. In the middle of the former is a large shed for depositing and drying the coffee and pepper. A rivulet passes through it, which has a sluice to distribute the water, by subterraneous channels, into two great basons, one of which, opposite the shed, is entirely of brick, and into gutters which water the roots of the pepper-trees. A third of the distance from each end of the principal avenue of this plantation are huts built of bamboo, and covered with cocoa-leaves, for those who have the care of it. A river runs at one side of the indigo-house, on which are sheds and other houses, also a building in which the Malays employed there, reside.

A league beyond, at Sacoradaija, are an extensive old brick-built house, hospital, and prison, for the Malays. Immediately in front of the house is a very large stove of flat, well-cemented, square tiles for drying coffee. So old is the plantation, that the branches of the coffee-trees completely fill up the avenues to it, and are not easily put aside to pass through.

The commandant, Wikermann, is also charged to keep up the friendly ties which subsist between the kings of Baly and the Company.

The Balyans who cross the Strait and come to Bagnouwangie, cannot be received until they are furnished with a passport, written on a badamier leaf.

This establishment is surrounded by a village of the same name, where the tomogon resides. It consists of thirty Chinese and forty Malay families. It is separated from Panaroukan by a desert, thirty-five leagues across, very mountainous, and covered with thick woods, full of tigers, buffaloes, and leopards; and being also one of the most unhealthy of the whole island of Java, all the malcontents of Samarang and Surabaye, as well European officers as soldiers, are banished thither for five or six months, according to the degrees of their offences. All the Javan and Maduran criminals, condemned to the gallies, are also transported to it for life, to work in the new plantation and in that of Sacoradaija.

The environs of the fort and village are surrounded by marshes, which frequently occasion putrid diseases among the few Europeans and natives who live there. The unhealthiness of this country, however, is mostly owing to a volcano, a league and a half within the western part of the isle of Baly, opposite to the establishment. This volcano frequently emits a shower of ashes which cover both the establishment and its vicinity, as happened in 1804, and soon afterwards occasioned a great number of mortal diseases.

Before quitting this part, it should be observed that all the geographers, ancient and modern, err in placing a town of this name in the eastern part of Java ; describing it as a city too, which, according to some, contains 10,000 inhabitants, carries on a considerable trade, and whither all the ships of the East resort.

Balembouang Bay, the entrance of which begins at Gounong-Ikan point, in the Strait of Baly, is entirely desert and full of thick woods down to the water's edge, where, at every step, may be seen tracks of the wild beasts, which haunt there in great numbers. In fact, in this extremity of the island, there is no establishment whatever, except the campong of Palankang, a league and a half inland, to the right on entering the bay : it is true that, forty or fifty years ago, the India Company had a battery and tent, round which was a small Malay and Chinese village; but that establishment, which was only intended for the refreshment of ships passing the Strait, and to keep up the amicable relations with the Balyans, for the slave-trade, has been abandoned ; six European officers, who successively commanded them, having all died of the dropsy, from the unwholesome water of two rivulets, the mouths of which are at the side of the place where it stood. This post has subsequently been transferred to the Bagnouwangie stream, whither the natives have also followed it.

CHAPTER VII.

*Catapang.—Caravan into the Interior of Java.—
Desert of Balembouang.—Panaroukan.—Prin-
cipalities of Besouki, Banger, Passourouang and
Bangell.—Reception by Javan Princes.*

Iro-Gounon, tomogon of Balembouang, ordered
a hundred Malays to attend a caravan, of which
M. Tombe formed a part, into the interior of
Java; twenty-five as a personal escort, and seventy-
five to carry the baggage. They were all armed
with poignards, and one party also had lances
of eighteen feet long, and another carbines, to
protect them from the tigers, leopards, and, what
were still more to be dreaded, on account of
their ferociousness, wild buffaloes. Having three
days journey of desert to pass, they had, independently of their own horses, and those of the
escort, fifteen others laden with provisions for
the whole caravan.

On the 26th February 1805, it left Bagnouwangie for the little village of Catapang, two
leagues off, on the coast in Baly Strait. The
road is very fine and level, through a large forest,
in which were seen a great number of peacocks
and apes; the latter jumping from tree to tree to
catch the others on the wing.

Continuing along the coast for about an hour, the caravan halted at a spring, which flows from a rock, where every one refreshed himself. Previously to entering the desert, dispositions were made that the caravan might be always on the defensive. The party proceeded one by one, led by the first mandore, armed with a lance, which he carried horizontally over his horse's neck.

As, in these deserts, there can be no encampment at night, without being subject to be devoured by wild beasts, besides that the coldness of the night-air in Java is mortal, particularly to Europeans, the governor, resident at Samarang, has built, about twelve leagues apart, a shed and a house for travellers; they are constructed of bamboos covered with cocoa leaves, surrounded by hedges and ditches, and guarded by armed Malays, who constantly, and especially at night, keep up fires about and in the centre of the inclosure.

The caravan reached the first post, Bagnou-Matie, New Death, so called because some natives and Europeans have been devoured there, at three o'clock in the afternoon : here were some bad mattresses and mats of *rotang*. The inlets to the inclosure were barricaded, and great fires were lighted within and round it. The night passed quietly; some lowings only being heard, and several buffaloes coming to one of the en-

trances to drink at a rivulet which runs near.
Four Malays armed with lances kept guard during the night at the entrance of the dwelling.

The road from Catapang to the post of Bagnou-Matie, is merely a way known to the natives; even the trace of it is lost in many parts of
the wood. This path is scarcely wide enough for
one person, and is bordered on each side by very
thick grass, nine or ten feet high, which adds to
the danger of the journey, as the tigers often
conceal themselves in it, and can make their attack when it is least looked for; different places
were distinguishable where these animals had
been. The path is always up or down hill, and
the dead branches of trees crossing it make endless stoppages: it also crosses several small rivers,
the points of rocks in many parts of which render the fords extremely rugged.

On the 24th the caravan crossed a rapid river,
and after going up the side of it for two hours,
halted. Here Joudo-Nogoro's colleague, Massoura-Adijlaga, who accompanied the caravan,
dismounted his horse to purify himself, which
he did by dipping his head in the water three
times, notwithstanding the danger of stopping;
but his religion prescribed it, and he was
surrounded by his escort.

At two in the afternoon the caravan arrived at
the second post, Sonbourouarou, which is also

guarded by Malays: Massoura-Adijlaga has built several houses here for himself and his wives, as he sometimes spends a fortnight or month together at it. He has a flock of goats, herds of deer, and much poultry. The road was nearly the same as before, and still in the forest.

The baggage, it should be observed, generally sets out before daybreak. On the 25th the caravan followed it, as usual, about an hour after. Massoura-Adijlaga informed the party that he should take his leave at the river of Calie-Ticos, Rats River, which is at the extremity, and on the frontier of the kingdom of Balembouang, as he was not to go further. It arrived there at ten o'clock in the morning. This river, the water of which is whitish and unwholesome, is remarkable for its extraordinary rapidity. It is wide, and shut up between two very steep mountains. On the crest of the mountain, on the left bank, near the ford, is a small hamlet inhabited by Malays, who, apprized of the caravan, and having perceived it at a distance, came into the water up to their waists, and guided the horses to facilitate their passage. These wretched Indians, dwelling in the midst of tigers and leopards, acquitted themselves of the duty of hospitality on this occasion ; they had dressed some maize in the ear, spread it on bamboo mats at the river side, and set it before the company as the best they had, apologizing that, being poor orang-gounon, mountaineers, they had nothing else to give. They partook of this breakfast, and added to it some roasted fowls, which the minister brought from Sonbourouarou. The company drank some water preserved and carried in bamboos, mixing with it a little gin, which remained of two flasks which the commandant of Bagnouwangie gave the mandores for the purpose, and who carried them suspended in large cocoanut-shells.

The caravan continued its route, having taken leave of the minister, and, an hour afterwards, crossed a river, the sides of which are very dangerous from the tigers of the environs, which often go there, five or six together, to quench their thirst. Several extremely fierce tiger-cats were seen skipping about, which went off as it approached them. There were also many apes, two of which, from their size, might be orang-outangs, wild men of the woods.

At length, at three in the afternoon, the caravan got out of the desert, and entered an immense plain, dotted with thickets and rice-fields, forming a fine contrast to the preceding solitary gloom.

Leaving a village on the right, at five o'clock the party arrived at Panaroukan, the capital of the ancient kingdom of that name, of which a rich Chinese is the chief. He attended, and excellent beds were made ready in chambers.

He occupies a very large house built of wood, the front of which resembles that of a theatre. He immediately ordered tea and preserved fruit to be served. The arrival was no sooner known, than the paty, chief of the Malays, paid his visit.

At seven o'clock the company were most agreeably surprised with a grand supper, wholly in the European style, and in so great profusion, that they at first thought other guests were expected. The only deficiency was wine, for which was substituted gin and water.

Being invited to make some stay with the host, they consented, and the more readily on M. Tombe's part, as he had learnt that there was a small fort in this country, occupied by a dozen European invalids, commanded by a sergeant. The escort, in consequence of the intended stay, returned to Bagnouwangie, and a new one of a similar number of Malays and horses was ordered to replace it the next day.

Soon after the arrival of the caravan, one of the invalids introduced himself. He was a Frenchman, originally from Amiens, sixty-five years of age, and had been thirty years in the Company's service. M. Tombe told him his wish to see the fort, where he announced him, and he went there next morning with M. Jaussaud. The sergeant-commandant is eighty years old, though he did not seem sixty, and the youngest of the detachment is fifty-five.

The fort is unimportant; it is square, built with palisades and planks, which are falling down from age; mounts four two-pounders, and is surrounded by a wide ditch full of water. It has two entrances, with a good drawbridge—the principal entrance fronts the coast. It stands on a marshy plain, three quarters of a mile from the coast. The Dutch flag is planted opposite the fort.

Within it is a small barrack-house, the rooms of which are tolerably comfortable. The sergeant's apartments are at the entrance, and isolated. They consist of three compartments and a kitchen on the side of the guardhouse. These old soldiers, although their pay is but moderate, live tolerably well, and make no complaints, as provisions are cheap, and their food consists principally of fish, poultry, and rice, with which the vicinity abounds.

Panaroukan is situated in the Strait of Madura, near Cape Sandanna, upon a river which empties itself by several branches into the sea: neither of them is navigable even for canoes, except in great floods. It is said that there is a passage for coasting vessels, in the midst of the reefs which line the coast, and which gave rise to the fort, which it has long been in agitation to rebuild of stone, as it, at the same time, serves as a check on the natives and Chinese in the event of an insurrection. From this fort, when the weather is clear, can be seen Sammanapp, and the south-eastern island. It is a considerable village, inhabited by one third Chinese and two thirds Malays; and either nation has its own temple, priests, and bonzes.

On the 27th, the escort and horses being ready, the party set off from Panaroukan for Besouki, another Malay principality, where they arrived in the afternoon. The distance is about eleven leagues of extremely bad road, and continually in the woods to within a gun shot of the place. At noon they found themselves in an immense plain of rice, interspersed with thickets, exhibiting a delightfully picturesque view. The approaches to Besouki are very beautiful, on account of their variety of pleasant scenery. The whole plain was then animated by a multitude of Javans, male and female, employed in the plantations and other work which the rice requires.

Besouki is a very large village, about three leagues from the coast. The mandores conducted the party to the tomogon's palace, but he was from home. His people asked them to walk in and wait. The paty, chief of this campong, came soon after to inform them that the tomogon was gone to visit the prince of Sam-

manapp, his father-in-law, and that he would
not return till five o'clock in the evening. He
then led them to his own house, where he
showed every attention, immediately serving up roasted fowls, excellent broth, curry-
fish, rice, tea, fruits, and sweetmeats. At five
o'clock they were apprised of the return of the
prince, to whom they were immediately conducted, and presented by the paty. The tomogon gave them a civil reception under a shed
opposite his palace, in which they had tea and
preserved fruits. Mats were laid on the ground,
at the side and without, for the paty and his
suite, who were served with betel.

The prince is from forty to forty-five years of
age, a native of China, and never had but one
wife, with whom he still lives, although polygamy is customary with the Mahometans: he
has no children. He is reputed, by the Dutch of
Java, a well-informed man, of some knowledge in physics and mathematics. His grand-
father, a Chinese chief, having put himself at
the head of a party of his own nation and the
natives, in a war which one of the emperors of
Mataram had to sustain against several neighbouring kings, and having obtained great suc-
cesses, that emperor, in return, promoted him
to the dignity of tomogon upon condition that

he should abjure his religion; which he did, that his children might succeed him.

His dress consists of nankeen trowsers, in the French style, with yellow slippers, which forms a singular contrast to his moustaches, turban, and Malay jacket. The company took leave of him to visit the mosques and tombs of his an-, cestors.

Besouki is a considerable village, intersected, in various parts, by a small river. The tomogon's palace is built, in the European manner, of white stones: in front is a large court with a wooden gate. He appeared to be more reserved than the others towards his subjects who were about him.

The environs of this canton abound in rice; and game is very common, owing to the quantity of thickets which cover the plain.

On the 28th the party set off, at six o'clock in the morning, with a new escort and fresh horses. As they had a long distance to go, the paty of Besouki sent forward, over-night, to a petty chief of a village through which they must pass, some poultry, eggs, and rice, with an order to have them ready for their arrival. The road is in many places bad: it crosses several rice-fields, some small rivers, and an inconsiderable wood.

The village where they dined is unimportant, and a brook runs across it.

They reached the tomogon's of *Banger* in the evening, and were most courteously received. The paty immediately paid them a visit, and took tea with them, and betel after it. There were only three European beds in the tomogon's palace.

This young prince, being curious in regard to foreign articles, wished to see the form of the officers' trunks. After having closely examined them, perceiving that he had touched two cases made of pig-skin, on which some of the bristles yet remained (that animal is detested by these people, who are all Mahometans), instantly called for a basin of perfumes and aromatics, and washed his hands to purify himself.

His disposition seemed very gentle, and his subjects appeared greatly attached to him.

The table was elegantly set out, though the provisions were all dressed in the Malay fashion : it was spread with fine linen and beautiful silver plate, and was lighted by four large flambeaux in candlesticks of massy silver. The tomogon did the honours, and was surrounded by thirty Malays seated on the ground, except the mandore who waited. Excellent Bourdeaux wine was set before the company, and they drank several toasts with three, the Malays all joining in the huzza. Candles were necessary, although it was the middle of summer, for, in the latitude and longitude of Java, day and night are nearly equal throughout the year. At six or half past six in the morning day begins, and ends at the same hour in the evening: there is neither twilight nor dawn; at least they are not perceptible. The tomogon himself showed them to their rooms, where they had capital beds, beautiful linen, and very fine musquito-nets, ornamented with fringe, and almost new. Several Malays slept on mats under the bedsteads, and at the doors of the rooms, to be ready to give assistance, were it requisite, in the night.

The prince was preparing a grand entertainment for his father, who was expected the next morning: he was seventy years old, and, on account of his age, had recently abdicated in his son's favour, and retired to Surabaye.

On the 1st of March the party began their journey, after having breakfasted: every thing was in readiness for the old man's reception, and a rich carriage, drawn by two fine horses, went to meet him.

It is only nine leagues from Passourouang, and good travelling for the horses. The road, which is large and old, is in the middle of rice-fields, with some hills easy of ascent and well cultivated. The country from Besouki is most delightful. The vicinity of the villages presents picturesque views, from the feet of the high mountains, in the interior, to the sea. The plains are strewed with thickets, which seem as though planted expressly for their ornament, to render the view more fascinating; and a multitude of Malay men and women working at the ground, give life to the enchanting picture.

The escort reached Passourouang at noon, and was well received by the Dutch commandant Hesselaar, a captain of foot. He was many years lieutenant in the European cavalry, which acts as guard of honour to the emperor of Solo; and the appointment of Passourouang was given him to retire to. He has with him two officers, some subalterns and European soldiers, and some companies of Malays, to guard a small fort of masonry, rather intended against the natives, in case of revolt, than against an external foe. He also has the management of several considerable plantations of coffee and pepper belonging to the Company, and which are in the environs; likewise the direction of a yard for building the coasting-vessels necessary for the transport of those productions. The hill, and a mountain two leagues inland, are cultivated, almost to the summit, with all kinds of European garden-stuff, which never degenerate, whether from the situation or from the soil in which they grow, and which supply a great part of the civil and military administrations of Surabaye, whose environs produce little in this way.

This appointment is very lucrative to M. Hesselaar, being estimated to bring in 15,000 rix-dollars a year. His household consists of thirty Malay slaves from Baly and Macassar, ten of whom are musicians; a Chinese belonging to the chief has taught them music, having learnt it himself from a German in the Company's service, who lived many years at Passourouang. He also has four elegantly gilt carriages, and a one-horse chaise, with twenty fine horses richly caparisoned. His wife is a native, by whom he has several children. He always keeps a most splendid table.

On the morrow he introduced the party to the prince, with whom they took tea, smoked, and ate some preserved fruits: the prince afterwards showed them, in one of his yards, two immense tigers, in an inclosure of thick palisades. Three had been taken in traps by several of his subjects, but one of them died a few days before.

The principality of Passourouang is one of those, in Java, where these animals are common.

They next visited the Chinese campong, which is very considerable, this people forming a third of the population of the place : they also visited their chief, who set before them pipes and tea.

Passourouang is the capital of a very large

principality; it is crossed by a wide river, which is navigable some leagues up the country for coasting-vessels, with which it is always covered. A fine wooden bridge communicates from one side to the other: the commandant's house backs the fort on the right bank facing the bridge. This is a very extensive and commodious residence, with many offices; the boat-yard is near the mouth of the river, which falls into the sea a short way beyond.

M. Gauffe, surgeon-major of the 12th French battalion, was there, but had gone into the interior to propagate vaccination among the natives, and to give them the advantage of that inestimable discovery. On the 3d March they proceeded to Bangell, only seven leagues off. The road is wide and excellent, over a plain, cultivated with rice and maize: at some distance right and left are several villages, embosomed in papaya and bananas, and surrounded by cocoa-trees. The prince of Bangell is almost seventy years old; he received them with particular kindness, and the usual ceremony. He abstains from wine, as he unites the rank of high priest with that of tomogon. This old prince is the elder brother of the prince of Besouki, and consequently originally from China. He speaks all the oriental languages, particularly those of Madura and China, and has some ideas of European geogra-

phy : he conversed like one who had travelled,
and more particularly in Italy, and was at no
loss how to make use of a map of Europe, which
was laid before him.

His eldest son, a fine man, almost white,
speaks Dutch fluently, and is well acquainted with
civil architecture. He said that one of his legitimate wives was big of her sixty first child, of
which twenty-nine were dead, and of the remaining thirty-one, twelve were at Besouki, with his
brother, who took charge of their education.

The facility of procuring women throughout
Java is rather singular. No sooner were the gentlemen in bed, than a Malay came to offer
them ; and it is the more remarkable, as the
character of the people inclines to ferocity. The
sex are slaves, and the men jealous in the extreme.
It is also true that these sort of females, called
rouguins, are free girls, or belong to unfor-
tunate families, who thus give them up on the
demand of the prince, to whom they refuse
nothing, in the hope of obtaining favour and attention in return.

The next day the caravan commenced the first
day's journey to Surabaye, the principal Dutch
settlement in the Strait of Madura. The company were conducted in the tomogon's carriages
to Soutacarie, the frontier town of his principality, five leagues off, where their horses and es-

cort waited for them with provisions, addressed
to the chief, with whom they breakfasted. The
road from Bangell to Soutacarie is wide, even,
and very fine ; the country is well cultivated in
rice and maize, and full of large and populous
villages.

After leaving Soutacarie they were still three
leagues from their first destination. They crossed
the river of Bagiéram, over a large wooden bridge,
leaving, on the left, a chain of low hills of easy
ascent. They kept along the side of the river up
to Surabaye: it is very wide, with several little
islands, which, combining with the charmingly
varied country round Surabaye, render the approach to it extremely fascinating. A league on
this side of it, on the right, and close to the
river, is a very extensive palace named Simpang,
which one of the Dutch governors had built of
brick : it now belongs to the chief of the Chinese,
but is occupied by the present governor, who is
his tenant, and makes it his residence.

CHAPTER VIII.

Opasses. — Surabaye. — Environs. — Gressec. — Entertainments by the Tomogon.

Opasses are Maduran or Sammanapp soldiers always in waiting on the European officers, to whom they are at the same time servants. These Indians are naturally brave and intelligent.

The Dutch governor of Surabaye is subordinate to that of Java. The principality is governed by two tomogons, one of whom is allied to the emperor of Solo, better known as emperor of Mataram. The garrison consists of major Franquemont, commandant of all the European and Indian troops ; an adjutant, one hundred Europeans, including a company of the old Wurtemberg regiment ; six companies of Maduran infantry and two of the Maduran artillery, under the command of European officers, or officers born in the settlement. Here is a military hospital for one hundred and fifty sick.

The capital of the settlement is the depôt for the recruits, with which the princes of Madura and Sammanapp are obliged to furnish the Company.

Surabaye is a small town not mentioned in any

geography, although it is an establishment of
some importance and very healthy. It is crossed
by the river of Caliemas, not far from that of
Bagiéran, which falls into it a little higher. The
environs and their banks are full of villages inhabited by two thirds Malay and the remainder
Chinese.

The troops are quartered in a brick fort, containing a small arsenal, on the right bank of the
river. The hospital is on the same side, without,
and near the town.

The government and all the officers dwell
mostly on this side: on the opposite bank are
the principal Malay and Chinese campong, to
which there is a communication by two large
wooden bridges. Two moles are just completed
at its mouth, with batteries, independently of
those, previously there, to defend the entrance.

The river is navigable for all the country
coasters, of which it is always full. There are
several small yards where they are built to draw
ten and twelve feet water; they are sold to the
princes of Borneo and Baly; likewise others
for transporting the produce of the neighbourhood, which is only rice.

The ships destined for the Philippines and for
China generally touch at Surabaye, especially in
the season of the north-westers; they there find
every possible refreshment, except garden-stuff,

which the Europeans are obliged to procure from
the principality of Passourouang. Good native
sailors may also be had there, but it must be
under an engagement to bring them back to Java.

The mountains, in the vicinity, contain a tolerably hard stone, in colour and veins exactly like
box-wood. The natives work it very tastefully,
by a wheel, into candlesticks, plates, and goblets.
They also manufacture many little articles,
such as combs, brushes, &c. of the buffalo's
horn.

A league and a half from Surabaye, upon a hill
which runs along the left bank of the river
Bagiéran, is a saltpetre-house. This factory
might have been an important establishment, of
great utility, had it been kept up, on account of
the quantity of saltpetre-earth in the vicinity, which
is produced from the dung of a number of bats,
with which the country abounds ; but it is given
up, and was lately sold to a Chinese for the small
sum of six hundred rixdollars, although it cost at
least fifteen thousand. This seems the more in-
explicable, as an European officer has been sent
to look for saltpetre at Byman, near Sombawa
island. Some say it was owing to private pique
of the council to Baron Ogendorff, who originated
the saltpetre-house. The rural walks about
Surabaye are very pleasant, and so numerous,
that they may be varied every day for a month,

without going the same twice. They are all
wide enough for a carriage, and are shaded by
thickets and close hedges of bamboo, banana,
and other very high shrubs, which keep off the
heat of the sun. Within the circumference of
twelve miles is an infinity of campongs, so close
to each other that they appear to make one city :
another proof of the salubrity and fertility of the
country. One of the petty kings of the isle of Baly
paid a visit to this place on his return from Batavia,
whither he had been on behalf of the great king
of that island, to solicit the Company's protection and alliance, that he might be enabled to
put an end to the devastating scourge of intestine
war, which has long prevailed among the kings
and princes of his country. His suite consisted
of one hundred men, armed with their poignards
and klébans. One carried his parasol, another
his betel-box, and a third his square silk cap,
embroidered with gold. While he remained
with the commandant, these three Malays sate
cross-legged on the ground behind his state-chair.
He had two other Malays with him, probably
his ministers, or nobles, as they were seated, on
chairs, by his side.

The commandant engaged M. Tombe and his
friends on a water-party to M. Van-Harsen's, resident of Gressec, whither they went in a beautiful large barge belonging to the governor,

covered like the passage-boats of Holland; the cabin occupied its whole length, except that, at either end, was space left for the master, some rowers, and a small sail to hoist when the weather permitted. The cabin was very well furnished; the seats, which went all round, were covered with good cushions: a table up the middle, with small lockers for provisions, and particularly for pipes; and lastly, latticed casements with silk curtains, completed the floating saloon.

From Surabaye to Gressec by sea, is reckoned three leagues, which was performed in five hours, against wind and tide. The coast of Java, from the mouth of the Surabaye river, to Gressec, forms a large angle, with an island in the middle. A bank of sand and mud which runs along the coast, and is almost always visible, has rendered necessary a wooden mole, built on piles opposite the fort: it is six hundred feet in length: the boats are fastened to it, and the pier is ascended by a wooden ladder. Having gained the other extremity, we traverse a large room with neither door nor window over the abutment, probably intended for a guard-house, and, descending five steps, arrive at Gressec.

Gressec, the capital of an ancient Javan kingdom, is now merely a small town divided between the natives and the Chinese. The latter,

here, as every where else, have their own campong, temple, and bonzes.

The small fort is built of stones ; within it is
a barrack for the guards who have the care of it.

The principal street is along the coast : it consists of four or five large houses of beach stones,
inhabited by the resident, Dutch admiral, book-
keeper, some commissioners, and the Company's
surgeon.   The street is wide, and shaded by several rows of tall thick trees, opposite the houses,
which makes the entrance rural and pleasant. At
the end of, and behind the street are Malay and
Chinese campongs, also the grand square, in
which are the palaces of the two ruling tomogons.
There is neither river nor rivulet at Gressec ;
water for drinking is fetched from two springs,
half a league off, near the coast, or it is brought
from Surabaye.   The natives frequently use
brackish water, and such as they catch from the
rains.   Notwithstanding the difficulty of procuring good water, and in spite of the marshes
and stagnant pools which lie round the Malay
and Chinese campongs, and the mud-bank on
the coast, which, being dry at low water, continually exhales intolerable vapours, the air of
the place is very wholesome : sick persons are
seldom met with, and it is esteemed the most
salubrious of all Java : which would induce one
to think that the unhealthiness of the kingdom

of Bantam, Jacatra, and Balembouang, is rather
owing to the nature of the soil than to the
marshes.   The currents, however, in this strait,
which is very narrow, are so strong, that filth
of whatever kind cannot remain long.

A short league further, at the foot of the
hills on which Gressec stands, is a saltpetre-
house in full work, established, by the Company,
under the direction of the resident.

The administration of the country consists of
a resident, and some Malay companies commanded by natives.   A Dutch sergeant of the garrison of Surabaye commands them in chief, with
the title of military commandant.   To give the
latter some consequence among the natives, he
is often, particularly when there are any officers
at Surabaye, invited to the resident's table.
There are also some inferior officers and a
surgeon.   Lastly, two tomogons govern the natives.   The present princes are brothers, their
father having long since ceded half the principality to his eldest son, and subsequently,
owing to his great age, finally abdicated in
favour of the youngest of seven sons.

This prince was major of all the Malay
troops ; he had been promoted to that rank in
preference to his next brother, to whom the rank
fell, as being more capable of doing honour to
the situation.

Returning from the resident to the younger tomogon, whose name is Ardyo adi Nogoro the party were agreeably surprised, on entering the first court of his palace, to hear noisy music and a Malay play. The theatre was in a shed opposite his principal residence, and was nothing more than a transparent curtain of seven or eight feet high, and eighteen or twenty feet long, stretched on a frame, and kept perpendicular by two feet fixed to each end. The manager was behind this screen, and gave action to card figures of different kinds, representing cavalry, infantry, kings and princes at war. It was exactly like what we term Chinese shades. The Malay director at the same time sung of the different fights and victories of the ancestors of the emperor and other princes of the country, to the sound of a number of kettle-drums and gomgoms of different sizes.

The two-stringed fiddle, already described, was the principal instrument, and played by the leader of the band. The musicians * were placed on one side of the theatre; on the other were the tomogon's six brothers, seated respectfully on chairs. In front, at some distance from

* All the Indians, and consequently their musicians, seem to have some ideas of the different sounds of music. On the approach of the party to the palace the musicians played an adagio; when they saw them, an allegro.

the screen, state-chairs were placed for the Europeans and the tomogon, who sate in the middle. In the long square which the company formed, were thirty rouguins, fourteen to sixteen years old, ornamented with garlands of flowers. These girls danced round without touching each other, and turned very gracefully on one foot ; at the same time singing, in a languishing tone, the victories and praises of the emperors. They now and then sate down in a groupe on the ground to rest. In one of the angles outside the shed were two tables set out with Bourdeaux wine, gin, liquors, and pipes, and it is customary to drink every instant.

No sooner were the gentlemen seated than Ardyo adi Nogoro opened the ball by a kind of minuet with two of the rouguins ; after which, having placed them close together, he threw an handkerchief round their waist, and brought them for M. Tombe to do the same, which, in compliance with their customs, he did, and in the same way passed them to the next, and so through all the European visitors.

While the handkerchief was round the two girls, and before dancing commenced, a mandore brought two glasses of gin on a silver dish, one for the dancer and one for the tomogon ; it was no sooner taken hold of, than the whole assembly and spectators huzzaed three times, after which the dancer did the same, and drank.

At the opening of the fête the tomogon se lected, from the groupe of young girls, the one whom he thought prettiest, brought her to M. Tombe, placed her on his knees, and left her wholly at his disposal : he did the same to the other five of the company. They were, however, at liberty to change them if they were not to their taste; and when they were tired of having them on their knees, they sate at their feet.

This entertainment continued till half past five in the morning; at six they breakfasted, and at eleven arrived at Surabaye.

CHAPTER IX.

Sidaijo.—Strait of Madura.—Rembang.—Japara. —Javanna.—Samarang—Its Line of Defence.— Tagal.—Tcheribon.

SIDAIJO is a pretty village, which appears to great advantage from the mouth of the channel of the Strait of Madura, across Panka Point. On this point is always a military guard of three or four Europeans and some Madurans, sent by the resident of Gressec to protect the Dutch flag, and a small battery which is there. M. Loriaux, the engineer at Surabaye, in his plan for the defence of this part of the island of Java, has seen the importance of this post, and of the village of Sidaijo, where is a fine road leading behind Gressec and Surabaye. He consequently has erected a much more considerable work, to which a company of Madurans, commanded by European officers and subalterns, has been added for the defence of the landing-place.

At Panka Point are always Javan and European pilots, who, as soon as they discover vessels standing for the channel, go before to pilot them to Gressec or Surabaye. The master of the pilot-boat always has an order, from the resident at

Gressec, for the captains to give the name of their ship, their own name, what nation they are of, whence they come, and whither they are going. This declaration must be made and signed by the captain or one of his officers ; the pilot then stays on board, and the master resumes his post. The same custom occurs at the port of Ancere, in the Strait of Sunda, and at Bagnouwangie, in the Strait of Baly. Refreshments may be procured at the same time; for the master and Malay rowers generally avail themselves of the opportunity to supply the sailors and passengers, at very low prices, with fish, poultry, eggs, garden-stuff, and fruit.

The channel of the Strait of Madura, where it narrows, is only eighty-three fathoms wide ; its entrance is designated by buoys. Although, at the beginning, there are only three, three and a half, and four fathoms water, the largest men of war can pass it ; the bottom being merely mud, which is easily worked through, without the least danger, in the lightest breeze, and by the force of the currents.

After leaving this Strait and doubling Panka Point, is seen Rembang, a small settlement on the northern coast, in a spacious hollow ; then nearing and doubling Japara Point, pass in front of Javanna, another Dutch settlement, where ships moor somewhat at large: this settle-

ment, and that of Japara, being open roads, and
the coast not altogether free from danger to those
not well acquainted with it. The residents at
these places are commissioned to see the engagements of the princes with the Company fulfilled,
by causing the rice, sugar, and coffee, which the
country produces, to be deposited in the magazines, until the ships come to take them to the
general magazines at Samarang.

Samarang, only about sixty miles distant from
the residence of the emperor of Samarang, and
one hundred and five from that of the sultan of
Jóucki, the two most powerful princes in the
island, is rather a pretty town, on the northern
coast of Java ; it is situated about seventy-two
miles west of Surabaye, and ninety east of Tcheribon ; intersected by the Great River, so called
because it is the largest in the vicinity.

It is a free road : ships which draw four and
five fathoms cannot anchor nearer than a league
and a half from shore ; merchant-vessels which
draw two fathoms, and two and a half, may approach within about a league. At the mouth of
the Great River is a shoal, but it is marked by
buoys.

A short mile east of the mouth of the Great
River, is that of the river Caligawa ; they are
both navigable a good way up the country for
small boats ; of which that of Caligawa is always

full, because it runs through the large village of Torabaya, and the Javan and Chinese campongs, where all the small trade of the neighbourhood is carried on. They both take their rise in the mountains of the empire of Mataram.

The houses occupied by the Europeans are, in a great measure, built of small stones. The air is very healthy; and, notwithstanding the great heat, one may walk out at any hour of the day, without being liable to inconvenience from it.

The authority of the governor of Java, who resides there, extends from Tcheribon, exclusively, to the easternmost point of the island in the Strait of Baly. He is appointed by the high regency, and is subordinate to the governor-general of Batavia.

This establishment is very important to the Dutch. All the communications of the two empires of Mataram and Joucki, as well as the other kingdoms and principalities, bear upon it; wherefore it is the general depôt of all the produce of Java in rice, sugar, coffee, and pepper. The greater number of the vessels which fill the magazine of Batavia touch here.

On a steep rock, three quarters of a mile behind Bodijon, is seen, from a bamboo observatory, all the neighbouring coast, mountains, and ravines. On the same height, a short distance from the observatory, are several tombs of the Javan princes, surrounded by walls of small stones.

Observations on the Line of Defence of Samarang.

The line determined on for the defence of this important post, extends from the river Tawang-Trassie to that of Clayrang. The intermediate parts of the two extremities of this line are naturally protected by banks, which prevent all approach to them, and by impenetrable morasses, which do away every hope and possibility of turning the centre-works, and penetrating into the interior.

The part which forms the centre, and which is intrenched, commences at the Great River, and reaches to the mouth of the Caligawa, an extent of nine thousand six hundred feet. Many works have been constructed along this part of the coast and at the mouth of the two rivers, but time has shown that the greater part of the positions were wrong. These works were thrown too forward, and were not substantial enough to resist the waves which continually break against them; one part has been overwhelmed, and the other sunk down, and was swallowed up by the sea.

To remedy this, and to put the coast into as respectable a state as the nature of the ground

would permit, the governor, Engelhart, has
built,

1. At the mouth of the Great River, on the
left bank, the angular fortification, called the
Nieuwe-west-baterie, which, with the old redoubt, called the Oost-baterie, which has been
repaired, and is on the opposite bank, seems an
adequate defence for the mouth and entrance.
Four guns, placed on the platform of a destroyed
demi-bastion on the bank of the river, rather
behind the fortification, would not be unserviceable, as they would enfilade the mouth of the
river and sweep the great bank opposite, over
which all boats can pass at high water ; but it
would be prudent to construct a parapet to cover
the cannoneers attached to those guns.

2. A circular redoubt, called the Goedever-
warting, constructed at five hundred and forty
feet from the coast, which sweeps the intermediate plain, defends the grand communication,
parallel to it, and flanks the left part of the
work, which forms the centre of the front of the
defence. It would be more effectual if a little
wider. The face should be prolonged twenty-
four feet, at the side of the river, to flank the
Nieuwe-west-baterie, and batter the gorge of
the redoubt called the Oost-baterie, in case the
enemy should succeed in getting possession of
this second work, and wish to establish himself

there.   It would also be indispensable to destroy
the demi-bastion which closes this gorge on the
side of the plain ; for there can be no doubt that,
if an enemy got possession of it, he would be
protected by the same demi-bastion, which he
would raise with the earth in front of the works,
and would then be sheltered from the fire of the
circular redoubt, and might batter the communications on the plain.

The centre is defended by a work called the
Nieuwe-angelegte Gedette-van, a fortification
looked upon, by the governor and principal
military officers, as the citadel and bulwark of the
establishment, where should be the central point
collecting the troops, the post of reserve, and
depôt of provisions and stores, in case of any
attack.   But this work, which is seven hundred
and eighty feet in front, is far from possessing
all the advantage ascribed to it, although its
fire seems pretty well calculated for the defence
of the coast, the grand communication at the
back, and the length which it occupies.   It is
surrounded by two branches of the Caïmans
river ; the left flank is lengthened to cover and
enfilade the interior, which is seen.   It also
defends the Redan-oost of the old line, on
which it is proposed to mount some field-pieces.

A second circular redoubt, called Goede-
Trouwe, Good Hope, is erected, on the plain,

between the work above mentioned, and those on the river Caligawa, at nearly the same distance from the coast as the former. This redoubt completely flanks the centre work; and Zeemans-baterie, Mariners' battery, defends the communication, and would prevent the enemy from establishing himself in the old battery Poulus, in case he succeeded in making a landing on this front; but it also might be somewhat widened: on one side the fire would be more extensive; on the other it would have the advantage of defending the communication with Zeemans-baterie, the gorge of which it might batter, as well as the Torabaya battery, and consequently not only prevent an enemy from intrenching himself in these two works, but likewise defend the Caligawa river, and co-operate in supporting a retreat, which might be effected along the right bank of the river Torabaya.

The Zeemans-baterie, and battery of Torobaya, situated, one on the left, the other on the right, bank of the river Caligawa, near its mouth, are sufficient to defend the approach to it. The Torobaya battery is an old one rebuilt; with a demi bastion added, to prolong its right flank, so as to defile it, and cover the communication from Zeemans-baterie to Goede-Trouwe, the coast affording a space for landing of about two hundred and forty feet. As an enemy, wishing to attack Samarang, might attempt to force the passage of the mouth of the river Caligawa, possess himself of its defence, and establish himself there, to protect the disembarkation of his troops on the shore of the right bank, it is essential that there should be, at least, one battery, in the creek, formed by the junction of the Torabaya and Caligawa rivers. A small work in this place would defend the communication of the river Caligawa, impede an enemy's establishment in the two works situate at its mouth, and moreover drive him out of it when he was there.

The centre work, and two circular redoubts, have not the necessary relief. In the first place, they are on marshy ground, which daily gives way; in the next place, they ought to command the coast, which they are much too low to do.

Notwithstanding these different works, Samarang is far from being in a respectable state of defence. It has but six hundred troops, of which one hundred and fifty, including the officers of the old Wurtemberg regiment, and forty national grenadiers, are European. The artillery is only served by Madurans and Javans, on whose steadiness the governor himself says he could not place much reliance if he were attacked. He was even convinced, that if five or six transports or armed boats were to appear

opposite the mouth of the two rivers, the gun-
ners would abandon the works, and consequently
leave the enemy at liberty to take possession of
them, and penetrate into the country. Independently of this inconvenience, and supposing
these artillerymen to be staunch, an entrance might
still be effected by the rivers Tawang-Trassie and
Clayrang, although they are small and shallow,
and some large bamboos are planted in the
mouth of the former, to prevent boats coming
there, and one or two small guns at the mouth
of the other; for all these obstacles, not being
supported, would soon be removed.

A little more to the west of the mouth of the
river Tawang-Trassie, the coast is healthy and
ground firm, where troops may be landed without
difficulty, and instantly strike into a large hollow
way leading to the town by Caliebanter, a height
which commands the neighbourhood; in the last
war a fortification was there, in the middle of
which runs the road, surrounded by mountains,
woods, and inaccessible vallies, a league and a
half from the town, which would be reached
without any impediment.

The emperor of Solo is engaged to furnish the
governor with ten thousand men, on his first
requisition, in case of an attack; but the time it
would take to collect this number of Malays,
scattered throughout the country, and in their

families, to form them into corps, and organize them, although their chiefs and companies are already assigned to them, would afford the enemy an opportunity of doing great mischief, by possessing himself of the town, and small forts which defend the communications with the interior, and by increasing the fortifications, to maintain himself there, until the Company could ratify its contracts with the princes, or enter into fresh engagements with them by treaties of alliance.

To guard against such an event, there ought to be,

1st, Instead of the centre work, which is inadequate to its object, a capacious fort of masonry, which, supporting the advanced works, would defend and cover the town.

2d, An increase of the garrison by a company of artillery, and a complete battalion of infantry, all Europeans : these forces, added to those already there, and to which the natives would more willingly unite, would do away every apprehension for the safety of the establishment.

A fort has been ordered to be built on the road which connects the empire of Solo with that of the sultan of Joucki, from fear of an approaching rupture between those princes, naturally hostile to each other ; and which will probably be so contrived as to check whichever of the two may appear adverse to the Company.

The government of Java is the most lucrative, as the highest office, in India, next to that of the governor-general. M. Engelhart's annual income is said to be two hundred and fifty thousand piastres; and, at his house, Asiatic pageantry is seen in all its splendour. His situation, changed every four years, is reserved for the counsellors of India, who are not rich or have lost their property, the high regency being convinced that, before the expiration of their time, they will have re-established their fortunes.

Tagal is a small establishment, where is a resident, who carries into effect the engagements of the prince, by receiving, and depositing in the Company's warehouses, the productions of the country. It is not a military post. The village is large, and divided between the natives and Chinese; it is built at the bottom of a mountain, on which is a volcano, always burning. The mount is a remarkable object from the sea, for it appears to have, at the top, a very high tower, somewhat inclining, from the effect of the eruption.

The irregular positions of all the out-offices of the principal houses at Tcheribon, and of which some are at the side and others in the middle of a very extensive garden full of trees, basins, and running streams, make the situation truly picturesque from the various scenery round about it. The resident, who has for many years inhabited this delightful retreat, has made it a most enviable place. He has a good music-master, who has formed a band of fifteen of his slaves. In his garden, a short way from the house, he has built a bamboo orchestra : in one part of the garden is a large park of antelopes, male and female, and twenty sheds where he rears deer; also a dozen large China vases sunk into the ground for an immense quantity of gold and silver fish.

Tcheribon is a small town, or rather a large village, the capital of the kingdom of that name, divided between two princes of the same family, each of whom has the title of sultan, and reside in it. From external appearance, their palaces affect little of Asiatic show, being built only of planks and bamboo.

This place, one hundred and fifty miles east of Batavia, has only an open road, sheltered to the west by a large bank. It has four and a half and five fathoms water two leagues from shore, the distance at which ships are obliged to moor. Smaller vessels run along the bank to within three quarters of a league from land. As the river, near Tcheribon, divides into two branches, which fall into the sea a short distance

from each other, the country ships, which draw
but four to six feet water, are obliged, in coming
in and going out of the principal branch, to wait
for high tides on account of a small bank at its
mouth, with only two and a half feet water
when the tide is out. This river is always full
of the vessels of Java and of the surrounding
islands.

On the right bank of the river, and on the
sea-side, is a small brick fort, surrounded by a
fosse, over which is a bridge with a redoubt.
The fort is of little consequence; its embrasure-
parapet is but eighteen inches thick. It is defended by four bad small guns, which serve
rather to secure the Dutch flag and answer the
salutes of the ships which pass or come in, than
as a defence against an enemy, who might
choose to take possession of it and establish
himself there.

The mole is in a very bad state; on the left
bank it is entirely down, and has in a great measure disappeared.

On the right bank it is still in being, but the
piles are rotten, broken, or forced out. It was in
contemplation to rebuild it, with a battery at
the end, as well as two others on each of the
banks, as a defence against the pirates who continually infest the vicinity, and could easily at-

tack so weak and unprotected a place, and pillage and lay it under contribution.

The whole garrison is composed only of fifteen Madurans, armed with bad firelocks, and commanded by a sergeant and two European corporals.

This kingdom produces the best and finest coffee of all Java ; the grain is sound and small : it is also famous for horses ; they are small, and well-made, but vicious.

The elder of the sultans has a park of spotted deer, like antelopes *, which are taken in the adjacent forests.

In the woods and mountains of this kingdom it is that the rhinoceros is most commonly met with.

The air of Tcheribon is generally salubrious ; notwithstanding, leprosy is a prevalent disease, also disorders in the eyes, which are sometimes dangerous from April to December.

In this town are only the resident, secretary, book-keeper, surgeon-major in the pay of the Company, and three subalterns, who are Europeans ; the rest are natives, who make up two thirds of the population, and Chinese, who have a considerable campong, and are employed in

---

* This species is the axis, cervus axis.— *Sonnini.*

retail trade and agriculture. The establishment may bring in sixty thousand piastres a
year; it is independent of the government of
Java, and the resident corresponds directly with
the high regency.

FINIS.

S. GOSNELL, *Printer*, *Little Queen Street, London.*